# Hunger, Poetry and the Oxford Movement

# Hunger, Poetry and the Oxford Movement

## The Tractarian Social Vision

Lesa Scholl

BLOOMSBURY ACADEMIC
LONDON • NEW YORK • OXFORD • NEW DELHI • SYDNEY

BLOOMSBURY ACADEMIC
Bloomsbury Publishing Plc
50 Bedford Square, London, WC1B 3DP, UK
1385 Broadway, New York, NY 10018, USA
29 Earlsfort Terrace, Dublin 2, Ireland

BLOOMSBURY, BLOOMSBURY ACADEMIC and the Diana logo are trademarks of Bloomsbury Publishing Plc

First published in Great Britain 2020
This paperback edition published in 2021

Copyright © Lesa Scholl, 2020

Lesa Scholl has asserted her right under the Copyright, Designs and Patents Act, 1988, to be identified as Author of this work.

Cover design: Eleanor Rose
Cover image © Alamy

All rights reserved. No part of this publication may be reproduced or transmitted in any form or by any means, electronic or mechanical, including photocopying, recording, or any information storage or retrieval system, without prior permission in writing from the publishers.

Bloomsbury Publishing Plc does not have any control over, or responsibility for, any third-party websites referred to or in this book. All internet addresses given in this book were correct at the time of going to press. The author and publisher regret any inconvenience caused if addresses have changed or sites have ceased to exist, but can accept no responsibility for any such changes.

A catalogue record for this book is available from the British Library.

A catalog record for this book is available from the Library of Congress.

ISBN: HB: 978-1-3501-2072-3
PB: 978-1-3502-3741-4
ePDF: 978-1-3501-2073-0
eBook: 978-1-3501-2074-7

Typeset by Newgen KnowledgeWorks Pvt. Ltd., Chennai, India

To find out more about our authors and books visit www.bloomsbury.com and sign up for our newsletters.

*Dedicated in memory of
Charla Jim Killion-Hakimi
who understood what it was to give.*

# Contents

| | |
|---|---|
| Preface and Acknowledgements | viii |
| Introduction: Containing hunger and doctrines of reserve | 1 |
| 1 Economizing emotion and moderating hunger | 19 |
| 2 Looking outward: The moment of lyrical connection | 61 |
| 3 Embracing the community as one people | 99 |
| 4 Social action demonstrated | 135 |
| Conclusion: 'Seeing, touching, tasting are in thee deceived': Responding to the fragmentation of poetry, community and the senses | 171 |
| Notes | 177 |
| Bibliography | 195 |
| Index | 211 |

# Preface and Acknowledgements

This book began in February 2014 when I was on a research fellowship at the University of Exeter. One day, after busily writing, I went to Tesco to get some groceries. On the way back, I encountered a young homeless man begging on the footpath. It was a challenging moment for me: having spent the day writing about hunger and poverty in nineteenth-century Britain, what was I going to do when directly confronted by poverty in present-day Britain? I gave the young man some blueberry bagels, and for a moment I was happy with my actions as I went on my way. However, my contentment quickly changed to discomfort as I asked myself, what had I *really* done to help him? It was dissatisfying to assure myself that, being a transient member of the Exeter community myself, there was little I could do to help him long term. It was further disturbing that this thought process alone seemed to be taking this man's vulnerable situation and making it about myself and my feelings.

I was at a conference at Griffith University some time later when I had the opportunity to share this experience with Professor Chris Lee. To paraphrase Chris's wisdom, he told me that the problem of hunger and poverty is like a three-volume novel: it is unwieldy, daunting and overwhelming, and people don't want to go near it. It's too hard. However, my encounter with that young man was like a lyric poem: short, transient and in the moment; it might have been small, but in that moment I was able to intervene. This comparison of experience to form sparked within me a desire to study representations of hunger in poetry of the nineteenth century, and I found myself immersed in Tractarian poetics and the Doctrine of Reserve, which emphasized not only the transience I had experienced and the limitations on my level of impact, but also the importance of having done something even if it seemed insignificant to me. The reserve of emotion that the Tractarians held on to seemed to be something I needed to emulate in order to recognize the young man's subjectivity instead of being paralysed by my own emotional response.

Throughout this project I have had incredible support from many people who, to varying degrees, know the challenges that I have faced during its production. Linda Hughes has supported it from its inception, going above and beyond through many conversations and reading of material. Thanks in this regard also need to go to Joshua King and Andy 'Tough Brit' Tate, who have given me unfailing support and encouragement. Your thoughtful comments, time, help and expertise have meant so much to me.

I was privileged to have a Visiting Scholars Fellowship at Baylor University's Armstrong Browning Library, which helped enormously with my research into nineteenth-century Anglo-Catholicism. Jennifer Borderud, Christi Klempnauer, Cynthia Burgess, Melvin Schuetz, Melinda Creech and Mary Schrader gave me wonderful research assistance, as well as becoming my Texan family. Also at Baylor, I want to acknowledge the Texas Hunger Initiative, particularly Jeremy Everett, Kathy Krey and Erin Nolan, for their support of my research and for understanding its resonances with the twenty-first century. The staff at the Jesse H. Jones Library, especially Deanna Burks, were helpful when I needed to go back in time with the microfilm collection. At the other end of the technological scale, I'd like to thank Chris and the team at Google Books for making material available to me digitally that would otherwise have been unavailable, especially turn-of-the-century periodicals.

Over the last few years, I've had the opportunity to present portions of this work at various conferences and institutions, where I've received encouragement and support while testing my wings. These have included the Midwest Victorian Studies Association, the British Women Writers Conference, the North American Victorian Studies Association, the Australasian Victorian Studies Association, Texas Christian University, Anglia Ruskin University and the University of Exeter. During those occasions, I received many thoughtful questions and comments that spurred me along. At the risk of omitting people, I would particularly like to mention Deborah Morse, Kirstie Blair, Hilary Fraser, Regenia Gagnier, Mary-Catherine Harrison, Lizzie Ludlow, Kristen Pond, Mike Sanders, Charles La Porte, Ayesha Mukherjee, Mark Knight, Jo Carruthers, Sarina Gruver Moore, Duc Dau, Ann Gagne, Michelle Smith, Grace Moore, Karen Dieleman, Amy Coté, Corinna Wagner, Chris Stokes, Kate Hext, Laurel Brake, Marjorie Stone, Dino Felluga and Ann Donahue. I'd also like to thank David Avital, Lucy Brown and the team at Bloomsbury Academic for their enthusiasm and support for this book.

On a more personal note, I want to thank Charlotte Chambers, Myles Lawrence, Heidi Hakimi-Hood, Susan Harris, Paul Kogler, Katie Klein Booth, Emily Cody, Amelia O'Connor, Katie Pennycuick, Susanna Cramb, Jas Sandes, Elizabeth Travers-Parker, Loraine Pennycuick and my parents. Thank you for taking me into your hearts and homes: for being my community.

# Introduction: Containing hunger and doctrines of reserve

A poor man met me and begged for bread –
    Lira, la, la!
'Brother, take all the loaf,' I said,
I shall but go with lighter cheer –
    Lira, la, la!
And oh within my flowering heart
(Sing, sweet nightingale!) is my Dear.
              – Alice Meynell, 'The Joyous Wanderer' (1913), 9–15[1]

*We feel that [poetry] is sparing and merciful to the emotions that seethe within us, and that, for a while, we enjoy at least that solace which Dido once fruitlessly craved, to her woe: '… a transient grace | To give this madness breathing-space.'*
              – John Keble, *Lectures on Poetry* (1832)[2]

In his inaugural oration as Professor of Poetry at Oxford, John Keble referred to his move from parish ministry to the university as being 'recall[ed] from the battlefield of life to the training-ground of youth.'[3] In this manner, one who would go on to be one of the founders of the Tractarians, or the Oxford Movement, stipulates where real work lies: not in the academic study of theology, but in the practical outworking of knowledge and pastoral care in the community. Therefore, the Anglican revival of Catholicism that the Oxford Movement sparked needs to be understood not just in terms of its theological impact, but also in the way it directly addressed social concerns. Oxford, like other academic institutions, could be seen as an ivory tower, a place of escape: a means to remove oneself from the trials of life, including, for many, preclusion from war – choosing the cloth over the navy. It was also a potential space of decadence and excess. However, Keble is adamant that the space allowed in the university's halls is not an end in itself, but a breathing space in which individuals are trained to go out to the world. At a time when Britain was in a state of turmoil that would only increase throughout the century, Keble's vision of learning poetry as a practical tool for ministering to a traumatized community would become further entrenched through the Tractarian social vision.

This social vision was predicated on interrelated forms of reserve. The Doctrine of Reserve, in which 'God's word … should be available only to the faithful, and not to either unbelievers ill prepared to understand religious knowledge, or to Evangelicals who were considered too familiar with the mysteries of faith',[4] informed emotional reserve and poetic reserve, written in terms of economy in a way that had a significant impact on aesthetics as well as theology. In *Anglican Ritualism in Victorian Britain* (1999), Nigel Yates suggests that the ritualism that emerged in the century 'provided colour and order for those for whom the drabness of an increasingly commercial and industrial society … was profoundly disturbing',[5] and so in this sense, the aesthetic mode of ritual aligns directly with the motive of poetics. Furthermore, the 'tension between personal emotion and reserve' and 'veiled self-expression' that 'bring[s] relief and healing to poet and audience alike' in Keble's vision is directly related to the capacity of individuals to contend with the anxieties of widespread social and economic turbulence.[6] Isobel Armstrong notes that 'to constitute something as a gap is a strategy for concealing anxiety',[7] and it is within this kind of concealment or poetic silence that the reserve of Tractarian poetics is most persistent throughout the nineteenth century. Indeed, Alice Meynell makes a significant editorial intervention in her 1913 translation of Catulle Mendès's 'L'heureux vagabond' (1892) by moving the quotation marks.[8] Whereas the original has the poetic speaker declaring to the beggar the joy with which he will continue on his way, in Meynell's version the speaker keeps those feelings respectfully to himself: the bread does the beggar good; it does not do the beggar good, however, from his position of desperation, to hear another's cheer articulated. The feelings of Meynell's wanderer are acknowledged in the poem, but they are deliberately contained.

Meynell's translation epitomizes a lyrical response to physical and social hunger that resonates with the influence of Tractarian ethics and aesthetics throughout the nineteenth century: a reserve of one's own emotions married with proximate, immediate, personal social action that recognizes the subjectivity of the vulnerable other. The difference, however, is that the speaker in Meynell's poem is a transient figure – a wanderer himself – and therefore he does not have to be overwhelmed by the beggar's poverty. He will not have to see the beggar again the next day, or the day after that, and thus feel compelled to give again and again. Keble, however, like his fellow Tractarians and those who would be influenced by them, was not in this kind of luxurious emotional situation. Poverty was constant and pervasive in his community. Keble's battlefield was not just a metaphor for the state of the nation, or even Europe, but for the individual's heart and mind, in which one battles to continue to care for others when the need is chronic. Alongside the growth of 'industrialization, capitalism, and urbanization … which tended to isolate the individual psychologically, if not physically,'[9] the Victorian age was marked by persistent economic devastation that overwhelmed the social consciousness:

> By 1841, industrial Britain was deep in a serious economic crisis and this was contributing to growing social misery and unrest. Beginning in 1837, there had been a series of four poor harvests, which drove bread prices to famine levels. Rising food prices had been combined with a trade recession, which was connected to an economic downturn in the United States. From 1838 to 1842, tens of thousands were thrown out of work, while for those in work wages fell sharply. Conditions for many labouring people grew desperate – their gaunt faces, emaciated bodies and rages haunted the landscape – and there was a growing popular rage over the condition of England.[10]

The oscillations of human history show that this condition was not particular to mid-nineteenth-century Britain, but is the condition of modernity; and the oscillations are made possible by regulation – that is, by moderation, or social, political and economic reserve, revealed in checks and balances. Lauren Goodlad argues in *Victorian Literature and the Victorian State* (2003) that Victorian Britain was a liberal society in that 'throughout the century, centralized institutions and statist interventions were curbed to preserve the "self-governing" liberties of individuals and local communities,'[11] and it could be further argued that the Tractarians were on the forefront of this social mission. Fighting throughout the century against the dehumanizing effects of the 1834 New Poor Law, as well as the growing impetus of political economy, the Tractarian vision resisted centralization and institutionalization as mechanisms that distanced people from each other and isolated individuals within communities. Simon Skinner argues that this vision was directly connected to the Tractarians' concern for the poor and vulnerable in communities: 'Tractarians' fatalism towards the efficacy of human legislation, and their sense of opposition to the world's oppression of the poor ... patently inhibited them from engaging with secular notions of social or political equality.'[12] He further suggests that the 'church's special responsibility to the poor ... was, therefore, bound to embitter its relations with a secular state whose development was the historical expression of the powerful'.[13] Importantly, Skinner observes, the main criticism of the Poor Law was that 'the revision to the law had made the provision of poor relief a tax rather than a charity',[14] which meant helping one's neighbour was moved away from a community duty based on human connection to an institutionalized, faceless – and thoughtless – penalty. One did not have to think about the poor, except as an abstract encumbrance on one's income, like any other tax.

## Reserve and Tractarian poetics

*Hunger, Poetry and the Oxford Movement* asserts the influence of Tractarian thought within the Condition of England Question through the poetry of the nineteenth century. Taking my cue from Dominic Janes, who writes in his introduction to *Victorian Reformation* (2009) that his book is not about Roman Catholicism per se, but a study of the 'Anglican use of material, visual, and liturgical forms *inspired*' by Roman Catholicism,[15] rather than writing about Tractarianism or Anglo-Catholicism, I am more interested in the specific influence of the Tractarian idea of reserve as it permeated the broader social ethos, particularly within Anglicanism in opposition to the overt emotional fervour of Evangelicalism. The influence of reserve on Christina Rossetti has been well-noted, and of the poets I address, she is the only one who stayed within the bounds of Anglo-Catholicism throughout her life. However,

Coventry Patmore, Gerard Manley Hopkins, Alice Meynell and Adelaide Procter were all deeply engaged in the Tractarian mode of Anglicanism before converting to Roman Catholicism in their adult lives, Hopkins, Meynell and Procter converting in their twenties, while Patmore converted in middle age. Their relationships to each other poetically and personally, as well as their noted appreciation of Rossetti, tie these figures together within the heritage of Tractarian poetics and reserve, extending beyond the narrow idea of High Anglicanism. I argue that Tractarian ethics and aesthetics persist in their understanding of social responsibility, as well as their literary production. It should be noted, too, that although Hopkins is primarily figured as a Roman Catholic poet and Jesuit priest in current scholarship, the majority of his poems discussed here were composed during his Anglo-Catholic days at Oxford.

The inclusion in this study of Alfred, Lord Tennyson, who is generally understood as Broad Church, is less obvious, although scholars like Kirstie Blair have suggested the influence of Tractarian poetics on his work, as well as Roman Catholicism.[16] Blair notes, importantly, that even within dissenting and Roman Catholic poetics, 'poets from these traditions were at least in part forced to define themselves in relation to Anglican norms, including poetic norms. Anglican forms ... were the common cultural property of writers both inside and outside the Church of England'.[17] Yet Tennyson's position is even more complex, given that Roman Catholicism's influence on him predates the Tractarian Movement, beginning while he was a student at Cambridge, primarily in the first instance through his friendship with Arthur Hallam, but after Hallam's death with his many Romanist friends. Arguably the reserve that is enacted within Broad Church liberalism resonates with the intellectual and spiritual reserve enacted by the Tractarians: developing throughout the century, it adopts a middle ground or, in Tractarian terms, a *via media* position, between the seeming Romanist tendencies of the Oxford Movement's adherents and the excessive emphasis on sinfulness and divine judgment within Evangelicalism. The way Seth Koven articulates the pragmatism of the Broad Church in his discussion of the influential theologian F. D. Maurice resonates with the fundamental idea of reserve:

> The leaders of the Oxford Movement ... struck alarmed observers (Maurice among them) in the 1840s as a band of brothers devoted to dangerously papist ritual ... Nor was Maurice any more sympathetic to the influence

of Evangelicals, whose spirituality, politics, and social ministry among the poor grew out of an abiding sense of their own sinfulness and the doctrine of atonement. Maurice's God was loving and compassionate, less focused on judging the ultimate fate of men's souls than bettering their earthly lot.[18]

Maurice's perspective is innately *via media* in this sense: he is resisting the excesses of asceticism on both fronts. While it could be argued from this assessment that the Tractarians were not able to hold to their own principles of reserve, what interests me in this example is the way that the idea of reserve operates independently of a particular theological persuasion, and instead infuses all of the standpoints to encourage moderation of thought, even though it is associated specifically with Tractarian theology. Maurice himself was a convert from Unitarianism to Anglicanism, while founding Tractarian John Henry Newman experienced a spiritual and theological journey from Evangelicalism to Anglo-Catholicism, and then to Roman Catholicism. While Anglican, Newman was accused of Romanism, yet after he converted to the Roman Church in 1845, he was accused of trying to move Rome back to Anglicanism. Furthermore, throughout the century, liberal Roman Catholicism looked in many ways like Anglo-Catholicism in terms of social theory and practice, which was one of the reasons the Tractarians were distrusted from the start: the fears of 'secret popery' were apparently confirmed in Newman's conversion, not to mention the conversion of many others.[19] The Anglo-Catholics claimed, however, to be returning to the integrity of the medieval English Catholic Church, not Romanism. Yet as much as these different persuasions sought to distinguish themselves from each other, they were similar in maintaining a moderation that hinged on the Catholic ethos of reserve.

Throughout Newman's work, there was a constant desire to moderate belief and understanding, consistent with the Doctrine of Reserve: given the imperfections of the human intellect, one should not assume their knowledge to be complete. It is this kind of intellectual reserve in particular that resonates in Tennyson's work, and found its way into Broad Church thinking more generally. Dennis Taylor notes that Tennyson's empathy towards the 'unresolved complexities of the human condition' has led some scholars to accuse him 'of mediocrity or worse as a thinker' and of being dangerously open to the influence of Roman Catholicism.[20] However, Tennyson's mutual acceptance of and struggle with the complexities of humanity resonates with the intellectual reserve of paradox that would become entrenched in Tractarian thought. Paradox is at the heart of the Doctrine of Reserve, flowing beyond theology into intellectual and social practice. Taylor argues that Tennyson's relationship with Catholicism 'is a continual dialogue where he sometimes approaches and sometimes withdraws from close identification with the Catholic faith', adding that the 'Oxford Movement and the rise of Anglo-Catholicism complicate the picture';[21] and I would add that Tennyson's capacity to hold several different perspectives at once without clinging wholly to any of them aligns directly with the paradox of reserve.

In my argument, I do not suggest that the theological idea of reserve began with the Tractarians. Its history lies within the Roman Church and is one of the key aspects of Catholicism that the Tractarians sought to recover. It was, however, entrenched theologically and aesthetically in Britain by the Tractarian movement and was culturally associated with them, primarily through Isaac Williams's two tracts 'On Reserve in Communicating Religious Knowledge' (1840).[22] In 1844 Dean Francis Close, an opponent of the Oxford Movement, remarked that 'Romanism is taught analytically at Oxford; it is taught artistically at Cambridge',[23] and while predating Newman's conversion, this comment suggests the broader influence that the Tractarians had, which Mary Arseneau aptly describes as 'emanating from Oxford'.[24] What interests me in this study is not theology or hard-line definitions between the denominational practices of the poets whose work I address. Instead, my focus is specifically on the influence of reserve as a catholic mode – catholic, in this sense, as universal – but foundationally tied to the *ethos* (a term anglicized by Keble) of the Oxford Movement. In this way, the doctrines of reserve go beyond a theological understanding to structures of belief in terms of how to moderate emotional responses and how to intervene appropriately in society. It acknowledges human limitations as a way of preventing emotional burnout or overstepping one's place, not necessarily as a way of preventing upward social mobility, but more as a way of recognizing and respecting vulnerable members of the community who are often made invisible or clustered together as a mass, rather than being identified as individual, equally human beings. This idea is epitomized in Emily Harrington's paradoxical term in *Second Person Singular* (2014), 'impersonal intimacy', and by Derrida's Law of Tact, as explicated in *On*

*Touching* (2000). Derrida's Law engages with questions of when to touch, how to touch, and how to touch *upon* – how to be *tactful* – in a manner in which reserve is motivated by respect and a desire to define appropriate behaviour and emotional response. Derrida emphasizes what one cannot touch: 'one must touch without touching',[25] a paradox of proximity and distance that, when applied to social vision, can be read helpfully in terms of Tractarian reserve. It is this effect of reserve in particular that preoccupies my readings of the poems and their position within the context of hunger and poverty.

The Cambridge Apostles, with whom Tennyson was associated, upheld this kind of vision as much as the Tractarians would. The project of the Apostles, 'written with the sophisticated éclan of shared intimacy', was 'not political change but the "regeneration" of society, not revolution, as Arthur Hallam's sickened fear of the rick-burners round Cambridge indicates, but a transformation of the mind of the country'.[26] Further affinities with the Oxford Movement can be found in the Apostles' '[nostalgic belief] in tradition, in traditional forms of literature, in a cultural unity forged by poetry and in a Christian society'.[27] The importance of poetry as an ordering force, an undeniable influence of Romanticism on religious and social thought in the early nineteenth century, undergirds the capacity for human connection and community; and this doctrine of poetry is as much one of reserve – order, restraint, moderation and form – as much as the theological doctrine of withholding knowledge until an appropriate stage of understanding. The poetic motive of the Cambridge Apostles, as for the Tractarians, was to 'relat[e] the rhythms of poetry to the rhythms of social experience, which ... are often messy, complex, and overlaid'.[28] Caroline Levine recognizes 'meter as another of these social rhythms, not an epiphenomenal effect of social realities', and in this way, it is 'capable itself of exerting and transmitting power'.[29] This recognition reinforces the way in which Keble, along with other leading Tractarians like Newman and Williams, viewed poetry and poetic form as essential for ordering society and building communal responsibility. In both respects, reserve is the *means*, not the end in itself: reserve creates opportunities for individuals to seek truth actively, to make deep human connections, and to enable them to maintain their capacity to meet the needs of others, even when the need never seems to end regardless of how much is given. Poetic reserve is paradoxically facilitated to create and sustain community.

## Immediacy and proximity: The lyric mode

The Victorian poet was, in Armstrong's words, 'post-revolutionary, existing with the constant possibility of mass political upheaval and fundamental change in the structure of society, which meant that the nature of society had to be redefined'; and Armstrong suggests that because of 'its awareness of teleological insecurity, Victorian poetry is arguably the last theological poetry to be written'.[30] Yet going beyond the vertical relationship between the material and the divine, the Tractarian mode simultaneously explores the consequences of this insecurity on the horizontal community relationships. In 'Victorian Lyric Pathology and Phenomenology' (2013), Marion Thain interrogates the way in which the 'logic of degeneration at the end of the [nineteenth] century' led to 'a cynical deadlock between self and other'. Instead she argues for a 'route out of that deadlock' and, borrowing from Walter Pater, suggests that for the lyric subject – that 'solitary prisoner' – 'heighten[ing] our receptivity to the pulsations the body receives from without … can shock one out of one's own internal landscape'.[31] Thain's argument suggests a critical turning outward of the lyric genre in the late nineteenth century, away from the discrete idea of self-exploration or self-discovery, to self-discovery within the context of the external world. In a similar manner, Harrington notes that for Alice Meynell 'thou' rather than 'I' is 'at the center of poetic diction', therefore identifying poetry 'as an explicitly relational genre', one that recognizes the individuality of at least two poetic subjects and also, even more crucially, the human connection between them, represented in 'the convergence of poetic form and intimacy'.[32]

In my study, I trace this shift in the lyric back through the nineteenth century, linking it closely to the early Tractarians. As G. B. Tennyson writes in *Victorian Devotional Poetry: The Tractarian Mode* (1981), while Tractarian poetry was concerned with the relationship between God and humans in a devotional sense, it equally considered 'the expression of intense feelings about the Church in her relations with society and the world'. Yet while Tennyson sees this shift as 'the first crack in the wall of Kebelian and Tractarian Reserve',[33] I see this fusion as not only reinforcing but also necessary to the moderation (or reserve) of feeling within the context of the Tractarian social vision. As Emma Mason suggests, the reserve of poetry allowed for the exploration of three issues key to Tractarianism: the emotive effect poetry and religion produced on readers; the consolatory quality of such an effect; and the regulation of the consequent feeling in believers (too much feeling, it was feared, could unbalance the believer altogether).[34]

In this way, Tractarian reserve is embedded within a poetic mode that is both aesthetically and socially motivated, creating a tension between distance and proximity in a way that forces those who engage with the poetry to recognize their social context. It therefore follows that Tractarian poetry 'figures the individual and the communal as interdependent through … [the] strategic use of singular and plural lyrical voices',[35] a mode that appears throughout the century. Furthermore, the Tractarian engagement with the proximate senses of smell, taste and touch – and often sensory absence – married with reserve, enables 'the language of intimate physical connection'[36] for the lyric subject in late-Victorian poetry. The intensity of the poem depends on the visceral yet silent recognition of the sensory experience of the other that leads to active social intervention.

From this perspective, the space of the poem becomes one of transformative encounter, predicated on human contact that confronts each subject's understanding of the world and their position within it. Within the lyric mode, ideas of 'personal happiness, a sense of community, closeness to nature, sensory acuity and the physical health it presupposes' are condensed and intensified, 'all simultaneously experienced in the sweet *now*'.[37] The mutual immediacy, transience and illusiveness of 'now' in Kerry McSweeney's understanding of the lyric aligns precisely with the Tractarian conviction that one must act in the moment because of the shortness of life on earth; yet another aspect that can be drawn from his statement is the sensory reserve of that 'now' being 'sweet'. In Tractarian poetics, the absence of sensory experience is most obvious in the removal to metaphor and allusion, but it also operates in the figurative use of the senses. This removal can be termed sensory reserve. The most obvious, yet most pervasive and therefore often invisible, form of this kind of reserve is in regard to taste. Sweetness seems almost analogous to poetic aesthetics, and secondary to such taste references is the idea of touch – being touched, in terms of feeling or affect. Yet in these references, it is little noted that the literal senses are being restrained by an aesthetic mode. Furthermore, experiences of the distance senses, that is, vision or audition, are often absorbed synaesthetically in a way that is rarely noticed: air can be described as sweet, as can flowers. This kind of aesthetic reserve, as a derivative of emotional reserve, moderates the emotional response to material, abject senses, such as starving bodies, the stench of poverty or death, or the feeling of sordidness. Within the Tractarian social vision, these abject realities are likely to disgust and psychologically distance the very people who might be able to do something to rectify them; therefore aesthetic reserve operates through sensory reserve to moderate the flight response, allowing proximity to occur. In this sense, touch both literally and metaphorically challenges the affective desire to distance oneself from the want of others, working within the restraints of reserve for sustained release of action. Applied to poetic structures, this economy of reserve provides a sense of stability and order in light of the overwhelming, excessive nature of hunger and poverty in nineteenth-century Britain.

## Interrogating the Tractarian social vision

Tractarianism emerged in response to the 'dark shadows' of Britain's industrial dominance and 'grand visions of commerce and Christianity': 'Although their deaths were often concealed by the smoke of the factories, darkness of the mines or squalor of the urban slums, thousands died unnecessarily each year in industrial Britain through malnutrition, exposure, contaminated food or water, industrial accidents or overwork.'[38] Yet in their response, the Tractarians understood their own limitations. As Levine notes, 'each shape or pattern, social or literary, lays claim to a limited range of potentialities. Enclosures afford containment and security, inclusion as well as exclusion.'[39] Even removing themselves from the larger political debates regarding social reform, within their localized, community-based vision, the Tractarians understood that a battle remained in regard to those who were excluded. Even though their theology declared the spiritual equality of all before God, they recognized the problems of inequalities on earth, in each community. One of their key responses in this regard was to reject 'any relationship between poverty and moral failing, such as was suggested by the less-eligibility principle of the new poor law' or, as it became commonly known, the idea of the deserving and undeserving poor.⁴⁰ In an attempt to bring the sense of responsibility back home to the community, the Tractarian writer Samuel Bosanquet argued,

> There can be no stronger symptom of the growing harshness and unchristian state of feeling towards the poor, than the opinion now both hinted at and affirmed – that the legal provision for the poor ought to be a substitute for private charity: that the one interferes with the other. There is nothing more erroneous ... We assert that the *private charity ought to supersede the public provision.*⁴¹

It is most crucial to note that the Tractarian view was not to abolish public aid, but simply that individuals and communities ought to give even more. The provision for the poor and the vulnerable was meant to be a personal priority of every member of the parish; as Skinner notes, their message, although it has been construed as socially conservative, was 'an insistence on the duties of the rulers, rather than the rights of the ruled'.⁴² That is not to say that the Tractarians did not perceive the 'rights of the ruled', but rather their concern was to address the abdication of social responsibility by those who held social power. This criticism included not just the secular state but also the commercialization of the state church, evidenced in patronage and pluralism, the latter being in many ways a forerunner of the unionization of parishes resulting from the New Poor Law. What amounted to the 'stratification of worshippers' in these aspects of Anglicanism opposed the idea of spiritual equality and affirmed that the commercial spirit was as much entrenched in the church as it was in the secular state.⁴³

The Tractarians actively worked against this commercial ethos with their vision of pastorship, which they 'conceived as a reciprocal relation between morally equal actors, even as vast inequalities of wealth and power were tolerated and, indeed, stabilized'.⁴⁴ Of course, the stabilization of inequality remains problematic, but the Tractarians were able to address social disaffection to some degree through their parochial ideal. Through the example of figures like John Keble, not only were students seeking ordination 'very deeply serious about their vocation as priests and strengthened by their love of tradition and beauty of holiness', they were imbibed with a high sense of moral and pastoral responsibility: 'young clerics caught up in the Oxford Movement were often prepared to accept the most difficult parishes, including those in the urban slums, and commit themselves to serve the impoverished underclass'.[45] The criticism they received from their Evangelical counterparts for their emphasis on ritual failed to recognize how deeply entwined their understanding of ritual and form, not to mention aesthetics and poetics, was to their psychological capacity to meet the most abject of human social needs.

Apart from Gerard Manley Hopkins, who became a Jesuit priest, the poets in this study were laypeople. Even so, they were each deeply concerned about social justice and personal social activism, and were aware of their capacity as poets to influence their audience to extend that social vision. Poetry is facilitated in this sense to reconstruct community identity and personal responsibility in the face of institutional failure, while reasserting the human subjectivity of the poor. The immediacy of the lyric mode, combined with the way in which the rhythm of the poetry speaks to the material body to complement and extend both the sensory and the aesthetic moment, provides a radical response to physical and social hunger, emphasizing not just the capacity but also the duty to meet the needs of an individual in the moment, rather than being paralysed by the enormity of the broader social problem of poverty. This response reflects the Doctrine of Reserve, in which emotional and spiritual moderation is understood as economizing affect, in poetry as in life, for sustained action, rather than an explosive, short-lived emotional response. Ultimately the devastating effect of hunger is contained by spiritual optimism, manifested through the economizing aesthetic form of poetry, giving the poet a means of control over the chaos of hunger.

The poetic works of Rossetti, Hopkins, Patmore, Meynell, Procter and Tennyson are significant in the way they engage simultaneously with emotional and spiritual reserve, juxtaposed with a willingness to be proximate to the hungry. The affective consequences of this kind of connection can be traumatic. However, the reality that physical and social hungers resist connection is at the heart of the Tractarian concern. Poetic form, like ritual, provides a containing structure that moderates and frames emotional and sensory response. As Patmore suggests in 'An Essay on English Metrical Law' (1856), 'the language should always seem to *feel*, though not to *suffer from*, the bonds of verse',[46] and similarly the poet attempts to bring the audience to a place of empathy without crossing into the language of abject disgust or sensationalism. The point is to give the reader pause for thought, just as Patmore coined the term 'catalexis' for the pause in poetic meter, or as Rossetti or Meynell enact poetic silences. This structure of reserve affects and directs the way in which representations of social inequality and hunger are experienced through poetry. Hunger is thus contained within an aesthetic and religious discourse, which is designed to create a sense of communal experience – through shared literal meals, as in the Eucharist and the Agape Feast, and shared metaphorical meals through literary and ritualistic encounter – in a way that reinforces the sense of responsibility and belonging to the local community, defying the social complacency of capitalist individualism and trusting to faceless systems and political structures in order to mend social ills.

The four chapters of *Hunger, Poetry and the Oxford Movement* follow a trajectory from contending with inner struggles through to outward social action, and rather than focusing on particular poets, each chapter brings a selection of their poems into conversation with each other. 'Economizing emotion' focuses on the struggle to show restraint in the face of extreme human emotion, confronting grief, mortality and betrayal, and the necessity of economizing emotion for the sake of the individual as well as the community. Community is built and maintained, arguably, through the 'fellowship of patience', which Karen Dieleman sees as 'being in communion even across divides of time, place, and disposition'.[47] It questions how to maintain authentic feeling while reserving expression. Loss, absence and hunger bleed into each other in the way that the poet contends with the apparent need for reserve. Reserve and emotional economy are not positioned as denial or emotional hoarding, but as providing a channel for sustained release of emotion that allows for the process of grief without the subject being overwhelmed by it. The poems discussed reveal the way in which the poets challenge reserve in the moment of grief, kicking against the goad of restraint and questioning its appropriateness; however, within the Tractarian influence, calmness and productivity are found through gradual release, rather than sudden, exhausting explosions.

Whereas Chapter 1 maintains the conventional inward focus of the lyric mode, Chapter 2, as its title 'Looking outward' suggests, begins to examine the way in which the poets facilitated the popularity of the periodical press to engage their audience in affective, empathetic connection with the poor. By publishing in periodicals, they engaged in the kind of shared reading familiar to their nineteenth-century audience through Anglican liturgy and the Book of Common Prayer, as well as Keble's very popular companion, *The Christian Year* (1827). This form of reading implicitly engaged the readers in community; yet even more, the context of publication, placed in journals and magazines alongside articles on contemporary social and economic issues, brought the lyric mode into a new dynamic that impacted the perception of those issues. Whereas John Stuart Mill had suggested in 'What is Poetry?' (1833) that 'the peculiarity of poetry appears to us to lie in the poet's utter unconsciousness of a listener',[48] it becomes increasingly evident that the Victorian lyric poet was not only deeply conscious of a listener, but also sought to activate that listener towards social feeling through lyrical intimacy, to be followed by social action.

Maintaining the focus on community building, Chapter 3 turns towards representations of the Eucharist that demonstrate the breakdown of the ideal of the Communion of Saints and spiritual equality. The ways in which the poets engage with the organic elements that are aesthetically transformed into the Eucharistic elements expose the social fragmentation and the emotional distancing that exists between rich and poor. The fusion of materiality and spirituality within the Eucharist finds its clearest representation in the Tractarian mystery of the Real Presence doctrine: not moving into the Roman Catholic doctrine of Transubstantiation, Real Presence maintained that the elements could be, paradoxically, at once symbols and contain the actual presence of God. Furthermore, the understanding of the Eucharistic rite as consuming the divine and becoming like Christ in the process also suggests that the poor are also like Christ; in this way, acting charitably towards the poor recalls the biblical verse that is repeated throughout this study as central to the Tractarian social vision: 'Inasmuch as ye have done it unto one of the least of these my brethren, ye have done it unto me' (Mt. 25:40). In the moment of the shared tastes of the bread and wine, inclusion and exclusion are reinforced, and empathy and identification with the poor are suggested by the call to partake in Christ's suffering. As Blair suggests, 'the relationship between poetry and ritual is not one of imitation but of identity'.[49]

The logical direction from the Eucharistic moment in this sense is to move to social activism. 'Social action demonstrated', as the final chapter, goes further into the individual investment of each poet in social justice, looking specifically at poetry inspired by their personal activism, both literary and social, which are constantly in dialogue. The political, theological and social meet within poetic form. The pragmatism of meeting physical and social needs is drawn into conversation with the way the poets' literary work influences their broader understandings of poverty and the figure of the poor in the community. Blair argues that as religious practitioners, religious poets 'knew what was at stake in formal choices and were highly self-conscious about them, creating their own discussion of the ethical and political ramifications of form … They were aware that poetic form would read as shorthand for the poet's belief and allegiance',[50] and in a similar manner, their social activism inflects their poetic form. The 'interdependency of individual and community' that Dieleman notes in Rossetti's later devotional work, 'remind[ing] readers that individual and community can coexist',[51] speaks to the broader Tractarian aesthetic and social vision that persists in ideas of community throughout the nineteenth century as a reaction to the 'individual self-reliance' promoted by liberal capitalist narratives of political economy.[52] Interdependence and focusing on one's social responsibility, rather than being preoccupied with one's own emotions or economic situation, are asserted as appropriate responses to economic and social precarity.

As the parochial community envisaged by Keble breaks down throughout the nineteenth century, there remains a need to manage the persistent, chronic problem of hunger. The adage, 'the poor are always with us', corrupted and decontextualized from the biblical 'For ye have the poor always with you' (Mt. 26:11), most often results in a complacency towards hunger: familiarity breeds contempt. Yet the Tractarian lyric mode directly challenges such emotional distancing through the identification of the poor with Christ and the emphasis on acting in the moment. 'Always' on earth is transient, and while the problem will not be solved in any one generation, this enormity should not preclude feeding the beggar on the steps today. The understanding of human limits infuses the poems in this study as the poets seek to intervene in the complexity between emotions, economics and sociopolitical ideas of responsibility, undergirded by an emphasis on reserve in terms of channelled, sustained action. Intervention ultimately lies with individuals who can choose either to act or not to act. As Meynell concludes in her account of the charitable work of the Sisters of Nazareth,

> Whatever a riper justice than that of our own time may decide as to the general debt owed by the nation to its poor, ... [i]t is the immediate and fugitive succour of want so urgent that no reply is possible except that of the gift in an outstretched hand.[53]

# 1

# Economizing emotion and moderating hunger

> Nothing is our own: we hold our pleasures
> Just a little while, ere they are fled:
> One by one life robs us of our treasures;
> Nothing is our own except our Dead.
>
> – Adelaide Anne Procter, 'Our Dead' (1859), 1–4[1]

Writing in the centenary year of John Keble's Assize Sermon, traditionally used to mark the beginning of the Oxford Movement, Ruth Kenyon observes the little appreciated significance of the social landscape of nineteenth-century Britain on the development of Tractarianism:

> it would have been a strange thing if men of the intellectual brilliance of Keble, Pusey, Newman, and Hurrell Froude, living ... in an England undergoing political throes which gave birth to the Reform Bill of 1832, the Poor Law Act of 1834, the Municipal Reform Act of 1835, the Bristol Riots of 1831, the agricultural labourers' revolt of the same year, and the industrial horrors disclosed in the campaign for the great Factory Act of 1833, should have noticed none of these things, or noticed them only to dislike the reforming zeal associated with political Liberalism.

She thus argues that 'Tractarianism was no calm academic excogitation of a theory of the Church from a city dreaming of spires. It was a reaction to the whole situation, and a reaction which, in the phrase of Newman no less than Froude, was to be "fierce".'[2] Indeed, in his inaugural lecture as Professor of Poetry at Oxford, John Keble addressed the question as to why one would give up serving as a church minister in 'such political times' when 'with what zealous industry unprincipled men are doing their evil work; with what mischievous eagerness they seek out country seclusions, so that there is no cottage, however sequestered or remote, which they have not filled with scandalous and profane pamphlets, to serve as fuel for their seditions', stating, even had I the ability which one who speaks with authority from this chair ought to have, I would certainly never shrink from my task on the plea that at a time of national peril it ill becomes us to betake ourselves to the study of poetry; nay, I believe that, on the one hand, nothing is more effective than these studies in bracing citizens to all virtues; and, on the other, nothing is more helpful to the studies themselves than the sight of a true patriot quitting himself self-sacrificingly, strenuously and unweariedly in the service of the State in its hour of need. And, no doubt, I shall find some opportunity later of showing how closely intertwined are the functions of noble poetry and good citizenship.[3]

Good citizenship for the Tractarians meant countering what Isobel Armstrong has referred to as 'a crisis of individualism', in which 'spiritual individualism becomes a form of the economic individualism' that plagued ' "busy" England'.[4] There was a visible need, from the perspective of the Tractarians, to intervene in this concern:

Strictly speaking, the Christian Church, as being a visible society, is necessarily a political power or party ... since there is a popular misconception, that Christians, and especially the Clergy, as such, have no concern in temporal affairs ... In truth, the Church was framed for the express purpose of interfering, or, (as irreligious men will say,) meddling with the world.[5]

The Tractarians felt the trauma of a nation in crisis keenly; indeed, the social conservativism that has been attributed to the movement can be read as a pacifist response to that trauma, seeking calm in the face of a nation that had not only seen riots throughout its own communities, but had also been the ventricle for millions of refugees fleeing war-torn, famine-worn nations from Continental Europe as well as Ireland. The affective nature of poetry was seen as key to creating empathy towards the community, as opposed to the 'isolation [that] becomes the counterpart of the pursuit of private gain',[6] while evoking perspective on the temporality of the world, and the consequent valuing of earthly wealth, as Procter's statement 'Nothing is our own' suggests.

For the Tractarians, a return to the form and order of poetry – indeed, the discipline of poetry – was an aesthetic means to find calm, as well as to connect, not just to a literary and intellectual heritage, but to a cultural heritage that enacted stability. Keble was conscious of the seeming hypocrisy in his departure from active pastoral ministry; however, at Oxford he would be teaching those intending to go into the ministry, and therefore he would be able to impart to them the values (which would become known as Tractarian) of poetry and form in theological understanding. For Keble, as for many of the Tractarians, poetry and religion were inherently linked. Keble's inaugural lecture articulates the criticism that is still levelled at the Tractarians: that they did not address key concerns of poverty and social inequalities. Stephen Prickett, for example, has continued the accusation of Tractarians as parochial and not using their seeming social power to petition for reform:

> this is not to say that many of the Tractarians were not personally philanthropic, but rather that in many cases their vision of social reform tended to stop at *personal* philanthropy. For men whose minds were so quick to think ecclesiastically on a national scale, it is noticeable that their social thought was usually parochial.[7]

However, while Prickett, among others,[8] condemns this vision as conservative, he fails to give full credence to the widespread disaffection the Tractarians felt towards the social institutions that had failed to solve the hunger and inequality that still plagued Britain. They held, as Simon Skinner succinctly states, 'the distinct conviction that social ills were, ultimately, unamenable to purely legislative remedies'.[9] The New Poor Law, the workhouse and the Reform Bill *in practice* did little to alleviate immediate suffering; indeed, they could be seen to increase it, while at the same time psychologically distancing people from poverty. The unionizing of parish relief, for instance, introduced by the New Poor Law, meant that individual parishes were no longer held directly responsible for relieving distress in their own community. Poor relief was thus bureaucratized, centralized and sanitized, making suffering and starvation more palatable and acceptable by distancing the direct offense of poverty from the local community's reach. Furthermore, as much as the extension of suffrage in 1832 was a progressive move, the violence leading to this reform can be too easily ignored when looking through the distancing lens of history: a violence to which the Tractarians felt all too proximate.

Rather than merely writing from a distance about political and economic theory, many of the leading Tractarians were working in communities, ministering to individuals whose lives were impacted by unrest and trying to inspire their congregations to care directly for the suffering in their parishes.

Skinner cites B. M. G. Reardon's observation that Tractarianism was 'a revival of practical religion' and argues, importantly, that 'historians of Tractarianism … have dwelt on the theological and the abstract at the expense of the pastoral and immediate'.[10] Edward Pusey's sermon of 1875, cited by both Prickett and S. C. Carpenter, speaks satirically of communities abdicating their personal responsibility to the poor:

> 'True, Lord, I denied myself nothing for thee; the times were changed, and I could not but change with them. I ate and drank, for thou too didst eat and drink with the publicans and sinners. I did not give to the poor, but I paid what I was compelled to the poor-rate, of the height of which I complained. I did not take in little children in thy name, but they were provided for. They were sent, severed indeed from father and mother, to the poorhouse, to be taught or no about thee, as might be. I did not feed thee when hungry. Political economy forbade it; but I increased the labour market with the manufacture of my luxuries.'[11]

While Prickett is dissatisfied with the fact that Pusey addresses himself to a congregation rather than to parliament in his call for reform, I argue instead that the Tractarians made a deliberate choice of audience in this regard, seeing the local community both as the key solution to social inequality and therefore unrest, and also as the audience most likely to respond because of its proximity to the concern. Pusey, like his counterparts, recognized the ease with which individuals could distance themselves from being concerned for the poor: if one paid their taxes, it was no longer their responsibility; it was up to the government or the Poor Law unions to solve the ills. The Tractarian vision is not only spiritual – as evidenced in Pusey's satirical mimicry of Christ's words – but economic and political: true social reform is more effective if activated at the grass roots level, implemented by individuals, based on personal conviction. Faceless institutions are not capable of empathetic connection, yet it is through this kind of affective response that social change can most powerfully and lastingly be instituted. The affective nature of poetry was identified by the Tractarians as a key literary and cultural form that could break through the rationalized hardness of political economic theory and challenge individuals to care for the poor dwelling in proximity to them, taking in the stranger as well as the neighbour.

It is understandable that in the face of poverty, which governments and no amount of public aid are able to temper, distancing oneself from the problem and laying blame on institutions becomes an appealing option. The horror of not being able to intervene effectively has a paralysing effect. Doing nothing becomes a viable option. In *On Touching* (2000), Derrida describes a similar kind of response when he describes Jean-Luc Nancy being 'paralyzed by emotion' when encountering Freud's representation of Psyche's death: 'he starts off, then begins again, more than once, compulsively, always beginning by freezing'.[12] Psyche's death is powerful in the context of my study, given that Psyche represents the human soul, or human feeling, and thus this moment is the death of empathy. Nancy's response, in Derrida's words, mirrors the unanswerable question of poverty in nineteenth-century Britain, wrapped up in multiple ways by Derrida's simple question, '[h]ow to touch upon the untouchable?'[13] The impossibility of touching – of being able to impact hunger and poverty in a broad sense – psychologically leads to a failure to have any kind of impact on hunger in a local area. It is this latter failure that the Tractarians sought to rectify, focusing not so much on the impossible distance between the present and the dream of equality but on the transient moment and what can be achieved in it. The Tractarians were preoccupied with mortality – with the transience of individual human existence; yet rather than concluding that time is too short for one to do anything, they held the conviction that because time is so short, one must do something *now*.

The poets I address were concerned with questions of how to respond with human feeling to the overwhelming problem of poverty, given that the established social institutions were seemingly powerless to impact its extent and, indeed, seemed to make it worse. Within the context of an overwhelming number of deaths as a result of poverty, not only with high infant mortality but also young men and women continuing to die from both starvation and illnesses associated with malnourishment, there was also the fear of becoming poor, alongside feelings of guilt for having and desiring worldly goods in the face of others' lack. Capitalism encouraged the perception of hunger, regardless of how prosperous one actually was: poverty and need were relative. This response can be seen as the heritage of political economy, following Adam Smith's claim that '[e]very man is rich or poor according to the degree in which he can afford to enjoy the necessaries, conveniences, and amusements in human life',[14] and Thomas Malthus's view in *Principles of Political Economy* (1820) that a flowing market requires a given society to believe itself perpetually in a state of want: '[n]o country with a very confined market, internal as well as external, has even been able to accumulate a large capital, because such a market prevents the formation of those wants and tastes'.[15] Pusey argues against this drive as a miasmatic disease: 'A spirit of enterprise infects all; it is the very air men live in; prosperity is our idol, the very measure of good or ill, the very end to which they refer all other ends; and what is this but their god?'[16] One of the key Tractarian periodical writers, Samuel Bosanquet, observed the effect of this idolatry on the nation in his review of W. Palmer's *A Compendious Ecclesiastical History* (1841) and E. Bickersteth's *The Dangers of the Church of Christ* (1840):

> Where once was sociable and merry England, we have care and caution in the countenance of the rich man, in the working man discontent, in the poor man misery and depression. Hospitality is nigh well forgotten ... classes are more separated and distinct from one another; men are more solitary, selfish and individualized.[17]

What the early political economists' theories do not account for is the individualistic, self-focused drive of capitalism, predicated on a fear of losing capital: in Smithian terms, it would seem as much a loss to lose amusements for one, as losing convenience or necessity is for another; but his list raises questions as to how these levels of wealth definition are established. Indeed, the definitions are necessarily slippery in the capitalist agenda. Regardless of definition, however, within a paradigm of want, self-interest in the name of survival prevails; thus the ideal of 'moral restraint' that Malthus calls for in his earlier *Essay on the Principle of Population* (1798) fails to have psychological currency against the compulsion to accumulate.[18]

## Accumulation, excess and hunger for worldly goods

As much as self-interest has been read in terms of evolutionary theory and economic necessity, it is also, crucially, a visceral, emotional response to the fear of starvation – a fear that was very present in mid-nineteenth-century Britain. In *The Afterlife of Property* (1994), Jeff Nunokawa refers to the 'inevitable loss of property in the nineteenth-century imagination' and the

Victorian conviction that 'nothing gold can stay'.[19] The task for the Tractarians was to inspire congregations not only with empathy for the poor, but with enough faith in divine provision to overpower the fear of their own loss. The perspective of faith counters fear, moderating emotion as an outworking of the Doctrine of Reserve. While this doctrine is seen primarily as a theological tool, regulating modes of worship and the dissemination of esoteric rites and tenets, or as a poetic tool that regulated literary form, it also worked effectively in the context of nineteenth-century practical life by guiding individuals to moderate their emotional responses to the world. As much as reserve operates on the idea that God will only reveal himself to believers to the degree that they are ready, applied to emotion, reserve acknowledges the limitations of human intervention in the temporal world and encourages the individual to conserve emotional energy in order to sustain activity.

The Doctrine of Reserve does not deny the existence – or, indeed, importance – of strong emotion, but encourages appropriate channels for emotion that will bring about active social intervention. For the Tractarians, this intervention was crucial: for as much as they were engaged with doctrinal matters and matters of church form, these preoccupations were grounded in very real social issues. For example, while the debate over pew rentals was considered by some as being about the positioning of the altar in the church, it was also a matter of addressing the social inequalities between parishioners – without the boxed pews, all parishioners, regardless of their worldly wealth, had equal sensory access to the church service. Twentieth-century evangelical historians have looked back on this debate as one of elitism. G. J. Cuming suggests that box pews 'were censured because they prevented the worshippers from being able to see the altar',[20] and that therefore the spiritual experience of the wealthy who occupied them was compromised by their obscured vision. Yet, as Skinner points out, the contemporary texts of the debate speak more of the social inequalities created through divisions of comfort: the box pews provided a level of comfort for those who could afford it, creating a social divide that was at odds with Christian teaching:

> The area of the nave, choir, and aisles is choked up with high square pews only half occupied, where the richer parishioners recline in solitary state, while the poor are too often left to stand in the gangways. This, perhaps the most odious practical abuse introduced into the Church during the last

two centuries, the Anglican party has the credit of successfully combating. 'Equality within the House of God,' has been from the first their motto and their practice.[21]

Equal seating was a reminder of the community members' equal footing before God. Furthermore, the founding Tractarians, coming from a background in parish ministry, continued to emphasize the importance of local ministry: caring for the sick and giving alms to the poor. Giving alms is not to say they did not support the idea of enabling the poor to find the capacity to provide for themselves, but this was understood as a long-term project; giving alms enabled them to meet specific needs in the present, but certainly did not preclude more slowly achieved long-term solutions.

Giving alms also had the added advantage of tempering the impulse to hoard one's possessions out of fear of loss. In this sense, Adelaide Procter's statement, 'Nothing is our own except our dead', while on the surface seeming extreme, actually has a moderating effect. While dire in its expression of poverty, Procter's 'Our Dead', in the reminder of 'Cruel life' and 'Cruel death', and that 'Justice pales; truth fades; stars fall from Heaven' (7–9), evokes the understanding that none are immune to falling from God's good grace, as much as all are potentially at risk of falling into poverty. Importantly Procter's initial acknowledgement that 'Nothing is our own: we hold our pleasures | Just a little while, ere they are fled' acts as a reminder that regardless of seeming worldly wealth, from the Christian perspective, wealth does not belong to us; individuals are merely stewards. This perspective can be extended to governments and institutions, and can be seen as a further criticism of governments that seek to accumulate surplus rather than distributing funds to the needy, as well as questioning their authority to decide which recipients are worthy of aid. Procter questions:

> Is Love ours, and do we dream we know it,
> Bound with all our heartstrings, all our own?
> Any cold and cruel dawn may show it,
> Shattered, desecrated, overthrown. (29–32)

The 'cold and cruel dawn' that could arise any day, for anyone, mirrors the cruel life and death: in the face of death, all are equal. This grand equality then bleeds into the inequalities of the man-made world of society, emphasizing the transience of earthly wealth – not just because an individual's time on earth is so short but also because in that life, treasures can be lost. Importantly, the use of 'desecrated' warns against the idolatrous worship of worldly possessions that can be lost so rapidly.

Procter gives an antidote to the fear of this kind of loss through the Christian creed of giving in her simply titled poem 'Give' (1854):[22]

> And the more thou spendest
> > From thy little store,
> With a double bounty,
> > God will give thee more. (21–4)

Procter's doctrine of giving is expressed through reserve. The difference in Procter's reserve, however, is that although she does enunciate the aesthetic of 'poetry as the vehicle of hidden emotion',[23] her emotional reserve or distance is created through her didacticism. Karen Dieleman argues that in many of Procter's poems, 'a moral-didactic voice takes precedence over genuine dialogue', and while Dieleman sees 'social and emotional fervor' in the poems being more dominant than 'theological precision', I would still argue that the didacticism allows Procter to moderate her own fervour, as well as that of her readers.[24] She directly challenges her reader to contextualize their position: the 'little store' may or may not be small; however, the *perceived* smallness reveals the fear of loss – that one cannot afford to give. Procter's faith in God's provision moderates the fear of loss so that one can act and give from what one has in the moment, rather than fearing potential future loss, recognizing that because the provision is God's, the individual is merely the steward of that store.

As much as Procter entreats her reader to trust in God's provision, such faith is not always achievable in the temporal world, where the evidence of loss persists. The paradox between trusting in an invisible God's provision and understanding that 'there but for the grace of God go I' establishes an uneasy emotional reserve and contains echoes of classifying the deserving and undeserving poor in an attempt to moderate the threat of poverty. Further, just as political economy saw accumulation of wealth as a result of exertion and effort and poverty as the result of idleness, lack could also be seen as a result of not trusting God. Such a conclusion establishes a myth of control and distance: 'I will not be poor *like them* because I trust God.' An even more disturbing and distancing conclusion would be that *none* of the poor are 'deserving' of help, because their poverty is their own fault. The Anglo-Catholic poet refuses to allow such distancing to occur. Just as they force their reader to face their own mortality, they also compel them to face their tenuous state within the temporal world. In a similar vein to Procter, although allegorical where Procter is direct, Christina Rossetti's 'An Old-World Thicket' (1881)[25] contends with the tension between faith and fear, providing an extended exploration of the struggle to moderate the fear of loss.

In her epigraph, 'Una selva oscura' (A dark forest), Rossetti uses sensory deprivation to establish the pervasiveness of hunger. The hunger for the visual, the key distance sense, emphasizes the temporality of the individual's experience and an overall sense of absence and loss. Ironically, in trying to find ways to see when vision is depleted, the proximate becomes increasingly unreachable: 'ways of seeing are also ways of not touching'.[26] Indeed, the distance and proximate senses are inverted, with vision brought close in its limitations, while later in the poem, taste – the most proximate sense because it takes its subject into the body – is aesthetically distanced into the 'Sweetness of beauty' that moves the poetic voice 'to despair' (46). This removal to the visual and to metaphor creates a sense of dark isolation, while the loss of the visual also challenges its necessity. The inversion of the senses calls into question the individual's understanding of the temporal world, for the sensory experience is shown to be incomplete. The light that is available is limited, written in terms of shade and the 'unseen sun', suggesting the need to have faith that the light is there – that vision is possible – even if the poetic speaker cannot see it:

> The shade wherein they revelled was a shade
>     That danced and twinkled to the unseen sun;
>     Branches and leaves cast shadows one by one,
>         And all their shadows swayed
> In breaths of air that rustled and that played. (26–30)

That the indentations of the lines stretch the limits but return, following the compressed penultimate line, to the original point creates a visual representation of the space of poetic reserve, with Rossetti endeavouring to find the light beyond the shade. Similarly, the faith that is maintained through the rhyme scheme with 'shade', 'swayed' and 'played' provides a trajectory from darkness to doubt, before finally finding another sensory pathway to belief through the auditory rustling of leaves: playing returns to a kind of childlike trust and faith. Sound begins to mitigate the obscured sight, revealing a capacity to adapt to the limitations of the world.

The beginning thirty-five lines of the poem establish the tension of faith in the invisible eternal from the perspective of material, temporal doubt. While Kirstie Blair has argued that 'when Victorian poetry speaks of faith, it tends to do so in steady and regular rhythms; when it speaks of doubt, it is correspondingly more likely to deploy irregular, unsteady, unbalanced rhythms',[27] this delineation is complicated in Tractarian poetry that deliberately exists in a space of tension between faith and doubt. This narrow space becomes the channel of reserve that is typical of Tractarian poetry. In Rossetti's work, this space is created formatively through the way in which she maintains her tight rhyme schemes, designating faith, but it is disrupted by frequent irregularity of rhythm. This form relates to the 'tension between exploration and hesitation' that Andrew Armond identifies in Rossetti's poetry, which aligns with the tension between the material world and the unknowable God.[28] In 'An Old World Thicket', there is an attempt to reconcile the seen and the unseen world through visual obscurity, and this sensory confusion is complicated further by the uncertain consciousness of the poetic vision:

> Awake or sleeping (for I know not which)
>     I was or was not mazed within a wood
>     Where every mother-bird brought up her brood
>         Safe in some leafy niche
> Of oak or ash, of cypress or of beech,
>
> Of silvery aspen trembling delicately,
>     Of plane or warmer-tinted sycamore,
>     Of elm that dies in secret from the core,
>         Of ivy weak and free,
> Of pines, of all green lofty things that be. (1–10)

Not only is the poetic voice in an uncertain abstract dream space between waking and sleeping, the sensory materiality is doubly confused, not just in the 'was or was not' presence but in the temporal sense of being lost, or 'mazed' in the wood that might or might not have existed. In this way, temporally and spiritually, the poem opens with the anxiety of human vulnerability in an uncertain world. This vulnerability is accentuated by the excess of trees in which the birds dwell, while the obscurity of vision, the lack of trust in vision, speaks to the individual's awareness of their limitations of knowing. Because it is obscured, it is out of her control, and any perceived control is false. The visual compression formed by the indentation, in spite of the lines ending more or less in the same place, and the anaphora of 'Of' in the lines suggesting each of the trees, echoes the implosion of the 'elm that dies in secret from the core'. By juxtaposing the elm with the apparent moral weakness of the 'ivy weak and free', its sprawling branches overwhelming and imposing upon its surrounds, the elm's reserve in the face of death is honoured from a distance. The speaker seems to want to inhabit both: she longs for the freedom of the ivy, but remains drawn to the exquisite private death of the elm.

The excess suggested in the cataloguing of the trees brings Rossetti's reserve and spiritual purpose to the fore. Betsy Winakur Tontiplaphol identifies a similar 'spirit of accumulation' in the works of Tennyson and Hopkins as a powerful way to catalogue 'material pleasures, natural and commercial'.[29] The overwhelming variety of trees, and the way they loom over Rossetti's scene, provides an allegory for the overwhelming temporal world, allowing a comparison to be drawn between the birds that inhabit them and human society. Rossetti's poem becomes an extended reference to Christ's words:

> Take no thought for your life, what ye shall eat, or what ye shall drink; nor yet for your body, what ye shall put on. Is not the life more than meat, and the body more than raiment? Behold the fowls of the air: for they sow not, neither do they reap, nor gather into barns; yet your heavenly Father feedeth them. Are ye not much better than they? (Mt. 6:25–6)

Through observing the birds, Rossetti's spiritual and poetic reserve works to moderate human desire and fear: 'Such birds they seemed as challenged each desire; | … Such mirth they made … | They seemed to speak more wisdom than we speak, | To make our music flat | And all our subtlest reasonings wild or weak' (11, 16, 18–20). In an economic reading of the poem, these 'subtlest reasonings' can be seen as the excesses of capitalism: the compulsion to hoard or the unwillingness to share what one has with a neighbour (or stranger) in need. Such an understanding is justified by the lines that follow, which are a direct reference to the verses from the Gospel of Matthew:

> Their meat was nought but flowers like butterflies,
> >  With berries coral-coloured or like gold;
> > Their drink was only dew, which blossoms hold
> > > Deep where honey lies;
> Their wings and tails were lit by sparkling eyes. (21–5)

Reserve is maintained through 'nought but' and 'only dew', juxtaposed with the luxurious images of coral and gold, and the deepness of the blossoms. In this vision of godly provision, there is a tempered plenty: with daily access to food and drink, there is no need either to store or to indulge in immediate excess. Similarly the provision of water to nourish the land is presented as a constant stream, running deep, not given to the extremes of flood and drought:

> A sound of waters neither rose nor sank,
> > And spread a sense of freshness through the air;
> > It seemed not here or there, but everywhere,
> > > As if the whole earth drank,
> Root fathom deep and strawberry on its bank. (31–5)

The ideal of this vision is overturned, however, by the insertion of human experience from line 36:

> But I who saw such things as I have said,
> > Was overdone with utter weariness;
> > And walked in care, as one whom fears oppress
> > > Because above his head
> Death hangs, or damage, or the dearth of bread. (36–40)

Rossetti's delay in embodying the impoverished figure until this point plays with her reader's sympathies, reinforcing that 'damage' and 'dearth' are potentially as inevitable as death. She directly challenges Adam Smith's optimistic view in *The Theory of Moral Sentiments* (1759) that it is through 'looking around and admir[ing] the condition of the rich' that man is compelled to change his situation, leading to labour and productivity.[30] In Smith's view, the individual human nature 'rouses and keeps in continual motion the industry of mankind' out of his self-interested 'ambition' to acquire property.[31] Rossetti, though, shows instead the intense isolation for the figure observing the provision of the birds, leading to anger and despair rather than industry: 'Sweetness of beauty moved me to despair, | Stung me to anger by its mere content' (46–7). Rather than Smith's ideal, Rossetti reveals the cruelty of the world in 'Brimmed full my cup, and stripped me empty and bare' (50) and continues:

> For all that was but showed what all was not,
>     But gave clear proof of what might never be;
>     Making more destitute my poverty,
>         And yet more blank my lot,
> And me much sadder by its jubilee. (51–5)

The echo of the poem's opening obscurity brings painful clarity in 'all that was but showed what all was not'. Instead of Smithian progress, the speaker becomes self-isolating in Derridean paralysis and deliberate sensory deprivation: 'Therefore I sat me down: for wherefore walk? | And closed mine eyes: for wherefore see or hear?' (56–7). Crucially, the deprivation of the distance senses of sight and sound here holds further meaning for the poor: there seems little purpose in maintaining the ability to see and hear when one cannot touch or taste, except to punish oneself further: 'Self stabbing self with keen lack-pity knife' (45).

As the birds grow silent, Rossetti's impoverished speaker turns to an excess of despair: the constant ease of water becomes the 'drip of widening waters' that 'seemed to weep', and 'All fountains sobbed and gurgled as they sprang' (66–7). The agony becomes a 'universal sound of lamentation', with 'Nought else but all creation | Moaning and groaning wrung by pain and fear' (71, 74–5). In the seeming absence of divine provision, figured in the calls of the birds, the vision left is one of repeated 'Ingathering wrath' (79–80), with the speaker's heart giving in to 'the misery of its doom', arising as 'a rebel against light' (76–7). The moaning and groaning of Rossetti's diction evokes the desperation of hunger within the nineteenth-century context, in which without hope that hunger would be met, desperation in communities turned to violence – from the Flour Wars in the late eighteenth century to the machine-breakers and reform rioters of the 1830s, leading to the underlying, persistent fear of people movements, including Chartism, throughout the 1840s. Hope is necessary to temper desperation; yet in the absence of this kind of reserve, violence arises with bitterness against others and against oneself: 'All impotent, all hateful, and all hate, | That kicks and breaks itself against the bolt | … And vainly shakes, and cannot shake the gate' (82–3, 85). Such self-violence, which prefigures the social, collective violence in the mind of mid-century Britain, is unproductive: it provides no release or relief. In this state of excess, the poetic voice becomes 'A random thing … without a mark, | Racing without a goal, | Adrift upon life's sea without an ark' (93–5).

Rossetti's speaker is found in a paralysis between life and death, first questioning the purpose of her life, then why she should work, followed by why she should die (101–5). In this state, the materiality of breathing, working, or even dying, seems to have no place in her existence. In spite of an underlying, persistent hunger, figured in 'there gnaws a worm – | Haply, there gnaws a grief' (108–9), the overwhelming nature of temporality leads to emptiness and *ennui*. The 'ripe fruits' that 'Surely … tremble on their bough' are distant and abstract, not visible in 'the perpetual Now' (121, 124). The speaker seeks to dissolve into immateriality, becoming 'Birthless, and deathless, void of start or stop, | Void of repentance, void of hope and fear, | Of possibility, alternative, | Of all that ever made us bear to live' (125–8), yet the exhaustion of this excess is made evident:

> Rage to despair; and now despair had turned
>     Back to self-pity and mere weariness,
> With yearnings like a smouldering fire that burned,
>     And might grow more or less,
> And might die out or wax to white excess. (136–40)

It is important to note in the structure at this point that the indentations alternate and do not press as far, reflecting exhaustion and the inability to sustain an effort towards compression or reserve. The back-and-forth of this smaller movement mirrors the speaker's despair. In this way, Rossetti shows the dangers of giving into excess – the exertion of inner turmoil can be as debilitating as the external circumstances with which one is faced.

Rossetti does not allow the poem to end in a state of doubt. With the caesura after 'Then I looked up' (146), she returns to a vision of faith and likewise returns to the earlier formation of her stanzas, reflecting order and calm while figuratively looking up to the divine. The transition made at this point is not just a restoration of faith but a reconnection with community, and a new recognition of aesthetic sensory engagement as the treasures of nature are revealed: 'Each twig was tipped with gold, each leaf was edged | And veined with gold from the gold-flooded west' (161–2). This gold is the display of the wealth of nature, and therefore the divine, as opposed to the tainted wealth of the temporal world. Although this gold is seasonal, like divine daily provision, there is more order and surety in the natural flow, while the gold of the world is corrupted by capitalism's impetus to accumulate and hoard. The gold of nature is inherent, flowing through the leaves, and thereby ordered and moderated. Turning from the nesting birds, the speaker now sees a flock of sheep heading homeward, 'at peace | With one another and with every one' (169–70). This pastoral image (in every sense of the word) meaningfully acknowledges the importance that the Tractarian movement placed on the parish community. The 'patriarchal ram' that leads 'all his kin' (171–2), as much as it operates as a figure for Christ, can also be seen as the parish priest, emphasizing the importance of local ministry and local community. The last lines emphasize that the flock 'kept together, journeying well', 'Journeying together' and 'Still journeying toward the sunset and their rest' (175, 177, 180). Although an allegory of God's divine provision, Rossetti also moderates an excessive view of faith by ending with the important space of community in the temporal world: it is through community that divine provision is enacted.

Rossetti's vision of a tempered, engaged community resists the fear and self-focus of capitalist individualism. In a similar manner, albeit in a much darker, unforgiving conception of the dangers of selfish greed, Gerard Manley Hopkins's 'A Soliloquy of One of the Spies left in the Wilderness' (written in July 1864) contends with worldly desire and fear of loss in opposition to faith in God's daily (economized) provision. Hopkins calls for a more austere adherence to reserve and moderation, in response to the social hunger for worldly luxuries, which aligns with his growing asceticism. The language and forms of excess are also much more prevalent, evoking a violence and assault that mirrors, in Hopkins's view, the dangers of disobeying God or lacking faith. Importantly, there is no redemption in Hopkins's Old Testament poem, and his evocation of a pre-Christ world suggests his belief that nineteenth-century Britain has forgotten Christ. The spy in the wilderness becomes a figure for capitalist, imperialist Britain, hungry for excess and intent on the isolating qualities of doubt, mistrust and self-worshipping individualism. In a letter to Robert Bridges in 1871, the now Jesuit Hopkins wrote,

> Horrible to say, in a manner I am a Communist ... It is a dreadful thing for the greatest and most necessary part of a very rich nation to live a hard life without dignity, knowledge, comforts, delight, or hopes in the midst of plenty – which they make ... England has grown hugely wealthy but this wealth has not reached the working classes.[32]

Hopkins's disgust with selfish greed and the pride of an England that has little concern for the poor is evident in 'A Soliloquy', in which he asserts the dangers, isolation and tastelessness of individualism. David Howes and Marc Lalonde suggest that taste moves towards an 'emphasis ... on quality rather than quantity' in the social mobility of the middle classes,[33] enacted by capitalist endeavour; however, in the midst of this refinement of taste, the impetus towards greed that Hopkins sees reflects more the descent into barbarism that Mark M. Smith describes, in which taste is overlooked for the sake of mere satiety. As much as '[h]unger threaten[s] to catapult man back in space and time, rendering him more animal than human', and further that '[s]carcity of food peel[s] back civilized man's exterior and reveal[s] an animal that would eat anything to survive',[34] persistently overlooking or denying taste (in the literal sense, but also in the metaphorical sense of aesthetic judgement) represents a denial of human feeling for the sake of personal gain. It is a perversion of unnecessary hunger. Tastelessness, then, the rejection of sensory taste, is used literally in Hopkins's poem to express the unattractiveness and inappropriateness of the excess and emptiness of capitalism.

While Rossetti uses the biblical image of God providing for the birds of the air, which could be seen as God in nature, Hopkins begins his poem with a biblical example of God's miraculous intervention: the daily provision of manna from heaven as Moses led the people of Israel out of Egypt into the desert on the way to Canaan, the Promised Land. By evoking the narrative of the Israelites' disaffection with God, Hopkins calls into question capitalist democracy's use of happiness as the calculus for society's success. As Armstrong paraphrases Hopkins's perspective, 'A rational account of happiness is merely a materialist account of comfort and amusement for the masses and leads directly to cultural decadence.'[35] This assessment explains what Blair has referred to as the 'deliberate eschewal of excitement and individuality' in Catholic poetics[36] and what Tontiplaphol identifies as Hopkins's 'vexed regard for pleasure'.[37] The insatiable appetite of humans, which is the premise of Regenia Gagnier's *The Insatiability of Human Wants* (2000), means that happiness through consumption is not only relative but also impossible, and will therefore only lead to greed and dissatisfaction. Hopkins comments on Britain's insatiable appetite and lack of satisfaction with its wealth from the opening lines:

> He feeds me with His manna every day:
> My soul does loathe it and my spirit fails.
> A press of winged things comes down this way:
>     The gross flock call them quails.
> Into my hand he gives a host for prey,
>     Come up, Arise and slay. (1–6)

For Hopkins, the same attitude that crucified Christ – the host – is that which despises the daily provision of God. For Britain, daily provision is not enough; the quails, which God gave when the Israelites complained of only receiving bread (the staples to survive), represent the luxuries of the world – the desire for more, for an excess, which becomes a violent, self-destructive desire: 'Sicken'd and thicken'd by the glare and sand, | Who would drink water from a stony rock?' (7–8). The assonance of 'sicken'd' and 'thicken'd' is oppressive, grotesquely pushing against the limits of reserve, as does the prideful rejection of the taste of water that comes from stone. While in the biblical passage, the people of Israel drank happily from the rock that Moses struck to draw water, in Hopkins's poem the spy rejects this sustenance for the memory of Egypt: 'Behold at Elim wells on every hand! | And seventy palms there stand. | Egypt, the valley of our pleasance, there! | Your parched nostrils snuff Egyptian air' (11–14).

Thirst and hunger, distanced through olfaction, are made to seem insatiable. Hopkins figures England as the Israelites, who would prefer slavery in Egypt, the nation of luxury and excess, over spiritual and physical freedom. His disdain for excess is made evident with 'Wasteful wide huge-girthèd Nile | Unbakes my pores, and streams, and makes all fresh' (19–20), at which point he interjects his own voice: 'Ye sandblind! Slabs of water many a mile | Blaze on him all this while' (23–4). The spy fails to see God's provision because he is too preoccupied with remembering the luxuries of Egypt, while forgetting that even when he was in Egypt, because he was a slave, he had no more access to those luxuries than he does in the desert. Hopkins's questioning, 'Must you be gorged with proof? Did ever sand | So trickle from your hand?' (29–30) satirically appeals to the paradigm of excess from which the spy cannot escape. Reminding the spy of his slavery of Egypt, in which he was charged to 'Bring in the glistery straw' (34), Hopkins states: 'Here are sweet messes without price or worth, | And never thirst or dearth' (35–6), yet the latter line is ironic: certainly there is plenty, but the 'sweet messes' are disordered, sweet without substance. In this way, Hopkins speaks to an England that he sees as sacrificing heaven for the sake of worldly pleasures. The nation is enslaved by capitalism, greed and the fear of loss, just like the Israelites who complained of their freedom and sought to go back into slavery where they knew that their bellies would be filled without having to trust in a divine daily providence. Because of their excess, the provisions in Egypt are described as a sensory assault:

> The trumpet waxes loud: tired are your feet.
> Come by the flesh-pots: you shall sit unshod
>     And have your fill of meat;
> Bring wheat-ears from the loamy stintless sod,
>     To a more grateful god. (50–4)

The spy is lost in his blindness and pride, not even recognizing his own lack in 'Go then: I am contented here to lie' (55). Hopkins speaks prophetically to an England entranced by political economy's empty promise of progress: 'Sure, this is Nile: I sicken, I know not why, | And faint as though to die' (59–60). The danger at this point is in not recognizing the hunger that makes one ill. Rossetti's 'The World' (1854)[38] expresses a similar danger:

> By day she wooes me to the outer air,
>     Ripe fruits, sweet flowers, and full satiety:
>     But thro' the night, a beast she grins at me,
> A very monster void of love and prayer. (5–9)

As much as it can be dangerous for one not to recognize one's own hunger, and therefore the need to sate it, the other danger of complacency is that when one has enough, one does not recognize the possibility that others might be hungry or that it is necessary to do something to try to meet the needs of others. Both

Hopkins and Rossetti, in resisting capitalism through reserve, are resisting the complacency created by plenty that makes one blind to the rest of the world's suffering. However, they both acknowledge that this complacency is often a result of feeling guilt over what one has, as well as the sense of powerlessness in the face of overwhelming need. It is one thing to help a solitary stranger, but when there are hungry people on every street corner, the individual tends to draw back, feeling inadequate to contend with that extreme level of want. The Tractarian vision resists this withdrawal, focusing instead on meeting needs in the moment. By facilitating the Doctrine of Reserve, they seek to avoid being overwhelmed by the multitudes through intimate engagement and accepting their proximity to the poor.

## 'Impersonal intimacy' and economizing emotion

As much as Armstrong argues that empathy 'is the expressive poet's outwards flow of emotion which attaches to and elides with the solid external world,'[39] it is this same empathy that allows the individual to connect with society and, importantly, with the poor. Yet when the suffering is overwhelming, the problem remains as to how one is to remain engaged. In the *Tracts for the Times* (1833–41), Isaac Williams speaks of the Doctrine of Reserve in terms of 'the wonderful and mysterious economy of God'.[40] The idea of economy is much broader in this sense than financial matters, extending into ideas of the earth's economy, measured by seasons, as well as ideas of natural justice. Where this vision of economy differs from a capitalist economy is that while capitalism envisages an exponential trajectory, 'God's economy', or the earth's economy, is figured in cyclical, seasonal or oscillating terms, which creates a sense of moderation rather than excess. Restraint is valued in these economic terms and, crucially, strong emotion is brought under this remit. Indeed, throughout Williams's two tracts on Reserve, he persistently suggests that excessive emotional display is evidence of shallow feeling, while reserved expression suggests depth – a response to the feelings being too deep or profound to express adequately: '[w]hen that reserve is cast aside, there is a want of true and deep feeling; and this may be seen in the rejection of strong, typical, and figurative, and, therefore, half-secret expressions with which deep feeling is apt to clothe itself'.[41] Even more compelling, he suggests that the 'strength of ungoverned passion, ending in a total want of control, is emphatically called "adding drunkenness to thirst"'.[42] Although using the metaphor of thirst, rather than hunger, this reference speaks to uncontrollable appetites, hunger, addiction and excess, expressing an anxiety of unfulfilled desire and a lack of self-regulation. The Doctrine of Reserve acts to moderate this kind of insatiable chaos: rather than being written in the negative connotations of repression, reserve in this sense involves learning how to channel emotions effectively and economically. It is no coincidence that the metaphor of streams and channelling bodies of water is common in Anglo-Catholic poetry. Anglo-Catholic reserve is about economizing affect: that is, moderating an emotional response for the purpose of sustained outward action, rather than an explosive emotion that either burns out or paralyses the individual who feels it, thus rendering them ineffectual.

A specific problem identified within the ideal of reserve is how to *maintain* reserve, or even if it is appropriate to maintain reserve in extreme circumstances. Many poets influenced by the Tractarian movement were preoccupied with mortality, arguably the most extreme circumstance of humanity. They longed for heaven, but they also recognized the shortness of life, and therefore the short time an individual has to act in the world. In a very human manner, they also contended with grief, doubt and fear. It stands to reason, then, that as much as they sought to maintain reserve, they also challenge its value. Tontiplaphol provides a provocative example of this challenge in her discussion of Tennyson's *In Memoriam* (1850) as she describes 'the difficulty in maintaining a worldview so gentle and loose in the face of death's ostensibly all-consuming totality'.[43] Hunger is present in the representation of grief – 'heart and ear were fed | To hear him' – in what Tontiplaphol refers to as a 'multi-faceted gustatory metaphor'.[44] Similarly, grief in Coventry Patmore's 'A Farewell' (1888)[45] strains spatially against reserve through 'In our opposèd paths to persevere. | Go thou to East, I West' (8–9). The departure necessitated by mortality is depicted in this distance, but the resulting emotional pain is constrained by reserve in the regular iambic rhythm, as well as by the conceit of a compass – evoking John Donne's 'A Valediction: Forbidden Mourning' (1633) – which conveys both the cyclical nature of life and seasons and the never-ending enclosure of a circle:

> And even through faith of still averted feet,
> Making full circle of our banishment,
> Amazed meet;
> The bitter journey to the bourne so sweet
> Seasoning the termless feast of our content
> With tears of recognition never dry. (20–5)

Death and grief in the context of faith in life after death are bittersweet and paradoxical, with the bitterness and sweetness separated to the east and west of the line they share, as much as banishment and meeting are simultaneously made impossible. Double negatives pervade Patmore's poem, layering and nuancing grief, and the resulting disengagement from feeling becomes potentially disconcerting, as much as its mission is reserve. Patmore declares, 'The nursling Grief, | Is dead' (14–15), as though death perversely consumes what it has nourished. Grief is strangely lost, then loss is compounded in the loss of tears: 'no dews blur our eyes' (16), poignantly suggesting that in the passing of grief the loved one is lost anew in an aestheticized distancing of emotion. The conceit of a feast continues the tense paradox of the sensory and aestheticized consumption of death, depicting the desire to use reserve to find a way through the tensions between having faith in reuniting after death, while experiencing the very real and immediate pain of loss. Instead of losing feeling entirely, the speaker seeks the never-ending 'tears of recognition' rather than the tears of grief that cease.

Reserve provides a channel between fear and grief, while a differentiation between fear and grief is used as a means to reserve. This idea is evident in Tennyson's 'Supposed Confessions' (1830),[46] in which fear and grief ironically moderate each other in the face of mourning and the recognition of one's own mortality:

> And at a burial to hear
> The creaking cords which wound and eat
> Into my human heart, whene'er
> Earth goes to earth, with grief, not fear,
> With hopeful grief, were passing sweet. (35–9)

Death's consumption of the griever's heart finds sweetness through the hope of eternity. Yet the hunger of death and grief inevitably devours; and in this mode, the poet clings to the tension between reserve and strong feelings by channelling fraught emotion through the restrictions of poetic form. As Blair acknowledges, while strong emotion has a place, it is 'always potentially dangerous and [has] to be handled carefully'.[47] Isaac Williams himself connected poetic feeling to reserve: '[s]omething of this kind always accompanies all strong and deep feeling, so much so that indications of it have been considered the characteristic of genuine poetry, as distinguishing it from that which is only fictitious of poetic feeling'.[48] In response to this assertion, I engage with the poetic techniques the poets use to aid reserve as well as the ways in which they push poetic boundaries to interrogate the definitions of authenticity, reserve, moderation and excess in emotional display. In this way they question ideas of authentic emotion and the value of affective restraint, as opposed to affective excess, while exploring the necessity of distance in being able to respond effectively to want and grief, for ultimately this is necessary in order to remain empathetically and intimately connected to the community.

F. Elizabeth Gray observes that 'the devotional poet's project to establish intimacy is undertaken through textual and technical means traditional of lyric', emphasizing the way in which the predominance of the first-person singular pronoun, in its '[s]ubjective, personal and particular' mode, 'allows the speaker to thematise her relationship with and emotions toward her God'.[49] However, while Gray acknowledges the 'communality' in the devotional lyric, she sees the poetic speaker's relationship with the reader as a 'secondary focus', even though she admits it is 'unignorable'.[50] In examining the expression of grief, though, I suggest that intimacy with the reader – this communality – is far more significant in understanding devotional poetry, particularly in the Anglo-Catholic context, in which shared reading, like the shared eating of the Eucharist, was central to devotional structures. While a great deal of criticism has focused on the dialogue evoked between speaker and God, my focus is more on the intimacy evoked between speaker and reader achieved through an emphasis on the 'you' in the poetry as much as the 'I'. In *Second Person Singular* (2014), Emily Harrington argues that there is an 'intimacy inherent in the use of the second person singular' that 'indicates the most basic elements of a relationship: it points to the simultaneous existence of an individual and of more than one' and that, crucially, this acknowledgement entails 'rapprochement, yes; but also distance'.[51] Harrington's perception of an affective connection that is formed ironically through a recognition of distance provocatively evokes both Derrida's Law of Tact and the agenda of the Doctrine of Reserve. Derrida's law states that

> one must touch without touching. In touching, touching is forbidden: do not touch or tamper with the thing itself, do not touch on what there is to touch ... *Respect commands us to keep our distance* ... The untouchable is thus kept at a distance by the gaze, ... or in any case at an attentive distance, in order to watch out carefully, to guard ... against touching, affecting, corrupting.[52]

Derrida's use of 'gaze' draws attention to the possible problematic assertion of power relations in the recognition of a subjective Other, and this difficulty must be acknowledged in terms of High Church philanthropy – it is not a problem easily contended with when thinking about the economic inequalities that necessitated their philanthropic role. However, if Derrida's Law of Tact is applied, the 'attentive distance' is crucial to creating respect, and therefore agency, for the hungry Other. Crucially, Harrington observes, 'only with that separation can they form a bond; otherwise, their link would be mere unification or absorption'.[53] Tact requires a distance that is respectful of the agency of the needy; and in this way, the reticence of touch prevents their corruption – they are not redefined in terms of the gaze but are interacted with in terms of an affective sensibility that is conscious not to abuse the recognized vulnerability of the Other: 'one should understand tact, not in the common sense of the tactile, but in the sense of knowing how to touch *without* touching, without touching *too much*, where touching is already too much'.[54]

Derrida's Law of Tact becomes even more intriguing as he directly relates tact to hunger and appetite:

> Touching ... *abstains* from touching on what it touches, and within the abstinence retaining it at the heart of its desire and need, in an inhibition truly constituting its appetite, it eats without eating what is its nourishment, touching, without touching, what it comes to cultivate, elevate, educate, drill.[55]

One cannot taste or eat without touching with the tongue; indeed, touch is understood by Derrida to be the most salient of the senses. For this reason, the way in which he writes of abstention – regulating, moderating and controlling touch in terms of appetite – becomes crucial to human interaction.

As much as physical hunger has been deemed 'the very fire of life, underlying all impulses to labour',[56] Derrida's use of the metaphor of appetite, and touch 'eat[ing] without eating what is its nourishment', essentially posits that tact, incorporating a certain level of spiritual and social hunger, is just as necessary to the formation of human understanding. Furthermore, the way in which he engages tact in terms of cultivation, elevation, education and drilling suggests a physical and affective restraint that echoes Williams's understanding of the Doctrine of Reserve:

> that reserve, or retiring delicacy, which exists naturally in a good man, unless injured by external motives, and which is or course the teaching of God through him ... It is the very protection of all sacred and virtuous principle, and which, like the bloom which indicates life and freshness, when once lost cannot be restored ... Every thing which has God for its end gives rise to feelings which do not admit of expression.[57]

Both 'impersonal intimacy' and the Law of Tact speak to Williams's 'retiring delicacy', which, revealing the Catholic influence on the Tractarian movement, emphasizes nature and an innate goodness in humans that can be 'injured by external motives'. This concept externalizes emotions such as greed and fear, relating them to perceivably corrupt ideologies (such as capitalism or political economy), but blame can also be attributed to external factors or circumstances, such as famine or the memory of it. Reserve can be read in terms of impersonal intimacy or tact, seeking to enable individuals to distance themselves enough from the suffering of others – past or present – in order to respond. The separation enacted through impersonal intimacy means that instead of identifying too closely with the hungry, or grieving through fear, thinking 'that could be me', the focus is shifted from the self onto the one who is actually suffering. In responding to others' needs, questions arise concerning the value of investing emotion when one could fail, either by not being able to change the other's circumstances or most dramatically through the other's death. The alternative, however, is to isolate oneself from the community, which ironically has the potential to create the very vulnerable circumstances feared. In the context of the Doctrine of Reserve, these fears are mediated by faith in God's daily provision in the temporal world and the eternal perspective gained through the hope of heaven. By regulating the fear of starvation and loss, and the fear of death through a doctrine of eternity, the Tractarian vision seeks to turn self-centred despair into community-focused action.

The poetry addressed in this section is not so much about physical hunger but about social and spiritual hunger, and contending with overwhelming grief. The fear of physical hunger is tied to social and spiritual hungers and, for the Tractarians, such fear always returns to the fear of death: the death of others as well as one's own death, and seeing one's own death *in* the death of others – an example of dangerously crossing the line drawn by impersonal intimacy. In a social and historical context of various famines and food shortages, death by starvation or malnutrition then becomes a double blow. Yet hope is positioned as the remedy for grief as much as the loss of hope is grief's cause. Hope then becomes the essence of Christ's Bread of Life (Jn 6:35), which is gestured towards in Williams's tract:

> And from one petition in the Lord's Prayer, 'Give us this day our daily bread,' taken in conjunction with our LORD's explanation of the 'only true bread', and with that His injunction of our not seeking the bread that perisheth, in another place, we are necessarily led on to seek for more than the letter through the whole of the Prayer.[58]

In response to the fear of physical hunger, the Tractarian model suggests a deferral to spiritual hunger, which moderates the material fear. Both the physical and spiritual on this point turn on the concept of death: physical hunger can lead to starvation but the resulting physical death leads to the spiritual satiety of heaven – eternal life. However, this dynamic does not necessarily mitigate the grief of losing a loved one. Tennyson's 'The Two Voices' (written 1833–4, published 1842) and Procter's 'Life in Death and Death in Life' (1858) both confront the grief of losing a very close friend. Procter's poem was originally published in *Household Words* as 'Two Dark Days', so it is interesting to note that both Tennyson and Procter deliberately evoke the binary of life and death to express the impossible divide from their loved one. This divide accentuates the intensity of grief and has implications for reserve and social action.

Although Tennyson began writing 'The Two Voices' before news of Arthur Hallam's death in 1833, with the title 'Thoughts of Suicide', his friend's death affected the ways in which he elaborated and concluded the poem. Whereas in the earlier 'Supposed Confessions' the dialogue is a much more direct Job-like complaint to a divine being, 'The Two Voices' blurs across the human and the divine, even perverting the divine in the face of grief. Both voices belong to the speaker, as he attempts to find a reason to continue living in light of the pain of his friend's death. Although Broad Church in persuasion, not only is the influence of reserve evident in Tennyson's work, he articulates with critical aesthetic accuracy the way in which reserve is achieved:

> 'I cannot hide that some have striven,
> Achieving calm, to whom was given
> The joy that mixes man with Heaven.' (208–10)

It is the mixing of temporal and eternal perspectives – mixing 'man with Heaven' – that enables the tenuous balance between faith and doubt that undergirds the Doctrine of Reserve. However, despair is still evident in that the joy that achieves this blending is seen as a gift bestowed, rather than something that can be cultivated. Tennyson seems to challenge the Doctrine of Reserve directly as he writes that such who have achieved this calm were 'by secret transport led, | Ev'n in the charnels of the dead' (214–15). As much as he shared many of the pacifist, anti-revolutionary (or, arguably, anti-reform) views of the Tractarians, Tennyson was sceptical of secret knowledge that appeared to deny access, particularly, in this case, to tranquillity. These lines cross over into a resentment of those who have mysteriously found out the impossible secret. However, the voice struggling to retain faith still recognizes the necessity of this calm, especially in the way it enables productive action and channelled, sustained energy:

> 'Which they did accomplish their desire,
> Bore and forbore, and did not tire,
> Like Stephen, an unquenched fire.' (217–19)

While evoking Roman Catholic undertones in the adoration of the saint, Tennyson also suggests a despairing chasm of believing oneself to be separated from such agency and energy. Even so, the tightness of the rhyme scheme fights for reserve within, in opposition to the resisting irregular meter, which expresses a simultaneous despair and desire for reserve. Meanwhile, this pained response is accentuated by the way in which the doubting voice disconsolately and sardonically questions the value of Stephen's hope and restraint – what good did such faith achieve, given that he was still martyred: '"Not that the grounds of hope were fix'd, | The elements were kindlier mix'd"' (227–8). The doubting voice seeks to subvert any possibility for hope.

The subversive nature of the poem is established from the opening line, where the voice of bitterness is established as '"A still small voice"' (1). Tennyson evokes the prophet Elijah's encounter with God in the midst of worldly turmoil:

> and a great and strong wind rent the mountains, and brake in pieces the rocks before the LORD; but the LORD was not in the wind: and after the wind an earthquake; but the LORD was not in the earthquake: and after the earthquake a fire; but the LORD was not in the fire: and after the fire a still small voice. (1 Kgs 19:11-12)

By taking a voice traditionally attributed to God and assigning it to the voice of self-destruction, Tennyson displays an excess of grief: despair and destruction are lent divine authority. This psychological space is dangerous, causing the self-control of 'Dominion in the head and breast' (21) to give way to an emotional annihilation in which the individual no longer sees his value on the earth:

> 'Think you this mould of hopes and fears
> Could find no statelier than his peers
> In yonder hundred million spheres? ...
> Tho' thou wert scatter'd to the wind,
> Yet is there plenty of the kind.' (28–30, 32–3)

The lion's share of the poem oscillates between a desire to shut oneself off from life and an acknowledgement of one's own temporality in a world that will keep turning after one's death. In this case, then, the question of living in the moment is drawn into excessive vision. The answer is found in looking outward to see what one can do in that moment:

> I said that 'all the years invent;
> Each month is various to present
> The world with some development.
>
> 'Were this not well, to bide mine hour,
> Tho' watching from a ruin'd tower
> How grows the day of human power?' (73–8)

As the speaker attempting to hold onto faith adopts the outward perspective that denotes reserve, the rhythm becomes regular, aligning with the containment of rhyme. Capitulation with reserve is further expressed through the softening of the line breaks from a semicolon to a balancing colon, and hence an easier flow through the passage of the verse, rather than jarring against the limits of restraint. The references to time necessarily reduce from the overwhelming sense of the years of grief ahead, moving gradually to a perspective of months, days and hours, enabling an understanding of possible purposeful action. As much as the bitter voice threatens the speaker with perpetual hunger in '"'Twere better not to breathe or speak, | Than cry for strength, remaining weak, | And seem to find, but still to seek"' (94–6) and the speaker almost concedes through recognition of this hunger: '"Hard task, to pluck resolve," I cried, | "From emptiness and the waste wide | Of that abyss, or scornful pride!"' (118–20), it is through remembering a past when he was engaged with life and hopeful of intervening in the community that he finds a way through grief. Through reconnecting with his desire to be fruitful – to provide, to nourish and to contribute to the community – the speaker re-engages with purposeful life: '"In some good cause, not in mine own"' (148).

The meaning of living or dying is wrapped up in one's connection to or isolation from the community. Although the bitter voice persists that the way one dies does not matter, the speaker claims that the possibility of eternity gives value to the temporal life; and in that belief there grows hope in action: 'He seems to hear a Heavenly Friend, | And thro' thick veils to apprehend | A labour working to an end' (295–7). Furthermore, the understanding of life and death without an eternal vision is positioned as spiritual malnourishment – 'To feed thy bones with lime' as if already dead (326) – 'A life of nothings, nothing-worth, | From that first nothing ere his birth | To that last nothing under earth!' (331–3). This realization, alongside 'Whatever crazy sorrow saith, | No life that breathes with human breath | Has ever truly long'd for death' (394–6), awakens the speaker's perception to a hunger for life: 'Oh life, not death, for which we pant' (398). Upon arising within that moment, the speaker is drawn by the simultaneous connection to community and mortality, represented in the image of the church: 'On to God's house the people prest: | Passing the place where each must rest' (409–10). The focus narrows, as it does earlier with the references to time, by moving into the crowd to detail a family of three that exemplifies reserve: the father smiles 'gravely' (414), his wife is 'prudent' (415) and 'in their double love secure, | The little maiden walk'd secure' (416–17). In this vision, the speaker reconnects with life through the proximity expressed through taste: 'These three made unity so sweet, | My frozen heart began to beat, | Remembering its ancient heat' (419–21). Within this moment of reconnection, the 'dull and bitter voice was gone' (424), replaced with the sweet-sounding 'little whisper silver-clear' (426), a voice of hope, promising satiety: 'I see the end, and know the good' (432).

This new voice is the voice of reserve: 'A little hint to solace woe, | A hint, a whisper breathing low' (433–4). Furthermore, it is described as a 'sweet voice' of 'hidden hope' (440–1). As much as the poem engages with excess and disorder in the struggle with grief, it ends with the regularity of rhythm that designates faith, and a reserve that leads to action: 'And forth into the fields I went, | And Nature's living motion lent | The pulse of hope to discontent' (448–50). Furthermore, in the distance beyond the moment of intense grief, further distance is found through 'marvell[ing]' how he could have considered choosing the bitter voice over the sweet in the first place (468). The narrative of reserve is one of self-control, suggesting that one chooses faith or doubt. The authenticity of Tennyson's reserve in this moment must be questioned, as well as its value: there is a danger of a type of reserve that denies emotion rather than containing it; however, within the context of community connection, the 'pulse of hope' suggests a more sustainable purpose than the 'stirring of the blood' of youth (159), a conclusion that evokes Keble's views on poetry and reserve:

> For which of us, in middle life, does not complain that, little by little, the fire and vigour of his youthful spirit seems to cool and ebb; and, just as with advancing day the morning glories of the sky hourly fade, so, too, that keen pleasure which beguiles the young to study of the poets, becomes daily weaker and, as old age draws nigh, feebler. Who would tolerate a criticism of poetry from one whose own fount of inspiration has dried up and who has lost the sense of the Muses' charm?[59]

The value of the reserve found through life's turmoil is evident in Keble's response to his own posited question: 'it is the bridle rather than the spur which he needs who speaks to others about poetry ... too rashly and irreverently do we burst into these sanctuaries ... there is no delay, no sense of reverence';[60] and for Tennyson, it is this aesthetic of cooled hope as opposed to enthusiastic fervour that enables him to reconcile his expectations with the temporal world.

The two voices in Tennyson's poem, expressing the inward struggle with a divided self, also communicate the struggle between the temporal and the sacred that preoccupied the Tractarians: between the transient and the divine, and the paradox of combining both within the human frame. Alice Meynell's 'The Two Poets' (1901)[61] similarly conjures this idea through the image of the beech tree, identifiable by the way in which the one tree is made up of several major trunks. The question of the opening lines 'Whose is the speech | That moves the voices of this lonely beech?' (1–2) evokes a dynamic relationship between the different agencies of voice and speech – that the speech that is heard emerges from the dominant voice – in a way that resonates with Tennyson's earlier struggle between his doubt and desire for faith. In Meynell's poem, however, there seems more of a desire to reconcile the voices to each other, rather than finding a way for one of the voices to dominate the other:

> Two memories,
> Two powers, two promises, two silences
> Closed in this cry, closed in these thousand leaves
> Articulate. This sudden hour retrieves
>     The purpose of the past,
> Separate, apart – embraced, embraced at last. (7–12)

As much as the two voices are dispersed through the cries of the dense canopy of the thousand leaves, they are brought together in a whole through the caesura after 'Articulate.' In the willingness to acknowledge the definition of the cries in this way, mirroring a recognition of the 'purpose of the past' – that is, of the grief of the 'dumb gale' that 'struck' the tree (6), seeming purposeless in its inability to articulate reason – the tree is able to embrace itself in its own separateness, depicting perfectly an internal impersonal intimacy with oneself. The destruction of a tree that should have lasted for hundreds of years evocatively speaks to the loss of transient human life, but Meynell also creates hope through the use of a wind-pollinating tree: just as Tennyson's hopeful voice finds purpose in connecting with and working in the community, there is potential for Meynell's tree to live on through its seed spreading new life, if the mourner can grasp hold of the 'voice' or seed as it spreads, necessarily through reserve: '"Thy sky was pathless, but I *caught*, I *bound* thee, | Thou visitant divine." | "O thou my Voice, the word was thine." "Was thine"' (16–18; emphasis added). Meynell importantly brings the voices of the temporal and the divine together in the final lines as a reconciliation between life and death.

Adelaide Procter's understanding of the poetic connection between the sacred and the temporal is evidenced in 'Life in Death and Death in Life', in which the abstract notion of 'the dread day' (1) is connected to the material hunger suggested in the 'gnawing pain' (26) of grief. Whereas Tennyson's poem is framed as an inner struggle with grief after death, Procter's poem is positioned before death, speaking to the object of future grief. Therefore, grief is projected; yet it cannot be dismissed as imaginary, as it also speaks to the grief felt by those tending the ill, watching them slip into death. This different kind of grief is expressed in recognizing the moment of death as 'Closing in deadliest night and gloom | Long hours of aching dumb suspense' (3–4), a precursor to 'leav[ing] me to my lonely doom' (5). It is evident that the loneliness of loss is already present: indeed, the object of grief never speaks. In this way, the sensory deprivation already experienced in the 'aching dumb suspense' is a type of sustained death.

As much as it seems to exemplify emotional reserve through its expression of faith, Procter's poem struggles with impersonal intimacy, desiring a closer connection as the loved one is becoming more distanced from life. This desire is emotively expressed through the tactile, but in a way that also recognizes the absence of response:

> Could hold thee in my arms, and lay
>     Upon my heart thy weary head, …
> Could smooth thy garments with fond care,
>     And cross thy hands upon thy breast,
>     And kiss thine eyelids down to rest. (16–17, 21–3)

As death approaches, the sensory desire becomes more intense; and, as a result, the poem turns to metaphors of taste: 'Alone now – yet with earnest will | Gathering sweet sacred traces still' (32–3). However, even in Procter's assumed resilience, in which she surmises 'I think I could check vain weak tears, | And toil' (36–7), her certainty seems to arise in some part from her recognition of that which Tennyson initially struggled with – the acknowledgement of the individual's embodiment of a unique space:

> – although the world's great space
> Held nothing but one vacant place,
> And see the dark and weary years
> Lit only by a vanished grace. ('Life in Death', 37–40)

The 'vain weak tears' that must be checked – that is, held in reserve – are linked through rhyme to the 'dark and weary years' that are 'lit *only* by a vanished grace', which becomes an externally enforced reserve. The consonance of 'Weak and weary' doubly ties these lines, suggesting the futility and exhaustion of giving oneself over to an excess of grief. Instead grief must be moderated by memory. There is comfort in memory, which allows this space to continue, even though the light is not as bright.

The fear that threatens Procter's equilibrium is the fear of losing her loved one's love: that loss would be greater than death, severing them eternally even beyond death because it would be a loss of community, of relationship. This fear is written explicitly in terms of gnawing hunger, the type of hunger that consumes from within:

> If loving thee still more and more,
> And still so willing to be blind,
> I should the bitter knowledge find,
> That Time had eaten out the core
> Of love, and left the empty rind. (56–60)

It is the loss of the soul that is greater than the loss of the physical body: 'The soul gone, that was once so sweet' (62), through which reconciliation Procter comes to terms with death. Yet this fear preoccupies the poem, juxtaposing the loss of physical touch – 'If I should loose thy hand' (71) – with the fear response of lost love – 'the dull throbbing of my heart' (75). This fear then becomes a fantasy, a possible escape from the pain of losing a loved one:

> If not to grieve thee overmuch,
> I strove to counterfeit disdain,
> And weave me a new life again,
> Which thy life could not mar, or touch,
> And so smile down my bitter pain. (81–5)

Procter contends with the same question as Tennyson regarding the importance of how one dies, but takes it further in a dream of rewriting history to save herself from grief: if her friend is dead, she has no agency to prevent such an act, a lack of agency that echoes the physical crossing of her arms on her breast. In death, the world becomes untouchable. Procter does not entertain this fantasy for long, however, instead pulling back from the terror of imagining a future without her friend, and how she will cope, to focus instead on the present moment, in which her friend is still alive:

> But see, thy tender smile has cast
>    My fear away: this thought of mine
>    Is treason to my Love and thine;
> For Love is Life, and Death at last
>    Crowns it eternal and divine! (96–100)

Procter is drawn back from the proximity of touch by the distance sense of sight, from the exquisite, yet excruciating, synaesthesia of 'touch' and 'bitter pain', to her friend's 'tender smile'. The proximate senses here are imaginative, forming an aesthetic excess that feeds fear, while stepping back to the visual brings Procter back to the present. This change in perspective is a form of sensory moderation that enacts reserve. Like Tennyson, Procter ironically finds reserve through the perspective of the infinite human soul; although less willing than Tennyson to entertain the possibilities of extremes – of falling into the abyss of grief – Procter similarly finds the answer to grief in community connection and individual action. The shortness of life in the temporal world bestows meaning, but only within an eternal context. It is this tension between the eternal and the temporal that continues to speak to the Doctrine of Reserve, finding a way to simultaneously connect deeply with the world, while remaining distant from it: touching the untouchable, and in touching, not touching. The challenge remains to touch with meaning and intimacy without touching too closely.

## The value of restraint

Emily Harrington argues that Christina Rossetti's poetry 'epitomises the impersonal' and that her 'patient stance set the stage for the impersonal intimacy' of the nineteenth-century lyric:

Her embrace of silence, distance, and a paradoxically submissive power served later poets as a model ... [T]his reserved approach is not only a hallmark of Rossetti's own style but also a trend that other poets develop over the course of Rossetti's lifetime and beyond ... Rossetti's impersonal poetics and concomitant embrace of silence also gave poets who came after her license to find poetic power in often devalued concepts such as silence, pause, distance, and waiting.[62]

While Harrington writes specifically of Rossetti's influence on other women writers, it is evident that her influence goes beyond gender, participating in a broader Anglo-Catholic aesthetic. Significant work is emerging on Rossetti, most recently from critics like Andrew Armond, Kirstie Blair and Emma Mason, that focuses on the influence of the Doctrine of Reserve on her poetry, which is a crucial development because it moves the perception of Rossetti away from ideas of female repression to an acknowledgement of her religious conviction: a move from passivity to self-determination. I agree with Emma Mason's position that 'it was a religious doctrine ..., rather than a broken heart or abused selfhood, that provoked Rossetti's reticent diction, reflecting her commitment to the Tractarian belief system'.[63] Joshua Taft has similarly challenged the way in which Rossetti's later devotional poetry has been characterized as 'exhausted, weary, and self-denying, revealing a poet who has traded vigor for dogma' and instead posits: 'we see how she embraces both restrained verse forms and a repetitive but resourceful style to create religious verse that moves from despair and resignation to determined activity'.[64] In a similar vein, Mason writes, 'the reserved poet is not passive or weak ..., but upholds a steadfast faith which is constant rather than excessive'.[65] The idea of determined activity being enacted by constant rather than excessive emotion, enabled by faith, is at the core of the Doctrine of Reserve; for the Tractarians, reserve was not an end in and of itself, but a means to action. Therefore, reserve must be considered in terms of holding back, as well as storing or saving, but as opposed to the excess of hoarding. By economizing emotional effort, expressed through poetic reserve, an outwardly focused action can be sustained for a longer period of time.

Rossetti's poetry is self-conscious in its reserve, deliberately showing that form and moderation of energy ironically require great effort. Her Anglo-Catholic conclusion is that such disciplined exertion is necessary and should be sought after over the physically wearying acts of excessive display. While acknowledging the difficulty of sustaining reserve at moments of crisis, the conclusions of her poems still assert the importance of trying to maintain reserve for the sake of stability and to conserve energy. At the same time, though, the threat of excess is what provocatively drives her poetry forward. 'Hope in Grief' (1845)[66] is a defiant challenge to emotional excess, but it conflates reserve and excess as much as it conflates betrayal with death. As much as the boundaries of reserve are very clearly defined, the poetic voice very clearly rails within that confined space. This is evidenced in the way the rhythm and meter kick against the goad of Rossetti's very tight rhyme scheme, maintaining its boundaries, but at the same time seeming to search for a weak point to break through. The poem then operates as both a challenge to the strength of reserve and a reinforcement of its necessity.

The first eighteen lines are contained by the rhyme structure, providing a foundation of restraint in the poem:

> Tell me not that death of grief
> Is the only sure relief.
> Tell me not that hope when dead
> Leaves a void that nought can fill,
> Gnawings that may not be fed.
> Tell me not there is no skill
> That can bind the breaking heart,
> That can soothe the bitter smart,
> When we find ourselves betrayed,
> When we find ourselves forsaken,
> By those for whom we would have laid
> Our young lives down, nor wished to waken.
> Say not that life is to all
> But a gaily coloured pall,
> Hiding with its deceitful glow
> The hearts that break beneath it,
> Engulphing as they anguished flow
> The scalding tears that seethe it. (1–18)

There is order, which, as noted earlier, is indicative of faith in Victorian devotional poetry. However, this containment becomes suffocating through the aggressive trochaic tetrameter of the first ten lines. There is an insistence on form through the repetition that speaks of the desperation of the poetic voice to maintain control in the face of grief and the frustration at grief's persistence. Yet this desperation proves exhausting as the repetition of 'tell me not' falls away into the weaker defiance of 'Say not', more sparsely placed, perhaps necessarily exhausted from the effort to enable quiet calming, until gradually finding a sense of control, with the poem eventually ending with the certainty of 'Surely the night will pass away, | And surely will uprise the day' (29–30). The grieving, tortured soul that rails in the opening is calmed by hope in the end; in this way, the poem reflects the human passage through grief, expressions of anger, betrayal and denial, before finding stability again. But importantly, although there is some room within, this passage remains within the boundaries of restraint. Reserve is not about static immovability in this poem; rather it is a *narrow* space, but a space nonetheless – the Anglo-Catholic channel – through which the feelings initially struggle, but eventually move smoothly.

While challenging boundaries, Rossetti never exceeds them. As much as, for example, the first five lines exemplify formal restraint, in doing so, they also express a polarizing chasm. Indeed, there is a double chasm created in 'Leaves a void that naught can fill, | Gnawings that may not be fed', alongside the extremes between the death of grief and the death of hope, both of which represent agonizing emptiness. The longing here seems to be for a moderation of grief – not its loss entirely, but also not losing hope, which does provide some satiety to grief's void. The changing rhyme scheme bleeds into 'That can bind the breaking heart, | That can soothe the bitter smart', and it is questionable whether the repetition creates restraint or demonstrates excess, particularly in the use of present tense. The blurring of the lines between restraint and excess marks the power of grief; and while Rossetti maintains the rhythmic and rhyme structures, the change of texture through the transition to the iambic and the enjambment of 'By those for whom we would have laid | Our young lives down' has a softening effect, suggesting that the betrayal felt by death has been softened by reflecting on the everyday nature of loss, bringing humanity into a community of grief.

There remains a tension between trying to find reserve by acknowledging the communality of grief as a form of comfort and the aversion towards the idea of accepting the pain as natural and common: to do so is to deny the singularity of the loss, which speaks back to Tennyson's claim in 'The Two Voices' of the unique space occupied by the individual. The engulfing 'anguished flow' of 'scalding tears' rejects the idea of patient acceptance and the impulse to hide the pain as if to do so were to deny the significance of the one lost, as though loss were nothing: as though there is no meaning or purpose in life's suffering. The idea of communal grief, then, becomes written as a form, not just of excess, but of waste:

> Say not, vain this world's turmoil,
> Vain its trouble and its toil,
> All its hopes and fears are vain,
> Long, unmitigated pain. (20–3)

Rossetti not only questions the value of restraint but that of grief itself. Yet to determine that grief is waste is not satisfactory from the Tractarian perspective, in which strong emotions are valued and affirmed through restraint. Furthermore, if one was to harden the idea of one's own grief as pointless and wasteful, it would then lead to failing to recognize the suffering of others. Rather than seeing the world's griefs as vanity, then – a part of the 'void that naught can fill' – Rossetti provides an answer through a hope established by an understanding and appreciation of communal suffering. There is a comfort in empathy that does not diminish the power of the loss: 'All in this world have been grieved, | Yet many have found rest' (25–6). In this revelation of hope, a channel of order is found, with hope in day surpassing the grief of night.

'Hope in Grief' is a significantly different poem from 'Sweet Death' (1849), arguably because while the former remained unpublished, the latter was published in the Pre-Raphaelite journal, *The Germ*.[67] While 'Hope in Grief' exemplifies the inward struggle towards order and emotional equilibrium, 'Sweet Death' presents a more outward vision, a call and question to its audience, rather than a questioning of self, although self-identification still plays a role. However, as much as 'Sweet Death' is ordered by restraint, the last lines are subversive in the way they encourage the reader to consider fullness and excess as opposed to moderation, or a brief taste: 'Why should we shrink from our full harvest? Why | Prefer to glean with Ruth?' (23–4). These closing lines echo the spiritual hunger established in the poem through synaesthesia and sensory absences, a kind of hunger for death that resists the hunger of grief. Synaesthesia suggests that the senses' response to the external world cannot be trusted – like hunger, the perception is out of control, chaotic. But at the same time, in Rossetti's poetry, rather than creating perceptive confusion, the blurring of the senses actually serves to prevent the poems from falling into excesses of affective response; the self-conscious blurring creates a kind of distance by acknowledging that the sensory experience is both flawed and lacking.

From the opening line of 'Sweet Death', taste, olfaction and vision are blurred in the advent of death. Olfaction, as the mediatory sense, aligns itself with the distance sense of vision rather than the proximity of taste in 'The sweetest blossoms die' (1), suggesting the desire to distance oneself from death. Similarly, in the last two lines of the first stanza, olfaction and vision are blurred as the perfume that rises is almost visible in its passing. The tensions between the senses as they struggle for definition against each other reflect the desire of the individual to come to terms with the inevitability of death. In the second stanza, the fall of the blossoms returns them to taste: they 'nourish the rich earth', becoming food for nature, creating not just richness, but further sweetness, the most desirable flavour: 'Sweet life, but sweeter death' (10, 12). Yet as much as the poetic voice seeks reconciliation with the temporal world through the continuance of nature, loss remains overpowering. In 'All colours turn to green' (14), there is an ironic loss; for while green is the colour of nature, growth and life, there is no other colour to give value to such life. The visible green is at the expense of the other sensory experiences: 'The bright hues vanish and the odours fly' (15). Moreover, while the green seems strong and eternal in comparison to the temporality of human life, represented in the blossoms, 'The grass hast lasting worth' (16) ironically evokes the biblical wisdom that the 'grass withereth and the flower fadeth, but the word of our God shall stand forever' (Isa. 40:8). It is only by displacing the fear of earthly, temporal loss into a spiritual hunger and a faith in a divine eternity that Rossetti is able to find significance.

'Sweet Death' is striking in its regularity, declarations of faith and the clear outward voice, aligning with Blair's assessment of poetry that speaks of faith. Yet this regularity requires an effort on the part of the poet that is meant to be transformative. The performance of faith is designed to speak not just to the reader but also to the poet through prayer. It acts as a reminder of the reward in heaven, recalling the parable of the rich man and the poor man in hell and heaven, respectively, and the idea that the rich have their reward on earth already. In this way, Rossetti works to moderate the desire for the world and what it offers. The reference to Ruth recalls the determination of the Old Testament figure who gleaned the fields although she had no right to the crops and who essentially scavenged behind the legitimate reapers. The taste of earth is compared to gleaning: this is not the Christian's legitimate field; their full harvest is in heaven. Given that perspective, Rossetti asks why her reader should shrink from death, preferring life on earth to heaven. Yet while 'Sweet Death' is more consistent in maintaining the rhythms and expectations of reserve, by ending with two questions, Rossetti creates space for uncertainty. In spite of the external vision and the desire to evoke faith, there remains a taste of doubt in the unknown, which balances and moderates the potential excesses of faith. This moderation of faith is just as crucial as the moderation of doubt or emotion because it tempers the flow of faith in order to sustain it, grounding it in the reality of uncertainty and giving it, in terms of the Doctrine of Reserve, depth of feeling in its awareness of the limitations of belief.

In *The Poetics of Luxury in the Nineteenth Century* (2011), Tontiplaphol refers to 'a sublime materiality bound by picturesque constraints' and suggests that in poetry in which 'the materiality is present, but the picturesque delimitation is not[,] [w]ithout the constraints imposed by the latter, the former can approach muchness but not too-muchness, plenty but not excess'.[68] This kind of sublime materiality resonates with the Tractarian project, in which the material world grounds one to avoid excess and exuberance, whether of religious fervour, of grief, or of any other kind of strong emotion. The 'why' of Rossetti takes on a different nature in this regard, expressed rhetorically in the end of 'Sweet Death' and formatively in the progress of 'Hope in Grief'. There is a necessity in gleaning, of moderating, of maintaining boundaries, so that one is not overcome by them: emotions can be used for what Taft refers to as 'determined activity', rather than depleting the individual of energy and will. In choosing reserve, Rossetti chooses to engage in oscillations of doubt, fear and grief within an essentially confined, psychologically safe space, which is defined and framed by calm, tempered faith.

Poetic form plays a significant role in reserve and economizing. It restrains but does not repress, and in doing so, moves towards beauty, using the aesthetic to transform the visceral response of fear, to a sense of order. In contending with one's worldly desires, and the quickness of death and grief, the poems discussed here become about the material and abstract desires that paralyse and distance individuals from their community. They are about loss, and the hunger such loss creates, whether physical, social or spiritual. The desire to distance oneself from the trauma of loss instead of facing it directly is written through the abstraction of the proximate senses of taste and touch, distancing them through memory, nostalgia and metaphor. Yet the material invades the abstract, bringing the poets back to the temporal world, albeit with a more eternal perspective of their limited space of action. The next chapter looks outward, examining poetry positioned deliberately in periodicals to provoke readers to look outside themselves in this manner, in order to address social injustice.

2

# Looking outward: The moment of lyrical connection

> A plague upon the people fell,
>     A famine after laid them low;
> Then thorpe and byre arose in fire,
>     For on them brake the sudden foe;
> So thick they died the people cried,
>     'The Gods are moved against the land.'
>
>           – Alfred, Lord Tennyson, 'The Victim' (1868), 1–6[1]

In 'On Lyric Poetry and Society' (1991), Theodor Adorno suggests that 'the lyric reveals itself to be most deeply grounded in society when it does not chime in with society'.[2] This connection pre-empts, to a degree, Caroline Levine's impetus in *Forms* (2015) to know 'how both aesthetic *and* social forms acted in the world, and how they interacted and overlapped with each other'.[3] Importantly, Levine argues for 'an alternative model for relating the rhythms of poetry to the rhythms of social experience, which, as we have seen, are often messy, complex, and overlaid'; yet while she argues that poetic rhythm does not 'carry the same material force' as social forms such as prisons, schools or other institutions,[4] Adorno's view seems to lend poetry an opaque materiality of its own through its very opposition to 'material things' and 'commodities':

> The lyric spirit's idiosyncratic opposition to the superior power of material things is a form of reaction to the reification of the world, to the domination of human beings by commodities that has developed since the beginning of the modern area [sic], since the industrial revolution became the dominant force in life.[5]

In particular, it is the lyric's willingness not to chime with society – the power to stem the flow of popular thought – that lends it the materiality and significance that embeds the aesthetic form within social forms. Using the same metaphor, but from a different direction, Hilary Fraser argues regarding Hopkins's religious poetry that 'not only does the interior life of the feelings take form in … poetry and lyrical prose, but the embodied writer who experiences those feelings is echoing, chiming with, and responding passionately to, something equivalent in the external world: the presence, or devastating absence, of Christ incarnate'.[6] This embedding, or embodiment, becomes even more material when poetry is positioned in the periodical press, alongside multiple authorial voices and generic modes.

While I do not restrict my poem choices in this chapter to lyrics in the traditional sense of form, I am interested in the aspect of the lyric mode that at once stands in opposition to the collective – the commodity-driven, individualistic, capitalist nineteenth century – and connects to a universal sociality. In this way I am aligning myself with Adorno's understanding of the 'universality of the lyric's substance' being 'social in nature' and the power of the lyric to convey shared human experience:

> Only one who hears the voice of humankind in the poem's solitude can understand what the poem is saying; indeed, even the solitariness of lyrical language itself is prescribed by an individualistic and ultimately atomistic society, just as conversely its general cogency depends on the intensity of its individuation.[7]

It is the lyric's capacity to assert the individual human face within a distanced, institutionalized society that provides a necessary intervention in the nineteenth-century context. I argue that the lyric responds to the problem of representation that Charlotte Boyce identifies in 'periodicals that targeted a readership with little direct experience of [hunger's] visceral pangs'.[8] In both visual and textual terms, there was a

> general challenge inherent in 'making present' a condition experienced by its sufferers in terms of diminution, absence or lack, while also contending with the specific problem of re-presenting the somatic experience of hunger to members of a social class largely detached from its miseries.[9]

Boyce usefully engages with Elaine Scarry's observation that 'when one hears about another person's physical pain, the events happening within the interior of that person's body may seem to have the remote character of some deep subterranean fact' that 'has no reality because it has not yet manifested itself on the visible surface of the earth'.[10] The problem of hunger lies, then, in that it is invisible until it is abject – shown on emaciated bodies. Poverty, connected so closely to hunger, can be seen as the visible effects of hunger, yet distanced again as symptoms and causes, not hunger itself. Poetry intervenes viscerally, creating a sensation that, while not simulating hunger, brings awareness to the bodily region of the stomach.

In response to the emotional distancing created through technology and economic discourse infused with moral rhetoric, the lyric mode encourages reconnection and intimacy. Marion Thain sees this connection occurring through the body of the lyric subject, written in terms of the material proximate senses of smell, taste and touch, arguing that this highlights 'a mode of transaction and connection with the world that is more somatic than vocal', so that even within the silences of the lyric, the poet foregrounds the intimacy of the sensory encounter.[11] Human connections are thus brought close, challenging the mediating, distancing modes of institutional forms. In the context of the Tractarian social vision, this move represents a return to community-based social responsibility and connection: a recognition of the human faces of the poor as a part of the community, rather than as a burden on a governmental or institutional system. It stands to reason, then, that the lyric was championed by the Tractarian movement and that as a poetic form it rose in prominence through much of the nineteenth century.

In *Poetry, Enclosure, and the Vernacular Landscape* (2002), Rachel Crawford argues that the re-emergence of the short lyric poem in the nineteenth century was a part of a movement towards 'democratiz[ing]' poetry, 'making it available to an ordinary audience of limited means and circumscribed prospects'.[12] The lyric represents, for Crawford, a return to containment. Speaking of space from architectural to agricultural, and to the space of the poem, she writes that 'contained spaces geared toward productivity, usually ... of smaller dimension, took hold of the English imagination', and thus the lyric reappeared 'after a century of neglect in dizzying numbers as a vernacular form in magazines, correspondence, and parlour games'.[13] Given the time period of which Crawford writes, the use of democratization to signify the expansion of access to poetry is particularly pointed: the turbulence of the late eighteenth and early nineteenth centuries in Britain and Europe can be attributed to the violent rise of democracy, from the Gordon Riots to the French Revolution, to the Reform Bill of 1831–2. Similarly, Emma Mason observes that 'the lyric offered the best route to the democratic dissemination of spirituality not only because of its ability to represent feeling but also due to its inherent opposition, and therefore resistance, to the increasingly material and reified world of the nineteenth century'.[14] While the Tractarians were perceived as politically conservative, it is important to nuance this understanding with their critique of democratic structures and institutions. In the same way that Pusey and Bosanquet challenged parishioners regarding their emotional distance from the poor, justified through their deferral of having paid their taxes, the expansion of suffrage through democratic principles was also a means to distance people from each other, through a myth of participation and having their voice heard. Isobel Armstrong, in discussing Thomas Carlyle's *Signs of the Times* (1829), presents what the conservative perspective saw as the problem of human distancing in the rise of democracy:

> Democracy was a form of alienation and mechanisation because in the same way that products were dissociated from workers outside their control, political representation was actually a way of dissociating people from relationships by depending on a depersonalised proxy form, the vote, which was empty of content. It is in fact a mere empty 'sign' of the times ... The vote is another example of a situation where nothing is done 'directly'. People leave a mark or sign on a voting paper, but nothing else. The paradoxical conservative argument that democracy is the most abstract way of conceiving of people enables ... oddly radical questions: what does representation represent? What are the signs signs of?[15]

In this view, the touch of the pencil to the voting ballot disconnects the individual from the representative, while providing a deceptive sense of engagement with a democratic process. Problematically, the abstraction of democracy diffuses the individual voice and ultimately disrupts communal ties by deferring individual communal responsibility into the act of marking the ballot, much as in the same way that the act of paying taxes seemed to remove one's sense of obligation to intervene personally in the face of poverty.

The subjectivity of the lyric mode stands in opposition to such deferral. As Adorno suggests,

The 'I' whose voice is heard in the lyric is an 'I' that defines and expresses itself as something opposed to the collective, to objectivity; it is not immediately at one with the nature to which its expression refers ... It is only through humanization that nature is to be restored the rights that human domination took from it. Even lyric works in which no trace of conventional and concrete existence, no crude materiality remains, the greatest lyric works in our language, owe their quality to the force with which the 'I' creates the illusion of nature emerging from alienation.[16]

In the context of what would become the Marxist understanding of alienation, the lyric mode is necessarily humanizing, materially, sensorially and aesthetically connecting human experience through communal affective response. It could be further argued that the democratization of poetry through its prolific publication in the periodical press provided a provocative elixir to dissociation and alienation by creating communities of readers. Joshua King goes so far as to suggest that between 1820 and 1870, Christianity as an institution 'retained its *public* and *national* force as an increasingly voluntary, competitive, and print-mediated phenomenon, rather than one *primarily* identified with any single group's site or institution' and that 'authors, educators, and clergy seeking to reinforce the nation's sense of spiritual unity' recognized the increasing extent to which 'reading, which eluded any institution's total control, was powerfully determining how Britons imagined themselves in community'.[17] The subsequent access to a broader audience and influence that Linda Hughes notes[18] enabled poets to facilitate the space of the periodical to disseminate political and social messages in a way that potentially held more power than petitioning members of Parliament or speaking from a pulpit.

The power of poetry to move groups and individuals viscerally as well as intellectually is inherently linked to 'shared human feeling' and, in the nineteenth-century context, an understanding of the connection between poetic order and social duty.[19] Susan Stewart asserts that poetry is a 'material ... force against effacement – not merely for individuals but for communities'.[20] She goes on to argue that '[a]s metered language, language that retains and projects the force of individual sense experience and yet reaches toward intersubjective meaning, poetry sustains and transforms the threshold between individual and social existence'.[21] Because poetry depends upon allusion and metaphor, shared human experience is necessary for its meaning to be conveyed. Therefore, as Stewart suggests, 'metaphor bridges the relations between individual human experiences'[22] by drawing individuals' experiences and understandings together in order to interpret the text. Through this understanding, rather than being positioned purely as personal, introspective and subjective, lyric poetry, through its capacity to create intellectual and emotional sympathy, when inserted into the nineteenth-century periodical press, becomes reconceptualized as a material, outward-looking genre that speaks to the contemporary world.

Within the proliferation and ephemeral nature of textual material in the periodical form, poetry played a significant role in containing and curating ideas. Rather than providing filler in periodicals, poems can be seen as thematic stops in the space and pace of the volume. Furthermore, while physically causing pause in the flow of the text, the poetic mode restrains and moderates the flow of ideas. As Hughes suggests, '[t]o the degree that poetry generically signified intimations of the universal, the spiritual, and the permanent, poetry could mediate the miscellaneousness and ephemerality of the periodical itself',[23] and the 'entanglement of poetry, periodicals, and fiction in print culture affected not only Victorian reading practices but also the conceptualization of poetry'.[24] This understanding seems particularly pertinent to the Tractarian perspective, first in terms of the relationship of poetry to the eternal and the temporal, that is, poetry's intervention (as the eternal) in the temporal world of the periodical press, and second in relation to the sense of containment within the poem alongside the poem's capacity to provide a means of moderation within the volume. Third, another kind of channelling or moderation is formed through the mode of shared reading, a formulation that resonated with liturgical culture, and was reinforced by other forms of shared devotional reading, such as John Keble's *The Christian Year* (1827), which was republished throughout the nineteenth century, and Christina Rossetti's *Time Flies* (1897) and *Verses* (1893).[25] The Anglo-Catholic ethos was one that valued shared reading – like shared meals, such as the Eucharist – as a way of creating a sense of community: sharing one another's spiritual and intellectual experiences and engaging with the needs of one's community. The literary form was, then, a means to create social form, to establish the boundaries of thought and to influence and contain ideas. Poetry in periodicals thus represents a double order or containment: the form of the poem within the form of shared periodical reading, creating a double bind as well as, potentially, a more powerful, if unconscious, influence. As King has argued in regard to Keble's *Christian Year*, poetry that 'trains habits of interpreting texts and the world as types of spiritual realities' provides 'the best agent', in Keble's view, 'for curing the infections spread by overindulgence in print culture – the "feverish thirst after knowledge," overconfidence in private judgement, and dismissal of ecclesiastical guidance'.[26]

The curation of ideas within a Tractarian social vision enables the poet to facilitate the overwhelming nature of the periodical press to create a channelled, sustained outward challenge to the dominance of liberal capitalism, selfish individualism and the deferral of personal communal responsibility. Editorial intervention adds yet another layer of moderation, for in the poet not necessarily having a voice in the positioning of their works, there is an overt limit and moderation exerted over the space and agency of poet, editor and reader. In particular, the placement of such poems within the secular press, or periodicals of other denominational persuasions, meant that the vision was disseminated to a broader audience, and often powerfully read alongside secular, socially engaged pieces. What links the contributions together is a practical desire to help the poor in real ways, as well as a desire to process the presence of hunger through literature, while challenging others to act. The serial structure of the periodical itself contributed to this motive by forcing readers to take their literary exposure into the context of their everyday lives. Hughes suggests that the voices of the members of the shared community 'augmented [the] understanding of literary works',[27] while at the same time reading was not 'enclosed' in the text; rather,

> readers repeatedly were forced to set aside a continuing story and resume everyday life. In that space between their readings, their world continued to direct a barrage of new information and intense experience at readers; and that context complicated and enriched the imagined world when the literary work was resumed.[28]

Poetry necessarily encounters the 'bustle and commotion' of society, from which Adorno refuses to distance the lyric.[29] It is therefore within the scope of lyrics and idylls, particularly those published in the periodical press, to speak to, augment and influence the readers' understanding of the world around them. In this way, poet and editor work to transform the personal of the lyric into a political mode of expression, challenging the order and 'chime' of society.

## Chiming against institutionalized complacency

Meredith Martin's claim that poetic form in nineteenth-century Britain was seen by poets as 'malleable and culturally contingent' invokes an interconnectedness between society, politics and poetry in which the destabilization of aesthetic form is inherently tied to a destabilized social structure.[30] Periodical publications, with their necessary ties to the everyday, brings this contingency to the fore, not just through serialization but through the context of the other pieces in the volume. A periodical piece is, according to Laurel Brake, 'instantly and always contextualized, embedded in a matrix of other pieces which make up the issue in which it appears, and extend to the issues before and after' and is 'self-confessedly historical, contingent, looking backward and forward, with a historical identity'.[31] Similarly, Hughes observes that

> [n]ot only did the real world intrude on individual fictional worlds, but many literary texts overlapped each other in their parts publication ... for subscribers certainly read much in each issue of their favourite journal, linking together in their minds not just specific continuing stories but overlapping ongoing presentations tied together by editorial principles.[32]

A journal volume, then, could become a manifesto, drawing materials of a variety of genres together with a particular agenda to appeal to the intellect, the emotions and the sense of moral duty. While the editor cannot control the way in which a reader approaches the volume, the capacity for the pieces within to speak to and inform each other necessarily has an impact on the messages of the pieces themselves. This factor is complicated even further in the nineteenth century, before the stabilization of international copyright laws, when it was common practice for poetry in particular, but also other periodical material, to be lifted and republished with or without the author's permission. This kind of lifting was rife across the Atlantic, but also occurred within Britain; and while it was problematic in terms of authors receiving their due royalties, it was also a means by which they could have their ideas disseminated to a broader, sometimes unexpected, audience.

Tennyson's 'The Victim' was first published in the London newspaper *The Examiner* on 28 December 1867, followed closely by its reprint in Alexander Strahan's evangelical illustrated magazine *Good Words* on 1 January 1868. In the same vein as Brake and Hughes, Kathryn Ledbetter argues that 'a Tennyson poem printed in a periodical voluntarily or involuntarily creates meaning outside of the solitary poetic text as the mind interprets the visual rhetoric of social and historical codes available from the page on which it appears'.[33] Ledbetter goes on to extend this conversation through discussing 'The Victim' as a response to Charlotte Yonge's *A Book of Golden Deeds* (1864) – an important connection given my argument for the influence of Tractarianism on Tennyson's work. However, I want to focus on the positioning of Tennyson's poem in these two early periodical contexts and the inflections of meaning derived from the surrounding material.

Set in a pre-Christian context, 'The Victim' opens with a kingdom racked by famine. The pagan priest declares that the gods will be appeased if the king sacrifices the thing he loves the most. The priest assumes this thing to be the king's son and heir, but at the altar of sacrifice, the boy's mother steps in and sacrifices herself in her son's place. The priest is disturbingly unconcerned with whom is sacrificed; his lack of human anguish is shown in the repetition of 'But the priest was happy' (61) 'And the priest was happy' (72). Yet perhaps the most significant moment in the poem regarding human anguish is when the queen tells her husband that the priest has taken their son. She asks the king, 'Is *he* your dearest? | Or I, the wife?' (51–2). The king responds:

> 'O wife, what use to answer now?
>     For now the Priest has judged for me.'
> The King was shaken with holy fear;
>     'The Gods,' he said, 'would have chosen well;
> Yet both are near, and both are dear,
>     And which the dearest I cannot tell!' (55–60)

Although the queen's self-sacrifice at the end of the poem is the most dramatic moment of anguish, it is this earlier exchange that reveals the crisis of emotional distress. It is a private moment between two very public figures, the outcome of which has the potential to reshape the kingdom. In this way, the personal and the public, and the individual and the communal, are powerfully conflated, and the personal anguish of the king and queen is amplified above that of the plague-ridden, starving kingdom. But in this amplification, emotional paralysis is outworked through the king's response. In the king's unwillingness to declare who is most dear, he inadvertently relinquishes his sovereignty, deferring his authority as well as his responsibility onto other systems: the institution of the priests. Although this is an ironic reversal of the Anglo-Catholic conviction that state government had usurped the authority of the English Church, it expresses a similar chasm created by emotional paralysis that allows institutional complacency to take precedence in social structures. The king, who is meant to rule the kingdom, does not feel his own power. Anglo-Catholicism's community-based approach was focused on individuals regaining their sense of power to intervene. In a way, although it is disturbingly gendered, the queen's last-minute sacrifice can be seen as her recognition of her power to do something, albeit small: she theoretically saves the kingdom (in the eyes of the uncaring priest) in the personal act of saving her son.

Tennyson's exposure of institutional and institutionalized complacency in 'The Victim' enters into the lyric mode of defying the chime and flow of society. However, his mythical setting arguably retreats aesthetically from the present day in a way that eschews the modern nineteenth-century world. This distance is emphasized in particular through the positioning of the poem in *The Examiner*, bordered by 'white space that demands attention',[34] yet hedged in and divided on the page by stories that are explicitly and temporally present. Tennyson's ancient, mystical world stands in striking opposition to the short reviews and advertisements on current theatre productions in London and the surrounding counties and an article on Colonel Merewether's 'Abyssinian Expedition' reported from Bombay. The discordance arises not just from the temporality of the surrounding material, but through the contrast wrought between pieces that hinge upon leisure, luxury and excess, bought at the price of imperialism, and the presentation of a myth rendered eternal through its connection to a past that deals viscerally with several layers of life and death.

Tennyson's poem does not seem so out of tune in *Good Words*, even though it is positioned within an evangelical context. It becomes in the slightly later publication a more stable, less transient piece, partly through the added value of illustration, but also through its discrete positioning on two pages alone, followed by an illustration of the mother's sacrifice. It is also followed by a C. J. Vaughan theological article entitled 'Earthly Things and Things Heavenly', which lends the preceding poem a more elevated authority than the advertisements in *The Examiner*. Its resonance with *Good Words* gives the poem a liturgical tone, much like a parable before the homily; yet it is in its discordant publication in the newspaper a few days earlier that 'The Victim' exerts weight as a social critique. In *The Examiner*, the poem is literally positioned within the everyday of London. The plague, famine and fire in the opening lines, while apocalyptic, would also resonate with living memory: cholera epidemics, famines throughout the 1830s and 1840s, machine breakers and reform riots. The 1867 Reform Bill and mid-century political protests evoked these memories, rewritten through fiction, political philosophy and journalism, and in the rhetoric of debate. Tennyson's idyll can therefore be read as entering into this context, with the poem's priesthood representing the capitalism of nineteenth-century Britain. Ledbetter observes the way in which 'Despair: A Dramatic Monologue' (1881)[35] 'criticized a society Tennyson viewed as materialistic and dogmatic';[36] and while this later poem more explicitly engages with the loss of faith in light of the selfish individualism of the age on the one hand, and the trauma of loss and disease on the other – 'a life without sun, without health, without hope, without any delight | In anything here upon earth' (7–8) – 'The Victim' similarly equates a loss of hope with the loss of authority. The king's fearful paralysis mirrors the priest's complacency; and while his emotional response demands more empathy, his paralysis is complicit in the human sacrifice that takes place. There is no evidence in the poem that the sacrifice was actually necessary, and so the poem centres on a pointless sacrifice, driven by hunger and fear.

Tennyson's poem expresses the human limitations in facing overwhelming earthly trauma, as well as the often unrealistic expectations placed on authority figures who are impotent to intervene. Yet these figures are not merely individual human beings; they represent larger institutional structures that ought to be able to do something. The biblical epigraph to Hopkins's 'Barnfloor and Winepress' (1865)[37] positions this earlier poem in a similar context: one in which a king is rendered impotent in the face of widespread famine. The King of Israel is travelling through Samaria, a nation devastated by famine. As he passes, a woman cries out for the king's help. When he asks her what the matter is, she tells him that another woman had convinced her to give up her son for them to eat, promising that the next day they would eat *her* son. The first woman agreed; yet when the next day came, the second woman had hidden her son to protect him (2 Kgs 6:24-30). Hopkins's epigraph is the king's response to hearing this account: 'And he said, If the Lord do not help thee, whence shall I help thee? | Out of the barnfloor, or out of the winepress?' (2 Kgs 6:27). The king rends his clothes, a signal of great grief, but does not do anything in either practical or legal terms to assist the woman. He was, arguably, emotionally overwhelmed by the extremes to which famine had driven these women; but at the same time, given that he is king, in his emotional paralysis there is an abdication of responsibility. This idea resonates with the Anglo-Catholic disaffection with a government ineffectual in addressing the extremes of poverty in Britain. Like Tennyson's king in 'The Victim', the biblical king that Hopkins references defers human responsibility to divine judgement without acknowledging his own earthly and material obligations.

The Anglo-Catholic criticism of such deferral was a significant point of difference between the Tractarian vision and the conservative Tory agenda with which they are often associated. In a sermon of 1841, given in Bristol, Pusey suggests that the fires and riots that occurred in Bristol ten years earlier when the reform bill was not passed were a direct consequence of the community's neglect of the poor:

> This cannot last; either our luxuries must destroy us, as they have every luxurious nation before us, or we must unlearn our luxuries, in order to learn the Cross and Christian charity; we must learn to sacrifice self, in order to Christianize our land, or the Heathenism of our land will destroy us. You have, in this place, already had an awful warning of God's displeasure upon past neglect; *the wealth, which a few years ago was here burnt up, because out of it none had been spared to extend the blessings of the Gospel to the poor.*[38]

In the preface to the published version of this sermon, Pusey criticizes his readers for their complacency, beginning

> We are apt to speak of the neglect of our immediate forefathers, of the slumber of the last century, of their neglect to provide for the growing population ...

yet while we acknowledge thereby both the misery and duty, we remedy it not: if they threw the duty upon the State, and shielded themselves under its neglect, we acknowledge that the State will not help us, and yet put not our shoulder under the yoke to help ourselves.[39]

Pusey's critique of the connection between wealth and social complacency lies at the heart of Hopkins's poem. On the surface it can be read in relation to the Eucharist and Christ's sacrifice, with references to 'the heavenly Bread' (8) and the 'sweet Vintage of our Lord' (20), but the epigraph creates a much more material, abject context, in which Christ's sacrifice becomes conflated with the suffering of the poor. The grain and wine, referring to the body and blood of Christ, refer just as much to dietary staples, but even more, the poor *become* the grain that is being threshed and the trodden grapes. This can be seen in the connection between the sheaves 'bruised sore, | Scourged upon the threshing floor' (5–6) and that 'He has sheaved us in His sheaf, | When He has made us bear His leaf' (29–30). Even more provocative, the Eucharistic sacrament is conflated with the women eating their own children in the final three lines of the poem, which disrupt the preceding ordered scheme of rhyming couplets:

> We scarcely call that banquet food,
> But even our Saviour's and our blood,
> We are so grafted on His wood. (31–3)

The lines look like they should be unified through rhyme, but they are not; similarly, the congregation should be unified through Christ, but they are not: they are separated through economic and social differences. The conflation of Christ's suffering with the suffering of the starving is so complete as to mingle Christ's blood and that of the poor, reinforced by another biblical image of being grafted into Christ. The Eucharist, then, could be read not just as a reminder of Christ's sacrifice, but as a perverse exposure of how the privileged in the community are actually consuming the poor.

The regularity of form and structure in the poem is crucial to Hopkins's emotional control. After the two 10-line stanzas, the shortening of the two final stanzas to six and seven lines respectively reflects the refining act, the threshing caused by life; and it is only in these last two stanzas that Hopkins breaks the form of rhyming couplets. It is important, then, that the transition into these two stanzas occurs in Gethsemane and Calvary:

Terrible fruit was on the tree
In the acre of Gethsemane;
For us by Calvary's distress
The wine was rackèd from the press;
Now in our altar-vessels stored
Is the sweet Vintage of our Lord. (15–20)

As much as Hopkins draws his reader into the accountability for Christ's crucifixion, he draws them into responsibility for the poor in the community. While through torture Christ's blood is aestheticized into ritual and sacrament, the sacrifice of the poor is diffused into the luxuries of the wealthy.

'Barnfloor and Winepress' was originally published in the *Union Review*, a Roman Catholic journal, the year before Hopkins's conversion. The structure of the journal reflects both the Catholic and Anglican liturgies, with a section of original poetry positioned as the readings, followed by a reprinted sermon, the homily, on the Feast of St Michael and All Angels. This liturgical structure reinforces the sense of connection and community by mirroring a familiar communal structure. The sermon, which addresses the topic of spiritual poverty, pertinently focuses on the heavenly table of the angels, and heaven itself is described in alimentary terms. The angels 'sit at the table of the Most High, where they are satisfied with the fulness of the house of God, and are drunk with the torrent of everlasting joy … They are satiated out of the fatness of the grain, while we feed upon a certain bran and upon a certain husk of the Sacrament'.[40] The language of excess and taste is provocative, given the material conditions of the world in which it was published, and the contrast is stark between the heavenly 'fatness of the grain' and the non-descript 'bran' and 'husk' of the earth. Each of the four poems that precede it contends in some way with the struggle of human life and a desire to look to the spiritual afterlife as a hope and means of surviving the material world. Where excess and feasting is permitted in heaven, the only excess for the human world seems to be 'the excess of our infirmity', which the angels 'cloke'.[41]

The sensory nature of the poems emphasizes their creation within the material world. In the yearning for taste, touch and hearing from the divine, though, there is a notable motif of absence of sight, undergirded by a Catholic awareness of the poet's own humble blindness rather than claiming to have vision, and thus poetic blindness enacts spiritual and emotional reserve. The paradox exists because the poet does not have the capacity to see. Affectively, this humility connects the poems to the poor and disenfranchised, who are required to believe in heavenly provisions when they can see nothing comparable in the earth. The violent haptic nature of 'Barnfloor and Winepress', with the 'cruel bands, bruised sore, | Scourged upon the threshing floor' (5–6), as well as the treading of the grapes (12) and the wine being 'rackèd from the press' (18) imposes Christ's suffering onto that of the poor, all the more so given that the preceding poem, taking the position of the Psalm, encourages the reader to take up their own cross. Hopkins's poem takes the place of the New Testament epistolary reading, which liturgically is designed to provide instruction for living in light of Christ's sacrifice. In this way, the poem becomes at once personal and communal: personal, as the poem wrestles with the response to hunger; and communal, as it looks outward and challenges the reader to consider the hungry.

## Psalter form: Speaking with the community

The material and sensory nature of liturgical-style poems is crucial to their capacity to speak to their audience. Susan Stewart observes that we need the externals of the senses to know ourselves, but also to understand the world around us, our position within it, and also to empathize with the position of others:

> The flux of sense impressions has a transitive and intransitive aspect. What propels us outward will also transform us, and it is only by finding means of making sense impressions intelligible to others that we are able to situate ourselves and our experiences within what is universal ... *poiēsis* as figuration relies on the senses of touching, seeing, and hearing that are central to the encounter with the presence of others, the encounter of recognition between persons.[42]

Borrowing from Levinas, Stewart further notes the importance of recognizing individual humans in light of the overwhelming nature of poetic existence: 'Levinas reminds us of another fear, a fear that the necessity of such activity is never-ending; that it will exhaust us and outlive us if it is not met by the acknowledgement and recognition of others.'[43] This understanding of poetry informs and illuminates the overwhelming nature of hunger: as a universal concept, one that persists throughout human civilization, it is never-ending and exhausting; yet the insertion of the human figure gives hunger a temporality that contains it and makes it seem possible to address. The sensory connection created through poetic form, and I would add the recognizable religious form of the Anglican liturgy,[44] undergirds the social authority of the poet, enabling them to turn the subjectivity of the lyric mode into an outward-focused social critique within the periodical press. While the Doctrine of Reserve was criticized as elitist and exclusionary in its emphasis on not revealing everything to everyone about the rites, rituals and theology of the church, hiding it through metaphor, allegory and paradox, for the poet, reserve was not about denying people *access* to truths, but challenging them to learn how to *decode* truths: to work hard to find it. Indeed, like Harrington's 'impersonal intimacy', the poet uses such reserve to create a respectful distance, trusting that readers, in their own subjectivity, would be able to discover meaning without it being imposed upon them. Writing in particular of Rossetti, Mason argues that her role as poet was not to hide the truth from her readers, but to use reserve in her poetic choices to 'invite the ... reader into Tractarian theology ..., enticing her to decode that from which she is barred and thus drawing a wider audience into a belief-system'.[45] Going further than enticing the reader into a theological persuasion, however, I would add that such poetry becomes a call to social action, and that this motive is enacted through the combination of the lyric and psalter modes – poetry and religion combined – which are closely related through their cultural position as communal songs.

For Rossetti, as for the Tractarians earlier in the century, social responsibility is as deeply personal as religious devotion; and this vision of practical religion is achieved most effectively through impersonal intimacy. Most of the work on Rossetti and reserve has focused on the way reserve is a tool to shape the self – that is, Rossetti's religious identity – and then how it is presented as a model and encouragement to others to embrace the Anglo-Catholic ways of worship, especially in regard to liturgical forms. Yet the focus on sacramental form has neglected the importance of acts of social justice as a form of worship. I argue that Rossetti, among other poets influenced by the Tractarians, sought to mobilize people to look and act outwardly, embracing not just church-based rituals, but tenets of faith like caring for the sick and poor within one's community and defending the vulnerable against injustices. Rossetti herself was involved in social activism through her work with education and fallen women, as well as her opposition to pew rentals. This latter objection was particularly important because it was not only about people's access to God through the sacrament of the Eucharist, but about access to the community of faith. The outward acts of charity and creating social awareness, then, are just as much a part of the Christian life espoused by Anglo-Catholicism as the rituals of prayers, readings and hymns.

The publication of religious poetry in the secular periodical press brings together the sacred and the social, with the readers consciously or unconsciously buying into the authority of the Anglican psalter form. Elizabeth Ludlow argues that Rossetti's familiarity with the psalter form – that is, when in the liturgy the celebrant and the congregation read or sing the lines of the psalm alternately, emulating a dialogue as a call and response – infuses her poetry: '[t]his liturgical practice brings to the fore the dialogic basis of the Psalter and the place of the individual in a community that reads together'.[46] In the liturgy, the practice of alternate line reading means that the members of the congregation are active participants in this part of the service and therefore complicit with its content. This complicity is borrowed through the mirroring of psalter form in the periodical press. Even the secular readership would be familiar with this form as central to the culture of the state church, and so it would influence the reading of the poetry. The poem itself enters into conversation with the material surrounding it. As Hughes notes, 'the relentless secularism surrounding the poem challenges the primacy it allots to mystery and eschatology, and introduces competing visions of what matters most to existence'.[47] Yet rather than seeing this as a challenge to the religious authority of the poem, I see this move as revealing the much more material and social vision of the poet's work.

Rossetti's 'Up-Hill' (1861)[48] and 'Amor Mundi' (1865)[49] both address whether one should take the seemingly easy way in life, focusing on one's own needs and wants, or face the uphill battle of living a life of labour and selflessness. In both there is a preoccupation with self and the need to subdue the self in order to look outward; and within this mode, both use poetic reserve to create understatement, deliberately diminishing matters of life and death through the poetic voice to provoke readers to react against their own complacency towards social justice. It is crucial, then, that both poems operate in dialogue – ultimately with each other, but also within the poems, in which the structure is one of two figures, a petitioner and a responder, mimicking the liturgical call and response. This structure within each poem constrains the poems within their bodies, and the tension between the speakers in terms of the dominance of the conversation is manipulated in both to provoke the reader to consider their own position in the journey of life: whether to embark on the uphill journey or to take the downhill path, which is easy, but from which there is no turning back.

In her 1876 collection *Poems*, Rossetti published 'Up-Hill' and 'Amor Mundi' next to each other, but with 'Amor Mundi' positioned first. It is evident that she considered them in dialogue with each other, but there is a further dialogue at play in their initial periodical publications, which reflect editorial intervention as much as poetic intention. 'Up-Hill' was positioned following J. M. Ludlow's article, 'Trade Societies and the Social Science of Association', which defends the relief that unions offer to the poor. Although Ludlow acknowledges that there has been corruption in unions, he posits a balanced view of their position within society: 'They have been led by selfish and designing spouters; they have had for leaders the most virtuous men of the class. They have thwarted the most benevolent employers; they have been their best friends, their main support against the unprincipled.'[50] He also goes on to criticize the lack of emphasis placed on the benefit of unions:

> The general public practically never sees them but through the heated and distorting medium of a strike atmosphere … For the working man on the contrary, it can never be too often repeated that the strike is but an accident in the history of his trade society. He looks to it above all as a hand stretched out to him in all his needs.[51]

While it might be a stretch to suggest that this article positions Rossetti's poem as a call for combination, it certainly causes 'Up-Hill' to be read as an illustration of the tensions between selfishness and belonging to a community. Furthermore, the role of the trade union in Ludlow's view seems to be fulfilling the role that the church is meant to fill, which therefore rouses a challenge to parish communities to care about their impoverished neighbours.

The four quatrain stanzas of 'Up-Hill', with their strict ABAB rhyme scheme, suggest a rigid containment and order, in spite of the questioner seeking answers contrary to what they receive:

Does the road wind up-hill all the way?
    Yes, to the very end.
Will the day's journey take the whole long day?
    From morn to night, my friend. (1–4)

It is significant that the questioner is given more feet, suggesting an indulgence in self, and over-concern with one's own comfort. The long vowels of 'whole long day' draw out the experience to hyperbole in its self-concern and indulgence, with the complication of rhythm and excess of syllables revealing an exhausting level of unrest. Their companion is noticeably calmer, responding in shorter, more regular lines that are more reserved. This speaker conserves energy for the journey, not wasting it on unnecessary speech. It is important that neither speaker is designated as a God-like figure, but that rather they seem to be companions on the same road.[52] The lack of quotation marks importantly obscures the regular distinction between the speakers, which suggests that either of them could at times take the other's place – both could be led into times of doubt or despair and need the other to respond with the levelling truths of death's inevitability. In the final stanza, while the questioner is still self-concerned, there begins to be concern for others: 'Shall I find comfort, travel-sore and weak? | Of labour you shall find the sum' (13–14) is followed by 'Will there be beds for me *and all who seek*? | Yea, beds for all who come' (15–16; emphasis added). The duality of beds and graves is an ultimate equalizer, although graves themselves are no more equal than beds in terms of nineteenth-century burial practice. However, death will be provided for all. Within the reference to graves for all, Rossetti speaks to the idea of community and the responsibility each individual has towards the other, either to encourage or to lead astray, to help moderate each other's emotional response, and to be alert and active in the process. Although reserved, the responder is not cold in their answers; rather the matter-of-fact boundaries are ironically comforting in their definitiveness.

In its initial publication in the *Shilling Magazine*, 'Amor Mundi' follows an article on horse racing. Horse racing epitomizes social privilege, luxury and decadence, and while gambling might not have been understood in terms of addiction in the nineteenth century, it was certainly understood as evidence of dissipation and self-destruction alongside alcoholism. The self-indulgence and waste of gambling is made worse when positioned alongside the want of so many, as well as the desperation of want that leads some to its path. In this context, then, Rossetti's poem depicts the epitome of being led astray: the nonchalant temptation of 'love-locks flowing' (1) and the potential adventure of 'the west wind blowing' (2), the wind that is known as the most pleasant and favourable, are simultaneously intoxicating and deceitful in the beauty of their representation. As the questioner asks the respondent where they are going in such luscious terms, the response seems particularly attractive, the internal rhyme enticing: ' "The downhill path is easy, come with me an it please ye, | We shall escape the uphill by never turning back" ' (3–4). To reflect that the downhill path is the easy way, the majority of the poem is a sensory embrace of the scent of heather and velvet flowers. But even in the seeming beauty of this description, Rossetti critiques this choice through the sensory experience. The senses are focused on the distance senses, especially sight, in a way that expresses a lack of engagement with the community. Olfaction is used, but selectively; there is the 'honey-breathing heather' (6) and the scent of velvet flowers is 'rich and sickly' (14), suggesting uncontrollable penetration and excess, but this excess of luxury is most potent in the capacity to choose *not* to smell: it is significant that the speaker does not smell the 'thin dead body which waits the eternal term' (16), but only glimpses it.

Importantly, there is no touch. The temptress, who embodies disconnection from the community, is described as having feet that 'seemed to float on | The air like soft twin pigeons too sportive to alight' (7–8). This physical lack of touch reflects her affective lack of touch: her nonchalance is shown in the anaphora of 'Oh' – her matter-of-fact dismissiveness of 'Oh, that's a meteor sent us, message dumb, portentous' (11) provides a false echo to what becomes the increasing concern of the first speaker, whose inquiries begin with the same 'Oh', but carry a tone of simultaneous wonder and ignorance. This conversation reveals the dangers of not being engaged with the world, of being blissfully unaware of social injustices. The 'grey cloud-flakes' (9) in the third stanza, another false echo, this time of the purity of snow, are a warning. The temptress describes the omen as 'An undeciphered solemn signal of help or hurt' (12). This line evokes Rossetti's call to her readers to work at deciphering and decoding not just poetry and the ways of God, but the hurt in the world around them. The sibilance of 'solemn signal' turns the awe of opulence to fear, leading into the thick, velvet flowers, whose scent is no longer pleasant. The 'scaled and hooded worm' (14) is an obvious allusion to the serpent in the garden, but it is not a sin of eating fruit that is revealed, but the social apathy that leads to the 'thin dead body which waits the eternal term' (16).

This line is the crisis point. It is a *thin* dead body, thinness speaking of impoverishment, starvation and neglect. It is this revelation that causes the questioner to want to turn around and go uphill again, desperation shown in the pleading to ' "Turn again, O my sweetest, – turn again, false and fleetest: | This beaten way thou beatest I fear is hell's own track" ' (17–18). The desire to turn, to move, but being constrained by panic, is reflected in the restraint of the verse, evinced through the consonance of the 'f' and through the internal, oppositional rhyme. Rossetti uses the revelation of complacency in the face of being too late to challenge her readers not to be swayed by the temptation to have selective sensory experiences: to choose not to smell the rot of death or, its forerunner, poverty; to choose not to decipher the signals 'of help or hurt'. The rhetorical effect of understatement in the last stanza has an effect of cold terror, as though the situation is inevitable. The wistful, nonchalant 'Oh' chillingly changes to the negative 'Nay', but with the same tone of complacency: ' "Nay, too steep for hill-mounting; nay, too late for cost-counting: | This down-hill path is easy, but there's no turning back" ' (19–20).

The agonizing hopeless despair, understated at the end of 'Amor Mundi', echoes the opening of the section of 'The Prince's Progress' that Rossetti had published in *Macmillan's Magazine* in 1863:[53]

'Too late for love, too late for joy,
    Too late, too late!
You loitered on the road too long,
    You trifled at the gate:
The enchanted dove upon her branch
    Died without a mate;
The enchanted princess in her tower
    Slept, died, behind the grate;
Her heart was starving all this while
    You made it wait.' (481–90)

In a similar tone to 'Goblin Market' (1862), 'The Prince's Progress' in its entirety is an idyll that explores the ramifications of the hero prince being delayed from rescuing the princess due to being led astray by a siren sorceress, who lures him with delectable food as well as her own beauty. Potentially, the prince can be read in the voice of the first speaker in 'Amor Mundi'. It is important, though, to read 'The Prince's Progress' in the context of what was published first, before Rossetti extended the backstory, as a short, anonymous dramatic monologue. There is no referent to define who is being spoken to or who is speaking; all that is known is that because of one person's delay or distraction – because of their complacency in having 'loitered' and 'trifled' – they are now too late to save a life. It is crucial that the princess's death is described in terms of starvation: not only was her heart 'starving', the language of hunger continues throughout the published stanzas: the corpse of the princess must be covered in a veil 'to shroud her face | And the want graven there' (507–8). The unidentified voice continues to berate and condemn the lackadaisical lover:

>'You should have wept her yesterday,
>    Wasting upon her bed:
>But wherefore should you weep today
>    That she is dead?' (531–4)

Although written as a love tragedy, the power of 'The Prince's Progress' lies in the evocation of starvation; and the use of romantic love can be extended to speak to social issues and the sense of common or communal love. Read alongside 'Amor Mundi', so similar in tone, 'The Prince's Progress' similarly confronts the dangers of selfish neglect and oblivion for the sake of pleasure and indulgence, in a temporal world with immanent need.

The positioning of these poems within the popular press, and their many reprints, makes a strong case for their capacity and, importantly, the vision, to impact a wide audience as a means to speak to the broader social apathy and disaffection of nineteenth-century middle-class Britain. Through the use of rhetorical understatement alongside sensual reticence, Rossetti presents the dangers of not touching: of not feeling; but at the same time, alongside other poets influenced by Tractarian ethics, she suggests ways *to* touch – to feel appropriately in order to be active agents in their communities. Indeed, it could be argued that by surrounding the emotional potency of the poems by secular articles and stories of the everyday, the periodical works as a form of moderation and containment that enables the message of the poem to be relayed without excess, bringing the spiritual into the material. The temporal context brings the universal overwhelming problem of hunger and poverty into specific communities and contexts in a way that is both challenging and helpfully containing: while the lyrical quality of the poems speaks to a broader metaphysic, the periodical provides a particular geo-social scope for action.

## Materiality, modernity and poetic critique

'Amor Mundi' in particular comments on dissipation in a way that connects to Rossetti's perspective on modernity and consumerism – a perspective shared by many influenced by the Tractarian social vision. In *Women Poets and Urban Aestheticism* (2005), Ana Parejo Vadillo reads Alice Meynell's 'A Dead Harvest [in Kensington Gardens]' (1901) as a critique of late-Victorian consumer culture. There is an irony in the beauty of the poem, in that 'such beauty is ... sterile and dead, because the crop is destined to be destroyed in the pyre and unlike Christ's body (the food of Christians), this crop will not nourish the city physically or spiritually'.[54] Vadillo's observation is particularly pertinent to social responses to hunger and poverty, evoking the sense of spiritual and physical nourishment within the sacrament of the Eucharist. The modernized city of London is depicted as an impoverished spiritual and material wasteland: it is unproductive, unable to provide the crops of food needed for the teeming numbers of people. London, a city overwhelmed by poverty, but also ironically the heart of the British empire's economic and political power, becomes focalized as a location of critique that is at once specific and universal, thus bringing together the temporal and the universal in poetic terms. Poetry set in, or about, London, positioned within the British periodical press, necessarily speaks to the temporal world, challenging the political and social structures that allow for the neglect of the vulnerable. Alice Meynell and Adelaide Procter, both as converts from Anglo-Catholicism to Roman Catholicism, reveal through their London poems the impact of the Tractarian social vision in their works, as well as their literary aesthetic as a means to convey their message. The poetry is at once personal and political in its lyric quality: it is indicative of a poetic voice seeking to reconcile its temporal existence, but it also turns outward to the readers, challenging their understanding of their world.

Procter and Meynell were key figures within nineteenth-century periodical culture, but in many ways have been marginalized into categories of women's writing or, more specifically, women's devotional poetry. Many of Procter's poems, due to their regularity of rhythm and meter, were easily translated into hymns for church services, while Meynell's reserved poetic style has been feminized within a narrowing nineteenth-century cultural context, more than recognized as a part of a Catholic poetic tradition that saw itself as playing an active role in shaping social feeling. But this marginalization does not account for the very real impact they had on society in terms of social justice, outworked through their publication in the secular press. It was recognized in their lifetimes, however, with Procter's prolific output in Charles Dickens's journals, especially *Household Words*,[55] and Meynell's journalism earning her the presidency of the Society of Women Journalists in 1897 and her poetry having her touted as the one who should succeed Tennyson as poet laureate.[56] Their scope of influence allowed them to have a critical impact on nineteenth-century Britain's understanding of the politics of material inequalities and injustices; and both women were highly conscious of the need for this voice, as well as their personal need to conduct their lives accordingly through their personal austerity and charity. Like the lyric mode, their focus was both personal and public.

Although both Procter and Meynell converted to Romanism in their 20s, the influence of Tractarian aesthetics, which feeds into both the ritualism and Romanism of the later nineteenth century, is evident in both their work and their social vision. Their poetry was heavily influenced by Rossetti, giving them a direct poetic lineage to the Tractarians. What develops in their work is a distinctly English rendition of Roman Catholicism that is, in form, very similar to Anglo-Catholicism, in spite of the adamant desire of the respective adherents to distinguish themselves. There is certainly more to unite them, particularly in social vision; and in the two poems to be discussed in this section, both positioned in the London context, Procter and Meynell locate themselves within an ethos and aesthetic resonant with that of the London-based Rossetti. In combining aesthetics and social critique, the loss of beauty is expressed through aesthetic form, and this irony creates the poetic reserve that stirs the reader: like Rossetti's use of understatement, Procter's and Meynell's London is aesthetically restrained, in ironic contrast to the explicit abjection of the poor. Given the sordidness of London, the historically entrenched 'romantic foreignness of the Catholic religion'[57] signalled a kind of hope or contrast to what they saw as the soulless modernity of their temporal world.

Procter's 'The Cradle Song of the Poor' (1855) was first published in Dickens's *Household Words*.[58] Most of the poem is embedded on the final page of an article entitled 'When London was Little', with most of the fifth and final stanza printed on the top of the next page, where it is followed by the final two chapters of Elizabeth Gaskell's *North and South* (1854–5). The preceding article discusses the growth of London throughout history, but finishes with a paragraph expressing current economic progress and seeming stability, juxtaposed with images of poverty that cannot be ignored:

> Then arose Portland Place, and Portland Square, and indeed most of the streets and places to the westward of Hanover Square, as far as Hyde Park. The nobles of the City rapidly filled up the vacant ground in Russell and Bloomsbury Squares, and similar localities. At this period the custom began of affixing name-plates to house-doors, and the names of streets to corners. These were improvements; but streets were wretchedly paved, with footways scarcely above the road: the lighting was very bad; and, in some of the best squares, which now are adorned with gardens, there stood heaps of filth and rubbish. The connections between the heart of London and the suburbs were of the worst kind, and the roads to Hoxton, Clerkenwell, and the Foundling Hospital, were impassable after dusk – dangerous even in the daytime – on account of the highwaymen by which they were infested.[59]

On one hand, there is a sense of stability in the placing of house names and street names, as well as the expansion of the city; but on the other, the 'bad pavements', the 'heaps of filth and rubbish', and the almost incidental reference to the Foundling Hospital operate as reminders of the very real poverty that persists in London, while the wealthy have the luxury of moving further away from what is described in hell-like terms as 'the sulphury fumes of the new fuel called coal'.[60]

This positioning situates Procter's poem within London; and in the intimacy of a mother trying to soothe her hungry baby to sleep, there is perhaps the threat that the mother, in her own desperate starvation, might leave her baby at the Foundling Hospital or that upon her death her child would be left there, evoking resonances with Dickens's own *Oliver Twist* (1837–9). In this way, the poem operates to move the reader from the distance of a city description to the very personal mother's monologue. Importantly, the chapters of *North and South* that follow Procter also begin in London, with Edith saying, 'Is not Margaret the heiress?' upon Mr Bell's death. Gaskell's text perhaps moderates the closeness of the emotional trauma that precedes it in the journal, with the narrative going on to Margaret bailing out Thornton's factory, which means she also saves the livelihoods of those who became unemployed when Thornton went out of business. Importantly, all of these people were members of a community in which Margaret feels deeply invested. Margaret's sudden wealth is an idealistic construct, but the narrative functions to provide an image of hope and action, of generosity in the face of poverty, which is crucial to Procter's social vision.

'The Cradle Song of the Poor' is notable for its persistent regularity in form and structure, which seems at odds with its content. The structure of two quatrains and a rhyming couplet, with an almost unbreaking trochaic tetrameter, shows the resolute and determined courage of the mother in spite of her despair. Indeed, the use of couplets resonates with the epic tradition, lending the mother heroism in her poverty. From a sensory perspective, the opening lines in particular are notable in the simultaneous desire *not* to see, and *to* touch – a desire for proximity, both physical and emotional, that is denied by their mutual starvation and loss of hope:

> Hush! I cannot bear to see thee
>    Stretch thy tiny hands in vain;
> Dear, I have no bread to give thee,
>    Nothing, child, to ease thy pain! (1–4)

The absence of bread stands at the centre of distress, the instrumental cause of the inability to touch. There is an exquisite intimacy in the mutual pain and distress of mother and child in this very close, personal scene. The haunting refrain of the rhyming couplet opens the scene out, however, through its repetition, bringing the audience into a communal chant of 'Sleep, my darling, thou art weary; | God is good, but life is dreary' (9–10), with sleep being used euphemistically for death.

The capitalization of 'Want and Fever' (13) in the second stanza recalls another Dickens tale, *A Christmas Carol* (1843), with the children Want and Ignorance haunting the text. The consonance of 'beauty fading' (11), 'Fever' (13), 'life' (14) 'Famine' and 'father' (15) connects to the 'left' hope (16) of the parents, who would be willing to 'suffer all' (17) had they 'but a crust' for their child (18). The sigh of despair through this repetition is counterbalanced by the deceptively soothing sibilance of 'strength sink' (12), 'Soon' (13), 'reckless' (15), 'suffer' (17) and 'sleep' (19). The recklessness of the baby's father suggests alcoholism; and in this space of absolute hopelessness, there is a hint of disruption in the meter of the third verse. And while the sibilance of 'Starve so soon' (22) and 'helpless sin and sorrow' (23) reflects again an ironically soothing tone, it also suggests the sighs of the mother and the sinister persistence of hunger. The helplessness is reinforced by 'Reckless, hopeless' (28), words that convey an emptying out, not just of the stomach but of the soul. Thus by the fourth stanza, the mother's focus has moved to herself: 'I am wasted, dear, with hunger, | And my brain is all opprest' (31–2). Her inability to press her child to her breast again emphasizes the dual physical and emotional inability to connect, to touch. Death is presented as the only hope, the only release from their oppression:

Patience, baby, God will help us,
    Death will come to thee and me,
He will take us to his Heaven,
    Where no want or pain can be. (35–8)

At this moment of abjection, once the readers have again joined the mother in the refrain of longing for the sleep of death, Procter changes voice, now addressing her readers directly:

Such the plaint that, late and early,
    Did we listen, we might hear
Close beside us, – but the thunder
    Of a city dulls our ear.
Every heart, as God's bright Angel,
    Can bid one such sorrow cease;
God has glory when his children
    Bring his poor ones joy and peace!
        Listen, nearer while she sings
        Sounds the fluttering of wings! (41–50)

This stanza epitomizes what Gill Gregory observes as 'Procter combin[ing] a Tractarian concern with ordinary devotions and duties with a more active urging of her readers to seize the moment or day',[61] although I would suggest that this active urging is not an addition, but central to the Tractarian concern. In recognizing that the city, in both its poverty and its luxurious distractions, is overwhelming in 'the thunder | Of a city dulls our ear', Procter also points out that the constant bombardment of poverty in that space desensitizes the viewer. Yet in compelling the reader to recognize the mother's cry in spite of this, she also reminds them that everyone can do something – can help 'one such sorrow cease' – encouraging the reader to focalize the individual figure among the dehumanized hungry, teeming crowd. The different rhyming couplet at the end is a call for the reader to become more proximate to the hungry, to listen to the song, which is conflated with the wings of angels. To help the poor is to serve God, recalling the biblical verse, 'Inasmuch as ye have done it unto one of the least of these my brethren, ye have done it unto me' (Mt. 25:40).

The need to encourage readers to see individual humanity within the excessive numbers of London's poor was as much of a concern to Meynell. Meynell holds up the Italian pastoral as representative of the Roman Church within a society that was still very anti-Catholic, and thus uses Italy as a foil to England's wasteland, and Romanism as a response to England's capitalist individualism. In 'Ceres' Runaway' (1906),[62] Meynell provocatively describes a graveyard in Italy in reference to London life: 'They slowly uproot the grass and lay it on the ancient stones – rows of little corpses – for sweeping up, as at Upper Tooting.'[63] Meynell's Italy is one of fecund overflow, where seeds easily find root in 'a little fertile dust the wild grass, wild wheat, wild oats!'[64] Her vision of London, however, is one in which the only abundance is in the dead bodies, which she compares to the persistent Italian weeds – weeds being, importantly, defined as such because they do not produce fruit. The weeds are like the late-Victorian consumer who, in Vadillo's reading of Meynell, 'produces nothing, but also … buries God's creation, i.e. nature'.[65] Yet in Italy, the weeds are actively kept at bay, while the abundant wild food is allowed to flourish. In 'Ceres' Runaway' Meynell writes,

> Italian grass is not turf; it is full of things, and they are chiefly aromatic. No richer scents throng each other, close and warm, than these from a little

hand-space of the grass one rests on, within the walls or on the plain, or in the Sabine or the Alban hills. Moreover, under the name I will take leave to include lettuce as it grows with a most welcome surprise on certain ledges of the Vatican. That great and beautiful palace is piled, at various angles, as it were house upon house, here magnificent, here careless, but with nothing pretentious and nothing furtive. And outside one lateral window on a ledge to the sun, prospers this little garden of random salad. Buckingham Palace has nothing whatever of the Vatican dignity, but one cannot well think of little cheerful cabbages sunning themselves on any parapet it may have round a corner.[66]

Meynell's parallel between the secular state of Britain and the religious state of the Vatican is expressed through the differing tastes of cabbage and lettuce, creating a nostalgia for the Italy in which she grew up. The 'savage savour and simplicity' of the Italian foods and the delight of sensory pleasure in their aromas feed into the way that Meynell argues that tilling and cultivating – that being the metaphorical work of modernity – has not destroyed Italy in the same way that it has destroyed England.[67] The nostalgic vision that Meynell sustains regarding Italy ties the fertility of the soil to her Catholic roots; and through this nostalgia, expressed through sensory absence and deprivation, Meynell challenges the effects of modernity in England, which she sees as social inequality, poverty and disconnection from community: problems that stand in opposition to her active Roman Catholic faith. The quaintness of the imagined 'little cheerful cabbages' in her essay expresses the inadequacy with which England has contended with poverty, while also creating a sense of unnatural contrivance in opposition to Italy's (and, by extension, Catholicism's) natural productivity.

'Ceres' Runaway' draws a contrast between the 'wildness' of Italy's vegetables and the ironic 'lands of liberty for all the tilling', in which Meynell suggests that the process of modernity has deprived those other nations of taste and fragrance. Perceived liberty comes at the cost of vital sensory, human experience. Meynell's argument clearly speaks in defence of Catholicism as a purer form of Christianity – less tilled, less cultivated, less interfered with by men – yet at the same time her argument is very much a political and social one. Indeed, the material and the spiritual are inherently mixed. John S. Anson describes the rows of dead leaves in 'A Dead Harvest' as 'symbolizing the spiritlessness of modern denatured life,[68] in a way that expresses the Catholic understanding of the intrinsic link between nature and spirit. For Meynell, this link is what brings about true productivity. The grass described in 'Ceres' Runaway' recalls the opening lines of 'A Dead Harvest':[69]

> Along the graceless grass of town
> They rake the rows of red and brown, –
> Dead leaves, unlike the rows of hay
> Delicate, touched with gold and grey,
> Raked long ago and far away. (1–5)

The regulated consonance of 'rake the rows of red and brown' expresses the metered violence of modernity, while the suddenness of the break before 'Dead leaves' is aesthetically softened by the enjambment of 'Delicate'. The aestheticized, regulated violence and death mirror the complacency of a society that, through the buried subjects and verbs, becomes invisible and passive in comparison to the active streets.

The streets that were raked long ago perhaps recall death by cholera and starvation throughout the earlier part of the nineteenth century in London, which is recollected in Meynell's 1921 essay 'A Modern Poetess':

> Every martyrdom of the past has ceased to be; it concerns no one how sharp, how insupportable it was in its day. There is no living pain now in all the universe to continue it, to answer it, to rehearse it, or perhaps to regret it. And if we complain that the past is not to be revoked or undone, we might rather confess the complete consolation of the passing of time, the undoing, the effacement, and the more than death. It is only by moments that we apprehend what it is to be past, or that we perceive how clean is natural oblivion; the uneasy human retrospection stirs nothing but itself, and wounds the now living heart with a present pity for that which is not. Nothing now on earth remembers.[70]

Meynell's understanding of the individual's relationship to the past, present and future is constructed through the Doctrine of Reserve and reinforced by the immediacy and transience of the periodical press, as well as the limitations she has as a poet in that medium. Although 'A Dead Harvest' was initially published in one of her volumes of poetry, therefore a material product that she had substantial control over, she did not have the same authority when her poems were reproduced in full in literary reviews. Often contemporary reviews focus on the sparse aesthetic of Meynell's poetry, rather than on the strong political and social messages she sought to convey. Emily Harrington observes that 'Meynell's writing importantly distinguishes between detachment and distance', and this distinction is at the heart of Harrington's impersonal intimacy.[71] This distance not only aptly describes the mode of Catholic poetry, it also expresses the Catholic response to poverty: aesthetics and ethics can only be understood in conversation with each other. The distance created is not designed to separate but to show respect for the poor as subjects, rather than sensationalizing or objectifying their position. Meynell's 'emphasis on distance acknowledges that it is never possible to fully know the other and thereby cultivates respect for the unknowability'.[72] It is this reticence, perhaps, that the reviewer for the *Athanæum* identifies: 'Every poem is like the hinting of a secret',[73] designed, in a mode similar to Rossetti, to encourage the reader to uncover meaning.

At the same time, though, secrecy and reserve are positioned as a necessary consequence in the material, consumerist world. Meynell's impersonal intimacy is designed to re-establish the subjectivity of the poor and vulnerable. It is a reserve that counterbalances the wilful blindness of society to the material persistence of poverty, which creates an unproductive distancing and breakdown of communities in which the poor are abandoned. The second stanza of 'A Dead Harvest' reflects such abandonment through the sensory deprivation of the visual and the auditory:

> A narrow silence in the park,
> Between the lights a narrow dark.
> One street rolls on the north; and one,
> Muffled, upon the south doth run;
> Amid the mist the work is done. (6–10)

The 'narrow silence' and 'narrow dark' bookend the street being 'muffled', and the people are buried completely in 'Amid the mist the work is done'. The bookending, enclosing structure provides a myth of containment and order within the verse, but what it actually contains is an increasing vacuum of human oblivion, emphasized through the fact that the scene is not just silent and dark, but that these sensory experiences are described as narrow. While narrowing dark could refer to the rising dawn, this, too, is obscured by the mist. The irony of this stanza could perhaps be what Meynell's reviewer refers to in *The Academy* as her 'exquisite sense of the inter-relations of words' and observes '[t]here is nothing so much beyond the reach of your plain man as the kind of truth which finds its most natural expression in a paradox'.[74]

From a Tractarian perspective, the recognition of this kind of paradox is a rational response to a world of contradictions: accepting that paradoxes exist, one is meant to act within the space of knowledge that one has, rather than ignoring that space to try to understand what one cannot. At the same time, it is the task of the poet to expose the realities of such paradoxes that run against social justice – such as the statistical prosperity of a nation juxtaposed with the poverty of so many of its inhabitants – and discover ways to overcome it. The final stanza of 'A Dead Harvest' is a jarring awakening, in both the abrupt opening and the return to materiality:

> A futile crop! – for it the fire
> Smoulders, and, for a stack, a pyre.
> So go the town's lives on the breeze,
> Even as the sheddings of the trees;
> Bosom nor barn is filled with these. (11–15)

Humanity remains obscured in the ashes of the smouldering fire in 'So go the town's lives on the breeze', depicting the emptiness of modernity. The ironic beauty is empty and unsatisfying. Vadillo aptly describes the roads as 'the indispensable vessels that circulate commodities',[75] for in the poem, the streets are more animated and present than the people. In this way, society becomes detached, empty and unproductive, in spite of the stuff – the commodities – that is the ironic lifeblood travelling through the busy, paved veins.

## Re-establishing community – Finding a common soul

Meynell's reviewer in *The Academy* recognized the significance of the way in which the poet fuses emotion and the intellect to speak to ethical issues:

> Primarily poetry is a purely subjective thing – the expression of emotion which the expression gives. The fact that the expression of the emotion

becomes at the same time the means of transmitting it to the consciousness of others is almost accidental ... What is essential in poetry is, firstly, that it should be charged with emotion, and, secondly, that the moods of this emotion should have aesthetic or ethic value ... This indeed is the crowning merit of Mrs. Meynell's work that, although it is highly intellectualised, the result of subtle and analytic meditation, it yet remains emotional. It is in the register, not of mere thoughts, but of a personal attitude towards thoughts.[76]

Meynell's reticent poetry is designed to move both hearts and minds simultaneously, creating a poetic voice that is at once 'intimate' and 'poignant', while being 'in the first place the voicing of high ideals, a criticism of life'.[77] Furthermore, her poetic convictions were generated through her everyday life, with June Badeni noting that in Meynell's home 'The food was frugal and usually bad, for luxury in eating seemed to her not only unnecessary but wrong', and that her austerity in general came from a place of wanting to relinquish luxuries: 'first by financial necessity and later by her conviction that the money was better spent on charity'.[78] Her recognition of community, and her place of responsibility within it, was central to Meynell's social vision. Her work, both literary and social, was founded on a desire to re-establish catholic communities in the broad sense as well as in terms of religious communities, and she also used the literary space to critique the failed outworking of ideas of community in her social context.

'The Lady Poverty' (1896), reprinted in its entirety in *The Academy* review as an example of Meynell's capacity to convey social critique with appropriately reserved emotion, challenges modernity through the presentation of religious communities. Meynell compares the idealized, mythologized poverty of medieval Italian Franciscan nuns to the communal behaviours of modern London. This comparison also resonates with Anglo-Catholicism, which was instrumental in re-establishing religious orders in England, including Franciscan ones. Pusey played a large role in this movement, while Rossetti was strongly associated with her sister Maria's Anglo-Catholic order, the Society of All Saints. The role of religious orders in serving the community in England through the nineteenth century proceeds from the Catholic emphasis on local community and local provision for the poor. From this perspective, Meynell also confronts the romanticization of poverty: rather than the sanitized, idealized poverty of the medieval Franciscan orders, or the mythologized, distanced poverty perceived by the middle classes, her depiction of English poverty is intrusive and violent, invading homes and sacred spaces where its sordidness cannot be ignored. There is no dignity in this kind of poverty, which pushes against nineteenth-century narratives of working-class honour and the possibility of social mobility.

As in her other works, Meynell's delicate irony contains 'The Lady Poverty'. Poverty has 'lost her looks' (2) due to a 'change of times and change of air' (3). Normally the English would go to Italy for an improvement of air; yet in Meynell's poem the movement has been from Italy to England. Poverty in Meynell's idealized Italian context is that of the medieval Franciscan nuns, and while the reality might have been quite different, the narrative was one of choosing poverty out of a spiritual conviction of desiring to give up worldly goods in order to serve the poor. Meynell's own domestic actions suggest the value of such conviction to the poet. This was a pure kind of poverty: one that can be expressed in 'when her pure feet were bare' (6), before commodities such as gowns and shoes were involved. Tying back to Rossetti's 'Amor Mundi', shoes and clothes in Meynell's poem are material means by which distance is created: because of the shoes, the feet no longer touch, and the communal response to poverty becomes more complacent through this distance. There is a sense of paradox in Meynell's presentation of poverty in that it is both relative – buying into the Malthusian vision of new hungers being created in order to sustain a market, which leads to the perspective of never having enough – and also the fault of the poor.

At first this vision seems contradictory; but Meynell takes the common idea of the deserving and undeserving poor and satirically turns it on its head: the poor in London are not on the streets in Meynell's poem, but in the parlours, where Poverty 'dusts and trims, | Watches and counts' (8–9). There is a spiritual poverty in the domestic space, where the poor are judged, while those who are housed, and have food, consider themselves impoverished and therefore having nothing to give. Meynell challenges this perspective through the Franciscan ideal:

>     Oh, is this she
> Whom Francis met, whose step was free,
> Who with Obedience carolled hymns,
> In Umbria walked with Chastity? (9–12)

The link to chastity not only evokes the vows of poverty and chastity as the Christian ideal, but challenges the social emphasis on female sexual purity over the command to care for the poor. By asking in the third stanza 'Where is her ladyhood?' (13) Meynell challenges the preoccupation with female sexual purity as the greatest moral imperative; yet she also overturns the gendered significance by adding 'Not here, | Not among modern kinds of men' (13–14). In a world in which charity was seen as a feminine domain, Meynell makes men as accountable as women for the loss of dignity for the poor.

Meynell's aesthetic turn at the end of the poem is deliberately disturbing: the ladyhood of poverty is

> But in the stony fields, where clear
> Through the thin trees the skies appear,
> In delicate spare soil and fen,
> And slender landscape and austere. (15–18)

The irony of aesthetic poverty is made evident through the 'thin trees', the 'delicate spare soil' and the 'slender landscape', which mirror the ideal of the wasted woman as feminine perfection. The poem feels unended, in spite of its containment, because poverty necessarily remains unresolved. This lack of resolution is due to the inability to reconcile the materiality of poverty with the ideal, and in this way, Meynell challenges not only the idealization and historicization of poverty, but the lack of community commitment in the burgeoning religious orders she saw to effect change in light of the struggles of the community.

Meynell's desire to confront middle-class domestic spiritual poverty was shared by fellow members of her circle. Her close friend Coventry Patmore, who also converted to Roman Catholicism, wrote of the dangers of selfish individualism in alimentary terms in 'The Zest of Life' (1863), provocatively using the language of food and taste to critique the society that allows hunger to persist:

> Give thanks. It is not time misspent;
>     Worst fare this betters, and the best,
> Wanting this natural condiment,
>     Breeds crudeness, and will not digest.
> The grateful love the Giver's law;

> But those who eat, and look no higher,
> From sin or doubtful sanction draw
> > The biting sauce their feasts require.
> Give thanks for nought, if you've no more,
> > And, having all things, do not doubt
> That nought, with thanks, is blest before
> > Whate'er the world can give, without.[79]

Like Meynell's 'A Dead Harvest', 'The Zest of Life' was originally published in a volume of poetry, but subsequently reprinted in periodical reviews. Reading this lyric as a 12-line sonnet turns the traditional unattainable love into unattainable food; and the shortening of the form also speaks to the lack within the figure of the poem: the lack of communal connection and the lack of concern for the disadvantaged. The volta of the poem, then, becomes a repetition of the opening 'Give thanks', but with the cynicism of 'Give thanks for nought'. This transition is Patmore's response to the attitude, persistent in social narratives, that one does not have enough to be able to spare for others; yet this is the perspective that leads to the disunity of a community. '[T]hose who eat, and look no higher' (6) reap the bitterness that they sow: 'The biting sauce their feasts require' (8). Gratefulness is the 'natural condiment' (3), the natural state of humanity rather than the perversion of selfishness, and in those 'wanting' in that flavour there is a 'breed[ing]' of 'crudeness' that 'will not digest' (4). In Patmore's terms, he cannot swallow the attitude that one does not have anything to give, not even thanks, and he explicitly confronts the false excuse that one will give more when the world gives something to them. In this vein, one will never have enough to give, and instead maintains one's own complaints of impoverishment.

The metaphor of not being able to stomach selfishness and self-serving links powerfully to the importance of the Eucharist in both Anglican and Roman Catholic terms, and the fusion of material and spiritual satiation through this rite. The vast majority of the community of shared reading, even of the secular journals, would be familiar with the significance of the Eucharist, both spiritually and socially. Historically excommunication meant separation from the community as well as from God, and throughout the nineteenth century, with the rise of Anglo-Catholicism and ritualism, parallel with religious dissent, debates regarding the role and significance of the Eucharist were reignited, particularly in regard to social inclusion and exclusion. Romanism and Anglo-Catholicism shared a suspicion of secular institutions and governments for their inability to effect real social change in terms of social justice, but at the same time, the literary figures influenced by these movements were not necessarily blind to the problematic structures within church institutions. Moving from the sense of community created through shared reading, and the facilitation of that community to mobilize social action, in the following chapter I focus specifically on representations of the Eucharist in simultaneous material and spiritual terms as a critical challenge to complacency towards hunger.

3

# Embracing the community as one people

*We hope that the* social relations *between all classes of our community are generally becoming* more close and intimate, *as the real character of our Spiritual Brotherhood is brought out by our frequent united acts of worship, and communion in the blessed sacrament of Christ's Body and Blood: for our parochial institutions are steadily working on for the promoting of our brethren's welfare, both physical and moral.*
– Robert Liddell, *Matins, Litany, and Holy Communion* (1852)[1]

Robert Liddell's way of bringing together the 'social as well as … liturgical vision' of the Eucharistic community in *Matins, Litany and Holy Communion*, an 1852 sermon delivered at St Barnabas Church, Pimlico, is consistent with Anglo-Catholic expressions of the role of the sacrament of Holy Communion.[2] Karen Dieleman observes that '[a]ll the elements of the Anglican Communion liturgy encourage the believer toward communal, contemplative, and receptive modes of *shaping* and *being*', not just for heavenly reward but 'for temporal, embodied human *community*',[3] while Julie Melnyk suggests that the centrality of the Eucharist for the Tractarians and those influenced by them was not only applicable to Church form and ritual but to 'Christian life'.[4] James K. A. Smith argues even more explicitly through a sensory, material reading of the liturgical 'display and performance' of the Eucharist that it is 'an episode that compresses the gospel into action'.[5] This expansion of sacrament into the material and tangible was at the core of inserting sacrament into everyday nineteenth-century Christian practice. Indeed, Dieleman points out that regardless of denomination, all Christian churches practised two sacraments, baptism and the Eucharist,[6] both of which involve fusing a material act with the spiritual, or, in the words of the thirty-third Bishop of Oxford, Francis Paget, an 'invasion and penetration of the material by the spiritual'.[7]

Dieleman notes that both baptism and the Eucharist, while being seen spiritually as 'intensified moments of God's grace', also function to narrate 'a religio-politico-social reality in which all believers are equal before God ... a reconfiguration of family beyond the sphere of the home ... and an affirmation of a fundamental antithesis in the world, between what pleases God and what does not',[8] and while the liturgy is designed to '[impress] upon participants a deep sense of community',[9] I focus in this chapter on the antithesis revealed in the Eucharist. While the spiritual narrative is one of an equality that is meant to translate into the temporal world, in practice, social hierarchies, privilege and unequal social agency work against such visions of equality. Importantly, Hilary Fraser argues that the 'Holy Eucharist is the climax of the whole unified system of Sacraments which Keble reinstated in the Anglican consciousness',[10] and apart from theological and doctrinal concerns, I argue that the centrality of the Eucharist is intrinsically tied to the Tractarian vision of social action. The Eucharist itself is predicated on violence and injustice, focused on the torture and crucifixion of Christ, not merely an aestheticized rite of religious practice. In consuming the material bread and wine, the Eucharistic sacrament becomes a nexus between the spiritual and the temporal, which reveals the failure of earthly society to live up to the heavenly ideal. Although the sacrament is meant to perform and narrate equality, it is evident that such equality fails to go beyond the church doors; and in this way, spiritual and social hungers become aligned with physical hunger, as the invisibility of the poor is entwined in the ritual. The Eucharist then becomes a prophetic statement, a challenge to the congregation, as the liturgical form reinforces the requirement on the church community to provide for the less fortunate. Importantly, in the Eucharistic service, the financial offerings of the congregation are placed on the altar next to the bread and the wine, thereby encouraging a parallel between their human offerings to their community and the divine sacrifice of Christ.[11]

Ritual was meant to influence and shape attitudes beyond the church doors, and the Eucharist in particular was envisaged as a means by which individuals could at once gain spiritual comfort and a renewed sense of duty towards their community. Joshua King makes this connection explicit in his reading of Rossetti's 'Because He first loved us' (1893):

Referring to his crucifixion in colloquial terms that directly apply to the Eucharist ('when Bread I brake'), Christ makes the heart of High Church ritual the empowering motive for everyday care in fulfillment of his parable of the sheep and goats, according to which love shown 'My hungry brethren' is love shown to him (Matt. 25: 31–46). Christ roots the speaker's love in his own love and in the communion of the new creation, of which the communion meal is a foretaste.[12]

This connection between the Eucharist and the Anglo-Catholic social mission is also tied explicitly to the art and form of poetry in Fraser's reading of Hopkins, in which art embodies 'the continuing "real" presence of Christ in the natural world', thereby resonating with the controversial doctrine of the Real Presence: 'God, having been made flesh, is mediated by the natural world and by the human body.'[13] The materiality of the Eucharist, tied to the divine representation of Christ's body and blood, embedded in the aesthetics of rite, 'brings together the human subject, the objective things of the world, and the spirit'.[14] In this way, the aestheticized, mediated state of the Eucharistic elements – as feeding one both spiritually and physically – provides a powerful medium through which to challenge the congregation's attitudes towards one another and their willingness to see, touch and acknowledge their inherent connection. While a comfort for some, this recognition of communion could also be a prophetic jolt to the self-serving consciousness, particularly given that the taking of the Eucharist follows a scripted requirement in the liturgy to share verbally 'The Peace of Christ' with surrounding members of the parish.

In the preface to the published version of the 1843 sermon that saw him suspended for two years for heresy, Edward Pusey writes, 'Nothing, throughout the whole Sermon, was further from my thoughts than controversy ... it was my wish ... to point out [the Eucharist's] comforting character to the penitent.'[15] He goes on to explain that since 'the very outset of this Sermon conveyed at once, that I believed the elements to "remain in their natural substances," and that I did not attempt to define the *mode* of the Mystery that they were also the Body and Blood of Christ, I had no fear of being misunderstood.'[16] The controversy arose through Pusey's *via media* Real Presence position between the Protestant Eucharistic elements being symbolic only, and the Roman Catholic belief in transubstantiation. The debates surrounding these divisions, and the fears of Romanism that the Real Presence doctrine evoked, are outside the scope of this study; however, what I want to draw attention to is, first, that by not attempting to define the Mystery, Pusey is enacting spiritual and intellectual reserve, thus deeply connecting two key doctrines, and, second, that the way in which the spiritual and the material are integrated in the Real Presence doctrine contributed to the social vision of the Anglo-Catholics and enabled poets to extend the ritual aesthetic into a question of social justice.

Pusey's concern for social justice is made evident through all his works. Two years earlier in his Bristol sermon he compared the social tenor of Britain to the selfish complacency that led to the Old Testament flood: 'We seem like those of old, who were "eating and drinking, marrying and giving in marriage, until the day when Noah entered into the ark, and the flood came, and swept them all away".'[17] For Pusey, the Eucharist is a symbol of all humans' equality before God – an equality that should be more evident in the temporal world. From his perspective, this equality is not present in the world because although some individuals have an outward vision, the majority of people do not take responsibility for their communities:

> Individuals, of course, feel and act upon this responsibility; but I speak of the age, and those things, in which its character, apart from God's grace to individuals and their use of that grace, expresses itself. Responsibility, except to obey the will of the majority, seems to be the thought the most remote from men's minds. In the pursuit of men's material interests, in the relation of nations to one another, in the education of the poor, the provision for their wants, the way of dispensing the abundance which God gives to any of us, the last thing which seems to occur to men's minds is, 'Has God any Will in this matter?' Men so forget God that they do not even think it worth while to deny Him. God is simply ignored. They are independent of Him. They live in the midst of the Gospel, which declares itself a 'power of God unto salvation,' and it does not even occur to them, that it is a duty to enquire whether their Maker (if it occurs to them that they have one) has revealed His Will to them, His creatures, or no.[18]

The way in which God is ignored parallels the way the poor are deemed invisible; thus Pusey indirectly reminds his listeners and readers of one of the most persistent threads through Anglo-Catholic sermons: 'Inasmuch as ye have done it unto one of the least of these my brethren, ye have done it unto me' (Mt. 25:40). Pusey's understanding of human responsibility resonates powerfully with Emmanuel Levinas's philosophy of responsibility, social justice and community connection: 'To maintain that the relationship with a neighbor ... is a responsibility for the neighbor ... is to find no longer any limit or measure for this responsibility.'[19] However, the limitlessness of Levinas's vision holds the danger of the emotional overload that the Tractarians and their descendants wished to avoid. Levinas's use of 'neighbor' seems to evoke the question in the gospels, 'Who is my neighbour?', which Christ answers with the parable of the Good Samaritan – a parable that has idiomatically forgotten the crucial element of the Samaritan's foreignness, and thus his own poignant exclusion from the community to which the man he saved belonged. Pusey's vision reduces the idea of the neighbour to the immediate parish community, not out of a separatist desire, but out of an impetus to challenge members of the community to recognize the poverty lying close to home. In this way, he circles back to a similar motive to Levinas, for whom 'Responsibility is a form of recognition – acknowledgement of a claim, an order, which is even constitutive of subjectivity – a summons to arise to be and to present oneself.'[20] Importantly, 'To be responsible before the other is *to make of my subsistence the support of his order and his needs.*'[21]

Whereas Derrida's Law of Tact emphasizes the untouchable, a distance like Harrington's impersonal intimacy, as a means to create subjectivity and dignity for the other, Levinas challenges this mode of creating distanced subjectivity through his emphasis on proximity. The Tractarians existed paradoxically in both modes, necessarily recognizing distance but also emphasizing proximity to the poor. This dual vision sought to challenge individuals to recognize the closeness of the poor and to acknowledge their visibility: seeing the poor as individual subjects who, due to their spiritual equality, were worthy of assistance in the temporal world's inequality. The individual took precedence over the collective. As Henry Parry Liddon contended,[22] 'It might seem that individuals die off while the nation remains; but the truth, the real truth is that the nation in time passes away, while the units who compose it live for ever. In the next world there will be no England: there will survive only souls of Englishmen.'[23] In a similar manner, King sees Rossetti's *Verses* (1893) as 'invit[ing] readers to imagine themselves in an ecumenical and international community of saints whose hope for citizenship in a resurrected nation under Christ would spur its members to acts of love and justice now'.[24] Although not all Anglo-Catholics were as egalitarian as Rossetti, this recognition of heavenly citizenship deliberately 'estranged them from total identification with any national society, branch of the Church, or reading audience',[25] while at the same time encouraging the recognition of proximate individuals. Similarly for Liddon, the figure of the Eucharist is used both to elevate the individual and to critique the commercial national vision, which worked against recognition of communal proximity: 'Yet how often do men speak as if commercial and industrial enterprises were a vast sacrament of regeneration, warranted to renew national life.'[26]

Levinas intervenes in this space through emphasizing that in order to be proximate, one needs to experience the sensation of loss in giving, rather than giving out of excess. Indeed, for Levinas, the essence of human duty lies in this experience:

> In corporeality are united the traits we have enumerated: for the other, despite oneself, starting with oneself ... in the duty to give to the other even the bread out of one's own mouth and the coat from one's shoulders ... If giving is proximity itself, *it takes on its full meaning only in stripping me of what is more my own than possession.* Pain penetrates into the very heart of the for-oneself that beats in enjoyment, in the life that is complacent in itself, that lives of its life. *To give ... is to take the bread out of one's own mouth, to nourish the hunger of another with one's own fasting.*[27]

The visceral nature of Levinas's pain confronts the complacency of an age that attempts to distance itself from suffering, much as the Tractarians confronted the complacency of the nineteenth-century British middle class. In the image of taking the bread from one's own mouth, Levinas appropriates the sacred role of bread in the Judeo-Christian tradition in order to interrogate the unequal supply of staple foods that persists in human history. Counter to capitalist individualism, it is the responsibility of those who have bread to give to those who do not, so that community can be sustained. Levinas's call for personal austerity requires one to rethink the limits of what one can afford to give, both materially and emotionally.

## The materiality of the Eucharist

The Eucharist gained increasing importance in nineteenth-century Anglo-Catholicism, from the influence of the Tractarians through to the development of ritualism. F. Elizabeth Gray notes that Alice Meynell's focus on the Eucharist – which Gray sees as resulting from Meynell's position as an '[i]nheritor of the renewed symbolic emphasis stirred by the Tractarians, as well as of the Catholic tradition to which she had pledged herself' – enables a paradox through which she can discuss 'the breakdown of difference between humans as she discusses the breakdown of difference between human and God'.[28] While Gray notes the egalitarian nature of Meynell's vision, suggesting that being 'one in Christ … means not just that we all partake in Christ's nature (that is, we *are* Christ) but also that we are, inescapably, *each other*',[29] her reading focuses on spiritual relationships rather than the implications of this theological stance for social justice: while the Eucharistic ritual emphasizes the construction of community, it also reveals the ways in which power relations and social privilege prevent such egalitarianism from going beyond the church walls.

The Real Presence doctrine, in the way it fuses the material and the spiritual, brings to the fore a challenge to church communities to acknowledge the disparity between doctrine and their everyday lives, not just on the personal level, but in the political and economic structures that reinforce social inequalities. Often this critique manifests not through direct references to the Eucharistic elements, but through the organic materials from which they come: references to corn or wheat, or wine, grapes or the vine, simultaneously allude to the body and blood of Christ as well as the staple foods of the nineteenth-century diet. Pusey's most controversial sermon on the Eucharist makes a point of connecting the sacred rite to its organic properties, while also cataloguing the representations of bread and wine throughout the Old and New Testaments, from the Garden of Eden, through to the Paschal Lamb, the manna in the desert, and the Shewbread, to the Last Supper and the Wedding Feast of the Lamb. The sermon is not only provocative in its transmission of the doctrine of the Real Presence, but also in the way this material connection to physical, earthly substance indirectly critiques capitalist structures:

'Wisdom,' that is, He Who is the Wisdom of God, in a parable corresponding to that of the marriage feast, crieth, 'Come eat of My bread and drink of the wine I have mingled.' Or, in the very Psalm of His Passion and atoning Sacrifice, it is foretold, that '*the poor shall eat and be satisfied;*' or that He, the good Shepherd, shall prepare a Table for those whom He leadeth by the still waters of the Church, and [']giveth them the Cup of overflowing joy;' or as the source of gladness, 'Thou hast put gladness into my heart, since the time that their *corn and wine and oil* (the emblem of the Spirit of which the faithful drink) increased,' and 'the wine which gladdeneth man's heart, and the oil which maketh his face to shine, and bread which strengtheneth man's heart;' or of spiritual growth, 'corn and wine shall make the young men and maidens of Zion to grow;' or as that which alone is satisfying, 'buy wine without money and without price,' for that 'which is not bread;' or as the special Gift to the faithful, 'He hath given meat unto them that fear Him;' or that which, after His Passion, He drinketh anew with His disciples in His Father's kingdom, 'I have gathered my myrrh, I have drunk my wine with my milk; eat, O friends; drink, yea, drink abundantly, O beloved.'[30]

In the heavenly economy, there is no question of deserving and undeserving poor – that is, who qualifies for externally funded provision. All are entitled not just to bare sustenance, but to an overflowing cup, of which they are instructed to 'drink abundantly'. Although Pusey speaks metaphorically of spiritual matters, it is difficult not to draw resonances with temporal, worldly provision in the references of corn, wine, oil and bread, and crucially that all these provisions are given 'without money and without price', consumed as a shared meal with Christ himself. In this way, he simultaneously rejects the capitalist economy of buying and selling, while creating an image of a community that is inclusive of the poor. Through the organic properties of the Eucharistic elements, Pusey not only challenges the selfish impetus of capitalism, but further challenges his audience to recognize the divine commission to care for the poor in their community, even to the point of self-sacrifice.

The poems I discuss here are not all obviously about the Eucharist. However, within the poetic tradition of analogy that the Tractarians upheld as a mechanism of reserve, allusions to bread or grain need to be connected simultaneously to Christ as the Bread of Life, God providing our daily bread, and the Last Supper. Through the lens of the Eucharist, the poets look through the spiritual aesthetic to the material beginnings of the Eucharistic elements: the organic corn and wheat. The poems constantly turn to grain and bread, or the lack thereof; and in this way, they conflate the sacred with the very real poverty of those who do not have access to daily bread. The poets perceive the ritual act of the Eucharist simultaneously as mystical and material, thereby at once evoking a sense of connection to the Divine, and also challenging their readers to connect with the community around them, especially the poor. While elevated by the mystical, they are grounded by the haptic and gustatory experience of taking the elements into their bodies, a sensory experience that grounds the participant in the tangible present. In this moment of satiating a spiritual hunger, they are potentially reminded of the daily physical hunger of their neighbours. Within this vision, the sensory materiality of the sacramental elements is intimately connected to the individual's understanding of their position in relation to God, or the spiritual, as well as the community, or material world. It is at once eternal and temporal in a way that reflects the Real Presence doctrine, and the adherence to ritual is emulated in poetic form. In the Anglo-Catholic vision, the shortness of one's time in the temporal world means that there is very little time or space in which to act, but the poet's understanding of one community of saints in heaven and earth creates a sense of ongoing dialogue that mitigates this limitation. By recognizing that one small act of help contributes to the communal effort, the dialogue is extended. Procter, Rossetti and Meynell, each heavily influenced by Tractarian theology and practice, build a sense of communal responsibility through their work, which informs this social vision. They challenge the restraint of poetry through pressing the boundaries of meter but being bound by tight rhyme schemes, but further, their use of anaphora and deixis reveals a mutual compulsion, not just to hold onto the moment, but to recognize the significance of the moment: a repeated desire to be awake in the now – Kerry McSweeney's 'sweet *now*'[31] – and able to act. Their allusions to the Eucharist undergird this vision, reinforcing and challenging their readers to understand their Christian responsibility to care for the poor, even if one person's actions seem small and finite.

In spite of the regularity of lines, the meter in Procter's 'Sowing and Reaping' (1856)[32] is surprisingly irregular for a poet who tends to adhere to a strict trochaic tetrameter; but the poem is held together by a rhyme scheme that reflects an exponentially increasing abundance that is grounded in, always returning to, something stable: *ab cb db*. The first stanza requires a trust in divine provision and a willingness to be generous to the poor, which this rhyme scheme reflects:

> Sow with a generous hand;
> >  Pause not for toil or pain;
> Weary not through the heat of summer,
> >  Weary not through the cold spring rain;
> But wait till the autumn comes
> >  For the sheaves of golden grain. (1–6)

The reference to 'golden grain' alludes to the spiritual fulfilment of the Eucharist, but also to economic provision. The Eucharistic allusion is not of the individual towards God, however, but of the individual facing outward to the community. This image is a break from Procter's Roman Catholicism, in which the priest would face the altar during the Mass, his back to the congregation, speaking in Latin at levels barely audible to the worshippers.[33] In a decidedly Anglican approach of 'community-consciousness … inextricably bound … [to] the sacramental act',[34] Procter looks out from the Eucharistic altar, alluded to in 'fear not, | A table will be spread;' (7–8), reminding her reader that a part of the communion of the saints is the common care for the saints:

> What matter if you are too weary
> >  To eat your hard-earned bread:
> Sow, while the earth is broken,
> >  For the hungry must be fed. (9–12)

Procter refuses to allow a question mark after 'hard-earned bread'; the question, even a rhetorical one, is denied, and the impetus is driven through the colon to forget about one's own concerns of provision and strength to keep moving in an outward direction to give to others. In terms resonant with Levinas's pain, the reader is called upon to sacrifice their own comfort in order to provide for those less fortunate; and while the broken earth speaks to its readiness for sowing, it also evokes the emotional and social trauma caused by war, famine and social unrest, made pertinent in the aftermath of the Crimean War and the Great Irish Famine.

Procter speaks peremptorily to a nation exhausted by its own socio-economic concerns and the press of migration. Following the trochaic accent on the repeated command to 'Sow', when the beginning of the fourth stanza changes to 'Then sow' (19), the emphasis turns to 'Then', the temporal moment. Following the caesura that emphasizes this moment, Procter reminds her reader of the shortness of time:

> Then sow – for the hours are fleeting,
>     And the seed must fall today;
> And care not what hands shall reap it,
>     Or if you shall have passed away
> Before the waving corn-fields
>     Shall gladden the sunny day. (37–42)

The moment of placing the seed before the starving ground is as fleeting as the moment when the Eucharistic element is placed on the tongue. Once it is swallowed, it can no longer be sensed consciously; however, the work is done beyond consciousness, and beyond death. As the sacred element feeds the soul in a way that cannot be materially felt, in feeding the poor, even on a small scale, one should have faith that the seed will turn into a crop, even if one cannot see its material benefits. Procter constantly looks to move her readers beyond 'the coward's doubting, | Or your own heart's trembling fears' (45–6), in order to trust that 'You shall reap in joy the harvest | You have sown in tears' (47–8). The Eucharist, as a symbol of Christ's sacrifice that the Church is meant to emulate, is drawn out through the material elements that feed people. Procter resists the fear of loss, which leads to selfish hoarding, instead embracing loss in order to call for generous giving.

Procter's resistance of consumerism and her preoccupation with the transience of time is similarly reflected in the poetry of both Rossetti and Meynell. Rossetti's 'Amen' (1862)[35] engages with the Anglo-Catholic understanding of human limitations, both in terms of transience and the extent to which an individual can have an impact. The poem's three stanzas show a passage through Autumn, to Winter, to Spring, reflecting the passing of time; yet even though the cycle is halted by the lack of Summer, the ending of time is questioned through the internal dialogue, which draws upon Christ's crucifixion seeming to be the end of life, but in the Christian perspective, it is the beginning. This paradox is at the heart of the Eucharist. The structure of the first line of each stanza with a definite statement followed by a question – 'It is over. What is over?' (1); 'It is finished. What is finished?' (6); and 'It suffices. What suffices?' (11) – appropriates the authority of Christ's words on the cross in order to buy into the Anglo-Catholic conviction that one small action can contribute significantly to a wider impact. The role of human beings in this act is asserted through the allusion to the call-and-response liturgical form familiar in Anglo-Catholicism. In terms of the structural representation of faith, the regularity of rhythm and meter in the poem reflects Rossetti's adherence to a faith in a divine, eternal picture that encompasses the temporal, yet faithful, work on earth.

At the same time, Rossetti is very much focused on the transient now as the moment in which one has to act. The anaphora of 'Now the sheaves are gathered newly, | Now the wheat is garnered duly' (4–5) intensifies the present moment, something that is made even more potent in the following stanza, where moving from 'Was the fallow field left unsown?' (9) she writes deictically, 'Will *these* buds be always unblown?' (10; emphasis added). The specificity of 'these buds' focalizes the work and effects of the individual with a powerful lyrical subjectivity: the work of each bud seems designated to an individual's responsibility, and if all work together, focusing on their point of responsibility, the work shall be completed successfully. Furthermore, each bud is individually significant. Therefore, to follow with 'It suffices' and 'All suffices reckoned rightly' (12) is a containment of purpose, a reminder not to be overwhelmed by the enormity of the field. With the hope of Spring, and the aesthetic pleasure of roses and the 'quickening sun' (15), the extended final stanza – a septet rather than the quintain of the first two – expresses the abundance of fulfilment in sensory terms, reflecting a faith that there will be impact: 'And my garden teem with spices' (17).

Rossetti's sheaves of wheat speak of a harvest of souls as well as the harvest that feeds the body, a duality that is represented in the Eucharist and echoed in her use of Christ's words on the cross. As Mary Arseneau observes in regard to 'Amen', the image of the harvest maintains a 'seamless identification of natural and spiritual fruition' and, just as Rossetti's 'devotional and non-devotional poetry modulate into each other', within the poem, the spiritual and material are inherently linked.[36] Meynell's poetry also embraces this duality of representation, incorporating the wine – or blood – as well as the body in wheat. The allusion to the Eucharist is therefore more direct, while Meynell, like Procter and Rossetti, uses this moment of ritual to focalize the moment of action. 'The Fugitive' (1907)[37] maintains a similar form to that of Procter and Rossetti through the use of tetrameter, although her rhythm is a mixture of dactyls, trochees and anapaests:

> Yes, from the ingrate heart, the street
> Of garrulous tongue, the warm retreat
>     Within the village and the town;
>     Not from the lands where ripen brown
> A thousand thousand hills of wheat;
> Not from the long Burgundian line,
> The Southward, sunward range of vine.
>     Hunted, He never will escape
>     The flesh, the blood, the sheaf, the grape,
> That feed His man – the bread, the wine.

The irregular rhythm is not used to reflect a lack of faith in the poetic voice of the lyric mode, but rather a reflection of the anarchical lack of faith in the community that the poet is representing. The deictic use of the French epigraph, 'Nous avons chassé ce Jésus-Christ', 'We hunted *this* Christ', brings the idea of the divine into the specificity of the temporal world, destabilizing an understanding of faith by critiquing the world for running after a range of ideas and passions instead of being grounded in the true Christian faith, which, for Meynell by this point, is Roman Catholicism. It harkens to revolutionary France throughout the nineteenth century, and the rejection of Christianity as a way in which the nation of France continually crucifies Christ.

The sense of Christ being hunted through the streets also alludes to the disjunction between the privileged and the starving, particularly through the reference to the 'hills of wheat' (5) and the idyllic 'Southward, sunward range of vine' (7) in stark contrast to 'The flesh, the blood, the sheaf, the grape' (9), using the Eucharist to refer as much to humans sharing in Christ's sufferings as to Christ himself. It is important that the last line, 'That feed His man – the bread, the wine' (10), is a reference to the people. Yet the poem is complicated as a criticism of the revolutionaries who are fighting the repression of 'the long Burgundian line' (6). It is difficult to identify where Christ is in this picture; Meynell reflects a similar longing to Hopkins in the desire to perceive Christ's inscape, the 'bridge' or 'stem of stress between us and things', the presence of Christ in the material world.[38] The materiality of the Eucharistic elements, in terms of either the Real Presence or transubstantiation, requires a literal acceptance of Christ's inscape; therefore, the anaphoric use of the definite article – 'The flesh, the blood, the sheaf, the grape' – particularizes Christ's presence in the world, and then 'the bread, the wine' becomes a deliberate link of the Eucharist to food provision, engendering the responsibility of the individual within the milieu of anarchy.

'In Portugal, 1912', first published as 'Christ in Portugal' (1911), is intriguing in the context of the particularizing deictic lyric. The revised title recalls the attack on Chaves on 8 July 1912, in which the Catholic royalist rebels were defeated by the secular rulers of Portugal. The change of signification moves from a lyrical Christ to a specific historical moment, rather than the repeated sharing of a perverse, violent Eucharist in 'The Fugitive'. The Portuguese rebels, who rose up on religious grounds, were also rebelling on the basis of economic and social dispossession, which inevitably involves lack of food security, an idea captured in Meynell's image of 'Scatter the chalice, crush the bread' (2). The 'Lonely unconsecrated Host' (8) emphasizes the division between God and man and, by extension, the mention of bread, vines and the wine press cannot be separated from the daily sufferings of the people. This poem is much more regular in meter: the lines are balanced, and the anaphora of 'In field, in village, and in town' (3) creates an internal structure that, mirroring in the next stanza 'His sun ... His frost' (6), creates order in the chaos of dispossession. The rite of the Eucharist is stabilizing, the repetition acting as a reminder that God is sovereign in a thoroughly catholic, universal sense: from country to city, from one extreme of weather to another, they belong to the Divine.

As a political poem, pressing the boundaries of the lyric, Meynell's 'The mill conceals the harvest's Lord' provocatively challenges the motives of the victors. Instead of the Lord of the harvest, they are ruled by the harvest (commerce) itself; yet within the poem's structure, while a political challenge, and while revealing devastation – 'The wine-press holds the unbidden Christ' (10) – there is an internal confidence through the regularity of the poem's form that suggests hope and resilience. In the preface to its publication in the *New Catholic World* in 1912, the editor writes that the poem 'not only bring[s] home to us the spiritual havoc wrought by the anti-Christian Government of Portugal, but with beautiful poetic mastery [it] reveal[s] to us through the light of revelation the wondrous integrity and harmony of God's entire universe'.[39]

This almost paradoxical juncture of material havoc amidst the integrity and harmony of the divine emulates the Real Presence in the Eucharist. The violence of the Eucharist is brought to the fore in Meynell: the aesthetic beauty of the rite is made possible through the violence of bloodshed. This paradox is at the core of the Doctrine of Reserve, which infuses the poetry of Procter, Rossetti and Meynell. There is a need to distance violence through the aesthetic (i.e. through aesthetic reserve) in order to avoid revulsion and abjection. This strategic aesthetic act reveals the role of the lyric in the political world, drawing readers into proximity with the inward subjectivity. Through the materiality of the Eucharistic elements, these poets speak with particularity to their social contexts, using their belief in the infinite as a poetic and spiritual means to counteract their finitude, and to challenge the retreat of society into a false belief of the inability of individuals to impact the temporal world.

## A taste of Christ in a hungry community

> As the manna is said to have 'contented every man's delight and agreed to every taste,' so He, the Heavenly Manna, becometh to every man what he needeth, and what he can receive.[40]

The Sacrament of the Eucharist illuminates the way that taste, the most proximate of the five senses, constructs and subverts social agency. James Smith provocatively refers to 'a sort of sanctified salivation' in the anticipation of taking Communion: '[the wine's] scent wafting across the place as our taste buds surprise us when, in an admittedly Pavlovian response, they begin to perk up at the thought of its bite on our tongue … and we slip [the wafer] onto our tongue in that weird moment of waiting for it to melt in our mouth'.[41] This account seems perverse because it is sensuous; yet the Eucharist is an extraordinary rite because it requires a merging of the most intimate physical sense – taste – with the deepest spiritual understanding: the idea of taking into one's body, and consuming, the divine. This is a point at which the sacred and the material meet: the eternal and the temporal. The act of the worldly consuming the divine exposes the failures of the world, revealing the inequalities and the distances between spheres of society that are meant to be one in Christ. By linking the Eucharist to the Old Testament manna, Pusey is suggesting that divine provision is meant to be equal across the Church community. The manna was dispensed so that every person would receive the same amount as each other every day, except on the day before the Sabbath, when twice as much would be gathered so they would not have to work on the Sabbath (Exod. 16:4-6). Similarly, early Christianity, which the Anglo-Catholics were drawn to, was predicated on communal living. Yet Christ's words at the Last Supper 'this do in remembrance of me' are evoked by Paul the Apostle to challenge the already emerging lack of communal spirit: 'When ye come together therefore into one place, this is not to eat the Lord's supper. For in eating, everyone taketh before other his own supper: and one is hungry and another is drunken ... despise ye the church of God, and shame them that have not?' (1 Cor. 11:20-2). This self-focus and social disparity, as well as the disregard for the poor, would have resonated powerfully in the nineteenth-century context, with the rise of capitalist individualism; and the presence of the tiny wafer or bread, and a sip of wine, although the congregation would not always be given the wine, presented as a shared meal enacted in memory of Christ could be seen as a perverse display of false equality.

In *Sensing the Past* (2007), Mark M. Smith connects the early-modern sumptuary laws with the Eucharist to critique not just the way in which Holy Communion functioned to regulate society, but specifically the way taste subverts the unifying myth of the sacrament: 'Bread, wine, taste: all served to establish the immediacy and intimacy of Christ's presence.'[42] Yet while there was bread, there was not always wine; and neither the quality nor quantity of bread were necessarily equal. The tension of 'taste and gustation ... arrang[ing] social authority'[43] persists well into nineteenth-century understandings of religious and social communities, brought into stark focus by widespread poverty and starvation. David Howes and Constance Classen connect taste and divine justice, pointing out that '[d]uring centuries when many people were hungry much of the time, the notion of divine justice (and more generally God) being "delicious food" had a powerful resonance';[44] and while this again is an early-modern example, there are clear resonances with the nineteenth century, from the memory of the Flour Wars, the food riots going into the nineteenth century, the Irish famines, and revolutionary Continental Europe. While the bread and wine seem to unite, it is taste that reveals social divides. Social inclusion and agency are defined by the tastes one can access and the foods one can consume; and while this was specified by law in early-modern England, in the nineteenth-century context it was determined by economics, politics and the response to natural and human disasters.

Levinas's perspective on taste is useful at this point because he emphasizes the importance of enjoyment in taste, as well as the necessity of sacrificing one's own enjoyment for the sake of others. At the same time, he acknowledges the visceral nature of taste through its fusion of taste and touch:

> Tasting is first satisfaction. Matter 'materializes' in satisfaction, which, over and beyond any intentional relationship of cognition or possession, of 'taking in one's hands,' means 'biting into' … It is irreducible to a taking in one's hands, for it is already an absorption of a 'within' including the ambiguity of two inwardnesses: that of a recipient of spatial forms, and that of an ego assimilating the other in its identity, and coiling in over itself … To bite on the bread is the very meaning of tasting.[45]

Without knowing satisfaction in what one is to give, there is no sacrifice, no sense of personal loss. In order to truly give, to 'take care of the other's need', Levinas suggests that one must not only incorporate 'his misfortunes and his faults', but also undergo 'a tearing from oneself despite oneself' and be 'torn from the complacency in oneself characteristic of enjoyment, snatching the bread from one's mouth'.[46] This violent vision of self-sacrifice resembles the motive of the Eucharist, in which 'the sacrificial elements of the Eucharist' suggest that 'the believer's "broken" body' ought to model 'the suffering of Christ'.[47] It seems even more pertinent, then, that Levinas refers to the 'vulnerability and paining' of sacrificing one's own enjoyment as 'exhausting themselves like a hemorrhage', in a way that evokes Christ's blood: one has to know the enjoyment of eating bread, 'not in order to have the merit of giving it, but in order to give it with one's heart, to give oneself in giving it'.[48] From this perspective, the satisfaction found in the rite of the Eucharist can be read as necessary in order to give of oneself, a visceral yet analogical reminder of the imperative to care for the vulnerable even at the expense of one's own worldly security.

Much current research through sensory studies looks at the Eucharist either through its spiritual purpose of connection with the divine, such as Finbarr Barry Flood's discussion of ingesting the sacred, which argues that this act 'point[s] to a desire to collapse a distinction between emulator and emulated', that has 'less to do with imitating than with becoming',[49] or through the distinction between the clergy and the laity. This latter perspective is perhaps particularly relevant in the Tractarian context, in which there was a push towards re-establishing the clerical hierarchy of the Middle Ages. In *The Deepest Sense* (2012), Classen draws attention to the fact that in early-modern Europe '[w]hile ordinary folk might bake the bread that became the body of Christ with their own hands, only priests were allowed to handle the consecrated host'.[50] She goes on to discuss that while the laity could swallow the host, there was great anxiety over how to do so appropriately; and furthermore, the wine – the blood of Christ – was 'limited to priests', apparently 'so as to minimize spillage'.[51] My perspective incorporates these arguments, but takes them in a different direction: rather than focusing on the division between the priesthood and the laity, I examine the way in which the Eucharist is used poetically to reveal class distinctions between members of the congregation. Excommunication, which excludes one from consuming the Eucharist, crucially not only denies the exiled access to heaven in the afterlife, it ostracizes them from their earthly community. Such exile can then be extended to socio-economic position. Again, Levinas is useful in his view that proximity 'is to enjoy and to suffer by the other', and most importantly, 'Proximity ... is responsibility'.[52] In a tone that seems to evoke the social vision of the Tractarians, Levinas adheres to a kind of Derridean Law of Tact in proximity remaining 'a distance diminished',[53] that is, exponential but never reaching a point of contact, but crucially forbidding cultural, social or emotional complacency: 'Proximity is not a state, a repose, but, a restlessness, null site, outside the place of rest.'[54] Given the violent origin of the Eucharist, taking the elements into one's body should be a paradoxical moment of comfort and discomfort: comfort in salvation and God's provision so that one is emotionally free to be uncomfortable enough about social inequalities to sacrifice one's own comfort for the sake of others. In the poems I look at in this section, the Eucharist features figuratively to expose economic and social deprivation. The bread and wine of the sacrament are again diffused into everyday food and drink, so that the idea of figures being deprived of the sacrament – of being excommunicated – is extrapolated into their social deprivation. The importance of community connection and spiritual equality in the act of communion is further exposed and critiqued through the materiality of social exclusion expressed through a figure's capacity to taste the bread and wine.

Rossetti's 'At Home' (1862)[55] has typically been read as the poetic voice speaking from beyond the grave, but for my purposes I am reading the death in this poem more metaphorically, used as a trope to convey the secularized excommunication of separation and distance within the community: the dead figure represents the impoverished and forgotten hungry. Rossetti's concern regarding social exclusion can be seen, for example, in her engagement in the campaign against pew rentals, a system that 'alienated the poor who could not afford a rented pew and thus felt they did not belong to the worshipping community' even though it was their parish church.[56] The use of death as the means of separation in the poem is even more subversive in this sense because in the Anglo-Catholic vision there is one family in heaven and earth, so there is meant to be a sense that there is no separation, only delay, in physical death. Rossetti held to the doctrine of the Communion of Saints, which upheld a belief in 'the mystical union in Christ of members in the visible Church militant on earth with members of the invisible Church triumphant who have entered communion with God after death'.[57] Yet in Rossetti's poem, separation is both spiritually and materially evident through sensory disparity, conveying economic and social distance. The living figures are intimately connected through their shared feasting, and their sensory experience is acutely proximate: together, they are able to enjoy the sensuality of taste and touch. The dead figure, on the other hand, is isolated and limited to the distant auditory and visual senses, a limitation that evokes a sense of physical and social hunger. What is even more poignant is the title of the poem, in that the speaker is 'At Home' and yet feels so isolated and hungry in that space: there, but not there, not able to connect.

The first and last stanzas provide a sensory bookending to the poem, the first containing the taste of the Eucharist, while the last emphasizes the lack of tactility available to the dead. The tactile is crucial because one cannot taste without touching; and the inability to connect with food as well as with the community is what undergirds my reading. It is one thing to be able to see, and even smell, food, but to be restricted from touching and tasting it, while others eat, is the salient torture of inequality. The hope of the poem perhaps lies in that the friends are feasting under orange boughs, which aesthetically recalls All Souls Day, or the Day of the Dead, a time when the divide between the living and the dead is seemingly lifted, also suggested in the speaker saying

'I passed the door' as if crossing a threshold (3). This connection is subverted, though, through the disparity of the sensory experience of the poem.

The Eucharist is suggested through the friends' feasting: 'From hand to hand they pushed the wine' (5). The communal partaking of that which represents the blood of Christ is transformed from a solemn spiritual moment to one of singing, jesting and laughing, a move to the earthly that is mirrored by the intense tangibility of the food they eat: 'They sucked the pulp of plum and peach' (6), fruits that are as soft and succulent as they are sweet. The sensuality of the consonance and assonance resonates with 'Goblin Market', and must evoke a similar response: the intimacy of eating, and eating together, not to mention the luxurious, decadent fullness of the types of fruit mentioned, brings the idea of communion back to a carnal setting, reiterating not just the spiritual separation of the observer, but a material one.

The speaker, however, can only watch, her hunger increasing emotionally (and potentially physically) as the alliterative 'friends | Feasting' (3–4) takes on an ironic tone through the line break that haunts the rest of the poem and is affirmed in the penultimate stanza with 'I, only I, had passed away' (22) and '"Tomorrow and today," they cried; | I was of yesterday' (23–4). The speaker is diminished through 'only': she is the only one who cannot eat, but also her passing is not significant; further, the fact that they exist in different worlds is shown in that because she is of the past, she does not figure in her friends' thoughts or imagination. In the final stanza, the speaker 'shiver[s] comfortless' (25) but is not even able in that act to have enough impact to send a 'chill across the tablecloth', let alone eat from it (26). This inability to make a tangible impression reinforces the speaker's inability to taste, and therefore her inability to be a part of the group that communally enjoys the plum and peach. At the same time, though, this inability stands as a critique of the group, whose complacency and enjoyment of their present tastes render them unable to be moved by their lost (starving) friend. The present, unsacrificed enjoyment prevents individuals, not just from having compassion for the struggles of others, but from having the capacity to recognize those struggles.

Just as Rossetti uses poetic opulence to describe the fruit denied to her speaker, Hopkins's critique of the grotesque excess and luxury found at a church altar in his poem 'Easter' (c. 1866) takes the idea further, for while Rossetti's wealth is spent on an excess of food while forgetting those who cannot enjoy it, it is at least something that is, in moderation, necessary for life. Hopkins's poem, however, has wealth spent on jewels and aromatic oils – the pearls, opals and spikenard used to 'deck [the] shrine' (7). These objects do little to sustain the human body. Subversively Hopkins evokes the tale of the woman who poured expensive oil on Christ's feet, an act that Judas Iscariot protested against with the reason that they could have used the money spent on the oil to give to the poor, although Judas was actually skimming the treasury: 'Reck not what the poor have lost; | Upon Christ throw all away' (4–5). There is a paradox in Hopkins's vision, however, as on the one hand, he sardonically positions the whole Church as a fusion of Judas and the Pharisees, espousing the need to provide for the poor while keeping that very provision for themselves, but at the same time evokes the first miracle attributed to Christ, when he turns water into wine at the Wedding of Cana (Jn 2:1-12): 'Ye have kept your choicest wine – | Let it flow for heavenly mirth' (9–10). In this duality, there is hope: God's provision is still possible in spite of the corruption of men. However, divine sovereignty does not justify human selfishness. The physical church has been built and decorated, but it is near empty of people, and those who are present enjoy an excess of literal and grotesquely metaphorical tastes – grotesque because of the distancing to aesthetic ornamentation when others are denied the literal taste of food – at the expense of the hungry, which should be anathema to the church. The allusion to Cana moderates the despair that could arise as a result of such perversion: although the church, represented by the Judas/Pharisee image, has failed, Hopkins maintains faith in God's intervention.

Hopkins believes that the church's wealth should be spent on providing for the poor, rather than exploiting the poor in order to buy more jewels for an empty building. The building is not Christ, so therefore the oil is wasted on a human structure rather than the divine. 'Crowded let His table be' (26) and the call to 'Make each morn an Easter Day' (30) explicitly evoke the foundation of the Eucharist. In an earlier sonnet, 'Easter Communion' (1865), Hopkins idealizes self-sacrifice in the context of Easter, a reminder of the fasting of Lent: 'Pure fasted faces draw unto this feast: | God comes all sweetness to your Lenten lips' (1–2). In stark contrast to the display of the Church institution, Hopkins draws out the virtue of individuals who participate in hidden spiritual integrity, including giving of themselves to their own pain, expressed through self-flagellation: 'You striped in secret with breath-taking whips, | Those crooked rough-scored chequers may be pieced | To crosses meant for Jesu's' (3–5). Although the extremity of Roman Catholic absolution is beyond Anglo-Catholic reserve, and at this point Hopkins was yet to convert to Romanism, what is important in this moment is the willingness to risk one's own suffering for the sake of God's will. In the physicality of the image of self-flagellation, there is a willingness to be proximate in Levinas's terms, which flows through Hopkins's aesthetic: 'Before language is a poetic harkening, it is a radical ethical sincerity: saying as "my exposure without reserve to the other"…, inspiration, witness, prophecy, risk, glory – "proximity and not truth about proximity".'[58] Just as rhetorical or aesthetic truth *about* proximity is not proximity itself, the church building is not the Church. Therefore, in order to be proximate to Christ, in Hopkins's view, the individual must become proximate to the people, rather than focusing on the adornment of a building.

Patmore's 'Victory in Defeat' (1877)[59] reflects a similar desire to embrace and emulate the suffering of Christ:

> Ah, God, alas,
> How soon it came to pass
> The sweetness melted from thy barbed hook
> Which I so simply took;
> And I lay bleeding on the bitter land. (1–5)

In evoking Christ's crown of thorns, Patmore also engages with the Crucifixion and Eucharist. The way in which the 'sweetness melted' is associated with the 'barbed hook' directly refers to the sweetness of the Blood of Christ, ironically recalling the beauty that emerges from the violence of the crucifixion. Importantly Patmore writes of the need for pain in life: 'And better than the insentient heart and brain | Is sharpest pain' (11–12), thus repudiating the lifelessness of not following Christ's command to love sacrificially. There is a sense of responsibility implied through this command. This attitude harks back to Hopkins's 'New Readings' (n.d.), a retelling of the Parable of the Sower (Mt. 13:3-9), in which the yield of the crop is determined not just by the type of soil on which the seed falls, but by the level of interference: while some do not prosper because of the stony ground, other seeds are eaten by birds. In Hopkins's poem, 'The wingèd fowls took part' (7). This could suggest the interference of institutions and organizations hindering social justice, which was at the core of early Tractarian disaffection with government, leading to a push for local government and the sovereignty of church authority, which Roman Catholicism took to a further extreme. Yet in this poem, Hopkins also expresses hope by evoking the literal fruitfulness of the Eucharist and Christ's sacrifice. The thorns on which the seeds fall in the second stanza link to the thistles and thorns in the first; importantly, these are the thorns that soldiers 'platt[ed] … around CHRIST'S Head' (4), from which, Hopkins suggests, 'Grapes grew and drops of wine were shed' (5). In the final stanza, the Eucharist is complete. This metaphorical provision of the Eucharist is directly linked to the material Christian duty to provide for the needy, and is reinforced through the reference to Christ feeding the five thousand: 'From wastes of rock He brings | Food for five thousand: on the thorns He shed | Grains from His drooping Head' (11–13). Further, to rebut claims that it is too challenging and too much to care for all the needy, that the problem is too overwhelming, he adds that Christ 'would not have the legion of winged things | Bear Him to heaven on easeful wings' (14–15). In the often hard line Hopkins draws, the reader is asked to put their own struggles into the perspective of Christ's, which turns upon the idea of taking up their own cross.

The constant return to fruit in these poems is not just about the grapes that become the Eucharistic wine, but also about signifying the quality of food available to the poor and the way those who have food should relate to their provision. Fruit has a moderating taste – it can rarely be bought or consumed in bulk because it will turn, and it can be sweet, sour or bitter, depending on its point of ripeness. Picked prematurely, it might never develop its full flavour. From the Anglo-Catholic perspective of having faith in God's provision (so therefore being willing to share what one has), fruit, of all foods, speaks to a daily, moderated provision. It resists hoarding. What one can taste and is able to taste is inherently linked to one's level of social privilege; and these poems challenge their readers to understand the privileges of taste that they have, as well as their Christian, human responsibility to enable tastes for others. As much as the bread and the wine are used metaphorically, the inclusion of fruit in this equation is both literal and figurative: there is the visceral need to eat for sustenance, but there is also the added pleasure of the taste of the fruit that is a luxury only to be had by a few, much like the fermented grapes used in the rite were often restricted to the priests. Yet there is also the biblical metaphor of 'bearing fruit', which is where the idea of Christian duty comes in, and the responsibility towards the poor in the community. Through the Eucharist, through fruit, and through the concept of taste, the spiritual and the material are brought together to challenge readers to take the taste (the flavour, the essence, the spirit) of the Eucharist beyond the church walls and into the community, providing for the poor with faith in God's daily provision for themselves, just as Christ was purported to feed the five thousand. This number pales in comparison to the number of starving people in mid-nineteenth-century Britain; however, from the Tractarian perspective, by focusing back onto community connections, the scope of need can be contained and met. Returning to Rossetti's 'At Home', home as a metonym for the community can become inclusive, enabling the isolated to share the feast under the orange bough.

## The fear of being too late

The Tractarian response to social unrest was to challenge individual parishioners to do what they could to help their neighbour and, in that way, build community. In this sense, the practice of the Eucharist becomes not just a reminder of Christ – or, at the other extreme, Christ's transubstantiated body and blood – for selfish individual consumption, but a reminder to the parishioners that it is also their duty to sacrifice themselves, and to give of themselves, for the sake of the poor. Self-sacrifice is the heart of the ritual, not the external elements of bread and wine. This message was most pertinent given the rise of capitalist individualism. Liddon's *Profit and Loss* hinges on Christ's words: 'For what shall it profit a man, if he shall gain the whole world, and lose his own soul?' (Mk 8:36), rewriting them for the nineteenth-century age of British imperialism, which arguably looked outward for conquest while neglecting those suffering close to home: 'A people may gain the whole world, and lose all those qualities of the head and heart which entitle them to possess it.'[60] He goes on to compare the moral state of Britain to the demise of the Roman Empire:

> The temperance, the courage, the justice, the patriotism of the earlier Romans had died out; and while, in the intoxication of her victories, Rome

grasped with one hand the sceptre of the world, she surrendered the liberties and lives of her citizens to the lusts and tyranny of the Cæsars with the other. A people may have been civilized, in the material sense of the word, for centuries, while it remains at heart and for ever barbarian.[61]

For Liddon, the British Empire had moved into the age of excess – the 'intoxication of her victories' – and a time of complacency regarding the vulnerable in society. Just as Christ's disciples fell asleep in Gethsemane, not understanding the significance of the moment of Christ's passion, nineteenth-century Britain is asleep to their moment of purpose. In this way, the 'tyranny' of the spirit of the age reveals the complacency at the heart of Britain, which Liddon sees as barbarism in a nation that prided itself on its global moral supremacy and claims of civilization as a justification for imperial conquest. It seems fitting, then, that a persistent motif in Victorian poetry is of the Odyssean epic journey, from which a near hero is delayed and returns too late to save a loved one from death. This concept is at the heart of Rossetti's 'The Prince's Progress', discussed in Chapter 2, but also in the works by Tennyson and Procter that will be considered here. The recurring reasons of distraction, ignorance and complacency used to justify the delay remain unmitigated in the face of death. In the end, such excuses become indicative of self-focus and arrogance, which is punished by social isolation in spite of increased personal worldly wealth or position.

Tennyson's 'A Character', written in 1829 and published in 1830, exemplifies this kind of self-focus. The 'half-glance upon the sky' in the first line suggests a lack of investigation, even though the character says 'The wanderings | Of this most intricate Universe | Teach me the nothingness of things' (2–4). This dismissal of the concrete for the sake of abstract thought is indicative of a lack of human feeling, an inability to care for the people seen before him: 'Yet could not all creation pierce | Beyond the bottom of his eye' (5–6). Tennyson's sketch of his fellow scholar at Trinity College, Cambridge, Thomas Sunderland, can be extended to represent those who are too busy trying to seek out metaphysical knowledge instead of looking at the ills in the world around them. In this sense, Tennyson reveals a sentiment of reserve that would come to be associated with Tractarian theology and poetics. Within his Broad Church views, Tennyson remained 'deeply attached to the language of the

Authorized version, the Prayer-Book, and the liturgy', a factor that contributes to his poetry both aesthetically and in terms of his social vision.[62] His critique of Sunderland engages indirectly with the theological idea of reserve in the suggestion that seeking knowledge detached from helping the community is a form of individualistic selfishness:

> He spake of beauty: that the dull
> Saw no divinity in grass,
> Life in dead stones, or spirit in air;
> Then looking as 'twere in a glass,
> He smooth'd his chin and sleek'd his hair,
> And said the earth was beautiful. (7–12)

The intellectual arrogance of the character is made more disturbing because his privileged idea of beauty is constructed to ignore the suffering of the world. Furthermore, the beauty of the earth he envisages is absolute narcissism. It therefore follows that the poem ends with a perverse, cannibalized image of the Eucharist:

> With lips depress'd as he were meek,
> Himself unto himself he sold:
> Upon himself himself did feed:
> Quiet, dispassionate, and cold,
> And other than his form of creed,
> With chisell'd features clear and sleek. (25–30)

The false meekness displayed on his lips – the orifice through which words and food pass, such as the elements of the Eucharist and the words spoken upon receiving it – contributes to the excessive baseness of his sacrament, which Tennyson conflates with capitalism: 'Himself unto himself he sold: | Upon himself himself did feed.' Not only are the two actions of selling and feeding equated through the colon, but the repetition of 'himself' is not only balanced but intensified in the second line, without another word to break it. The sense is of increasing self-focus, a turning inward upon oneself in a way that turns him 'Quiet, dispassionate, and cold' like a corpse, even though he lives. He is 'other than his form of creed', yet his hypocrisy is masked by the apparent beauty of his 'chisell'd features'. That these features are described as 'clear', as if transparent, and 'sleek', which suggests a kind of underhand sophistication, speaks to the deprecating way in which Sunderland's fellow collegians saw him as being like a politician, but in a broader sense to the falseness of a society of individuals interested in increasing their own wealth of capital and knowledge – that is, becoming more sophisticated – without having a willingness to use that knowledge and wealth to benefit the disadvantaged in their community.

As much as the Eucharist was meant to figure as a persistent ritualistic motive of remembrance of spiritual, social and physical hunger, there remained a disjunction between the self-focus of one's own preoccupation with the vertical spiritual relationship and a consciousness of the need to act horizontally through engagement with and commitment to the vulnerable. The Tractarian impulse called for a recognition of inequalities in order to rectify the disbalance, not to reinforce social disparity. Arthur Hugh Clough, who was influenced by the Tractarians although he later rejected the movement, and who would meet Tennyson in the 1860s, wrote in regard to the Irish famine in 1847:

> God, by a sudden visitation, has withdrawn from the income He yearly sends us in the fruits of His earth, sixteen millions sterling. Withdrawn it, and from whom? On whom falls the loss? Not on the rich and luxurious, but on those whose labour makes the rich man rich and gives the luxurious his luxury. Shall not we then, the affluent and indulgent, spare somewhat of our affluence, curtail somewhat of our indulgence, that these (for our wealth too and for our indulgence in the end) may have food while they work, and have work to gain them food?[63]

There was a strong movement, arguably with Catholic impetus, emerging from both Oxford and Cambridge that was willing to challenge their own privilege, inherent in their education and social position, in order to speak to their peers regarding those who are vulnerable and starving. However, given the overwhelming nature of famine, that a change in attitude would come too late was a very real possibility; and it is for this reason that the poems that articulated this kind of regret maintained a haunting reach over their audience.

Tennyson's Arthurian poems buy into the British medieval version of the Odyssean epic. In writing of the contrast between Tennyson's first volume of *Idylls of the King* from the 1830s and the later 1860s version, Linda Hughes notes that 'a poem with a medieval setting and descriptions of medieval ritual ... would in the late 1860s have implicitly invoked Roman Catholicism, Newman's conversion, and the controversial practice of ritualism in selected congregations of the Anglican Church'.[64] Hughes therefore remarks on the more overt symbols of Catholicism in the earlier poems, which aesthetically anticipate the Oxford Movement and are rich in the use of medieval Catholic ritual, especially of the Eucharist, in a way that resonates with what would become known as the Tractarian ethos. The exclusion of 'The Lady of Shalott' (1832)[65] from the canon of the *Idylls* inadvertently speaks to the social exclusion of its eponymous figure; and the world the poem depicts, so physically proximate to Camelot, is yet psychologically distanced through the ignorance of Camelot's inhabitants. The poem is aesthetically positioned to represent the capacity to use beauty, as in 'The Character', as a means to remain wilfully blind to poverty – social and economic poverty, as well as the poverty of one's soul. The poem enacts reserve in that it resists the abject: it is the Lady of Shalott's social hunger at the core, rather than physical hunger, but emotional and physical starvation are deliberately indistinct. Her social hunger and isolation stand aesthetically as a result of Camelot's ignorance of the very real poverty and physical hunger of the peasants the Lady observes in her mirror.

Betsy Winakur Tontiplaphol provides a provocative sensory reading of the woven tapestry in the poem:

> The tapestry brings the sensory wealth of Camelot into the tower, and Tennyson's prosody generates a luxe, permeable enclosure that mimics the not-quite-closed spatial experience cultivated in and by the Lady's airy weave. Shalott and Camelot are physically (and, perhaps, politically) discrete but aurally proximal; their shared final syllable establishes, every fourth or fifth line, a link between them, and when people cross en route to the other, they mitigate our sense of the Lady's isolation.[66]

This understanding is reminiscent of both Derrida's and Levinas's conceptions of proximity and importantly uses the sensory experience to depict distance. As in Rossetti's 'At Home', the only way the Lady of Shalott can experience the wealth of Camelot is at an aesthetic distance, not closely – neither gustatorily nor haptically. She will not be sharing in the feasts of the Round Table, an equality that enacts the equality of the shared eating of the Eucharist. The very aural proximity that Tontiplaphol notes is ironic because aurality is a distance sense, but this irony undergirds the entire poem in the way its evocative aural aesthetic, in its smooth regularity, belies the agony of social exclusion and potential starvation.

The mystical assonance of the first stanza evokes an abundance like that in Rossetti's 'Goblin Market', yet instead of the goblins bringing the fruit too close, the Lady of Shalott is separated from this abundance by a moat:

> On either side the river lie
> Long fields of barley and of rye,
> That clothe the wold and meet the sky;
> And thro' the field the road runs by
>     To many-tower'd Camelot;
> And up and down the people go,
> Gazing where the lilies blow
> Round an island there below,
>     The island of Shalott. (1–9)

Rossetti's later poem constructs a similar assonance with 'Come buy our orchard fruits, | Come buy, come buy' (3–4),[67] followed by the extensive list of fruits; yet Rossetti's poem is more tangibly present in the fruits it catalogues, even though they have been picked and are therefore no longer connected to the earth, while the fields of barley and rye, in their abundance, remain connected to the earth with the hope of future produce, but are aesthetically distanced. Rossetti's fruits are to be eaten, albeit forbidden; Tennyson's fields are to be looked at, and may as well be like lilies in the extent to which they are able to provide sustenance to Shalott. The reference to Camelot being 'many-tower'd' reflects a similar abundance, and so it stands to reason that the abundance of the field belongs to them – manifested in that the road in the fields goes to Camelot – because wealth belongs to the wealthy and increase is given to those who already have.

Most of the stanzas end with the line 'The Lady of Shalott', twice italicized to depict the writing on her boat, but the few that end differently emphasize her isolation: she lives on 'The island of Shalott' (9); the market girls 'Pass onward from Shalott' (54) as if her presence is unknown, or at least only thought of in passing; and the knight prays in a field 'Beside remote Shalott' (81). But perhaps most evocative is the line 'Sang Sir Lancelot' (108). It is this line that prompts the woman to abandon her tapestry:

> She left the web, she left the loom,
> She made three paces thro' the room,
> She saw the water-lily bloom,
> She saw the helmet and the plume,
>     She look'd down to Camelot.
> Out flew the web and floated wide;
> The mirror crack'd from side to side;
> 'The curse is come upon me,' cried
>     The Lady of Shalott. (109–17)

Lancelot, as a symbol of the prosperity of Camelot, sings, unaware of the poverty and isolation, represented in that he is unaware even of the existence of the Lady of Shalott, who watches him through her mirror in the same way she watches the poor: they are ironically equal in her vision. The previous knight who had knelt praying was too far away to be heard, but Lancelot has come closer. It is the sound – the aurality – of Lancelot's singing, rather than merely watching the figures in the mirror, that compels her to turn, and thereby remove the extra element of distance in the visual (the reflection) to see directly with her eyes. It is at this point that the Lady of Shalott speaks, and it is important to note that the assonance in the second half of this stanza mirrors the first half of the first stanza, but the difference is that here the assonance is closed by a consonant. To this point, ending with assonance suggested a magical hope; now the curse is the realization that the separation is real, not just a reflection, and it can no longer be aesthetically distanced.

It is through listening that curses are conveyed. The Lady of Shalott's fate is sealed by hearing Lancelot; yet attention must be given to the curse that comes not upon her, but upon the kingdom of Camelot, those who have heard *her* sing but are powerless to assist her out of her isolation:

> Only reapers, reaping early
> In among the bearded barley,
> Hear a song that echoes cheerly
> From the river winding clearly,
>     Down to tower'd Camelot:
> And by the moon the reaper weary,

> Piling sheaves in uplands airy,
> Listening, whispers "Tis the fairy
>    Lady of Shalott.' (28-36)

Morning and night, those responsible for the harvest – the reapers – hear her song. The barley being 'bearded' suggests it might be going to seed, and therefore no longer of use for harvest. The produce goes to waste, as may the abundance of sheaves piled in the uplands, a kind of waste that could not help but evoke the unnecessary starvation and consequent social uprisings attributed to the Corn Laws. The reapers take no notice of the Lady of Shalott except to mythologize her: she is potentially demonized, buying into traditions of fairy curses that must only be whispered about, much as Rossetti's Lizzie would tell her sister 'You should not peep at goblin men' ('Goblin Market' 49), but Laura 'whispered like the restless brook: | "Look, Lizzie, look, Lizzie, | Down the glen tramp little men"' (53-5). In Tennyson's poem, the Lady of Shalott becomes a figure for the marginalized in society who are made invisible, and even otherworldly: the peasants themselves. If she is not real, then her situation does not need to be addressed, much as if the statistics show that the nation is prosperous, poverty must not be real, or people are poor due to their own choices. The transience of time figures in a perverse way, then, with the fleeting presence of other figures in the Lady of Shalott's vision, shown in the repetition of 'sometimes': 'Sometimes a troop of damsels glad' (55); 'Sometimes a curly shepherd-lad' (57); 'And sometimes thro' the mirror blue | The knights come riding two and two' (60-1). The lack of connection felt by the Lady of Shalott is most poignantly depicted the first time she speaks: ' "I am half sick of shadows," said | The Lady of Shalott' (71-2).

    Maintaining the role of the visual aesthetic in Tennyson's poem, the structure of the poem's parts is created through a transition of the quality of the visual: Part I is grey; Part II, colourful; Part III is glistening, while Part IV is ironically pale, yet intense and storm-like. This movement not only reflects the seasons of a year, but also the Lady of Shalott's movement away from the visual and towards the tactile. For her, the curse comes when she sees Camelot and everything it represents: an equality, abundance and order to which she cannot belong. The tactility of Part IV exists not just in the 'straining', 'waning' and 'complaining' of the wind and stream (118-20), but in the Lady of Shalott's transition from weaving – an artform that in itself is distanced through working from behind – to writing directly on the prow of the boat. There is an ironic freedom in the tactility of her 'loos[ing] the chain' that kept the boat moored (133), while her lying down in the boat, her acceptance of cold death, makes her again passive to the elements' touch:

> Lying, robed in snowy white
> That loosely flew to left and right –
> The leaves upon her falling light –
> Thro' the noises of the night
>     She floated down to Camelot. (136–40)

As she floats down the river, the Lady of Shalott abandons herself to her exclusion from society, and the more she listens, the more proximate she physically becomes to Camelot, the closer death comes to her, as she joins her song to theirs:

> Heard a carol, mournful, holy,
> Chanted loudly, chanted lowly,
> Till her blood was frozen slowly,
> And her eyes were darken'd wholly,
>     Turn'd to tower'd Camelot.
> For ere she reach'd upon the tide
> The first house by the water-side,
> Singing in her song she died,
>     The Lady of Shalott. (145–53)

As Tennyson lists the aristocratic figures whose revelries are disturbed by the intrusion of the Lady's boat – knights, burghers, lords and dames, who are now forced to recognize her not as a myth, but as a tangible corpse – the questioning in the disruption reveals their oblivion regarding the impoverishment – physically on the part of the peasants (perhaps representing the nineteenth-century working classes), and socially or spiritually on the part of the Lady who operates as an aesthetic figure for them – that had existed in such close proximity to their prosperity. The intrusion of the Lady's corpse is like that of the 'thin dead body' (16) in Rossetti's 'Amor Mundi', discussed in Chapter 2. It is crucial that the Lady's corpse not only intrudes the geographical space of Camelot, but that its entrance disrupts a feast. Writing of *Idylls*, Charlotte Boyce notes the way in which food is a 'potent source of male energy and power' and 'the fuel necessary for knightly action, while commensality strengthens the fraternal bonds that underpin Camelot's civic society'.[68] She goes on to argue that 'Feasting and fasting thus function as important and complex signifiers in *Idylls*, intersecting not only with the poem's gender politics but also with its broader anxieties regarding duty, morality, civilization, and decline.'[69] This idea is just as pertinent to 'The Lady of Shalott', in which Shalott fasts while Camelot feasts. The corpse enters, just as in Rossetti's poem, but in death it is too late for Camelot to rectify the wrongs; they can merely express fear and what seems to be empty spiritual generosity:

> Who is this? and what is here?
> And in the lighted palace near
> Died the sound of royal cheer;
> And they cross'd themselves for fear,
>     All the knights at Camelot:
> But Lancelot mused a little space;
> He said, 'She has a lovely face;
> God in his mercy lend her grace,
>     The Lady of Shalott.' (163–71)

That it is Lancelot's musing that ends the poem is a double blow, given that he was the impetus for the Lady of Shalott's demise. The emotional distance created by his admiring her beauty in death links back to the aesthetic distance of the first stanza, reinforcing the divide between social privilege and isolation. The appreciation is not only too late, but it is misplaced; in the focus on aesthetic beauty, there is no evidence of questioning how she came to die. In this way, the civilization of Camelot seems doomed to extinction and barbarism, much as Liddon wrote of the Roman Empire and, by extension, the British.

Lancelot's empty prayer for God's mercy seems an exploitation of the Catholic practice of prayers for the dead: a few words are spoken when it is too late, instead of trying to do something to help the person before they die. A similar sentiment is expressed in Adelaide Procter's 'Too Late' (1860),[70] without the aesthetic distance offered by Tennyson. In this way, Procter brings the horror of delay much closer, a move that resists the desire not to be held responsible for the death of the starving and downtrodden. The first stanza of the dramatic monologue deliberately invites the reader close, initially positioning the reader as the one who has delayed, or been ignorant of the necessity to pay attention or return. Indeed, the poetic voice could be speaking to one like Lancelot, who comments on the beauty of the corpse:

> Hush! speak low; tread softly;
> > Draw the sheet aside; –
> Yes, she does look peaceful;
> > With that smile she died. (1–4)

The comment on the dead looking peaceful is quickly exposed as a deliberate visual lie, constructed through bland clichés of what one ought to say or think. Instead of looking from a distance, the poetic voice beckons the listener to observe more closely:

> Yet stern want and sorrow
> > Even now you trace
> On the wan, worn features
> > Of the still white face.
>
> Restless, helpless, hopeless,
> > Was her bitter part; –
> Now – how still the Violets
> > Lie upon her Heart;
>
> She who toiled and laboured
> > For her daily bread;
> See the velvet hangings
> > Of this stately bed. (5–16)

Procter's ironic juxtaposition of the unnamed woman laid out in an appearance of wealth alongside the recognition that she had suffered through poverty in life is a morbid extension of Lancelot's aesthetic appreciation in Tennyson's poem. The poetic speaker in Procter's poem constantly instructs one to see, and even to diminish oneself in order to do so from the first line's instruction to 'tread softly'. The use of second-person singular forces a proximity, not just with the woman in death, but with the life that led to the 'wan, worn features': a life in which, instead of being given her daily bread, she 'toiled and laboured' for it. Her labour stands in contrast to the implied leisure and previous complacency of the listener, only now approaching the woman in her demise.

Procter's poem turns to a mode in which the woman seems to have died for perceived unrequited love: 'If she had but lingered | Just a few hours more' (33–4), she may have received the letter from her lover. This move distances the listener from the action of the poem, as well as the language of hunger, which turns to a metaphorical hunger of the heart: 'Though he let this anguish | Eat her heart away' (39–40) and 'For one word she hungered' (47). Yet the fact that the speaker is not speaking to the lover, but a third party, is significant. The poem ends with:

> She needs no more pity, –
>     But I mourn his fate,
> When he hears his letter
>     Came a day too late. (57–60)

There remains a question, then, as to why the speaker requires the listener to draw near, as to why they should feel a sense of responsibility towards the dead woman. The lines between physical and emotional starvation are blurred. While the absent lover is held in a degree responsible through his delay, there is also the delay of the unknown listener. Within the woman's emotional demise, there is the decay of her body leading to death. If the woman's hope of escape from drudgery and labour lay in marriage to the absent lover, there is an accountability to be found in a society that does not provide another way for her to be able to survive the harshness of the world. There are many unanswered questions regarding the woman's state in life – whether she was a fallen woman, perhaps dying in childbirth, or if she had suffered from fever or another kind of illness leading to a weakened state – but also in how she finds herself in the bed of the wealthy in order to die. The compassionate speaker is also unknown; yet she (this gender also an assumption) is positioned as one who evidently tried to help the woman, only finding herself limited both in time and resources. In this poem, Procter urges her reader to come close to devastation, to be willing to be proximate to suffering, and even to have the courage to face failure in the endeavour to intervene. In the following chapter, I will examine poetry emerging from a pragmatic desire to meet the needs of physical and social hunger, and the ways in which the poetry addresses social action. The social activism of the poets themselves informs this work and speaks to a grounded, proximate aesthetic that maintains reserve in order to move as closely as possible to suffering without being disgusted by the abject. Being able to embrace the abject as a part of the community, or seeing through the abject to appreciate the beauty of humanity, is at the core of the social vision of the Doctrine of Reserve, as well as the cohesion of the Communion of the Saints, epitomized in the rite of the Eucharist.

# 4

# Social action demonstrated

*To recover this conviction was to recover that which is the great principle of a social faith, the principle that we exist in a permanent communion which was not created by human hands, and cannot be destroyed by them ... the effects of this teaching were assuredly very remarkable. We saw young men, who had been previously giving themselves up to selfish objects, making great personal sacrifices, devoting themselves humbly and zealously to the cause of their fellow-creatures: we heard of noble women not a few, who had learnt that charity and devotion should be the especial characteristics of their station ... Professional men, lawyers especially, said that they had at last found a faith which was calm, orderly and practical, one by which they could govern their lives.*

– F. D. Maurice, *On Right and Wrong* (1843)[1]

In his assessment of the Oxford Movement, F. D. Maurice, one of the most prominent Anglican theologians of the nineteenth century,[2] recognized the dangers of social hierarchy undergirded by what Joshua King refers to as a 'nostalgia'[3] for apostolical succession and an exclusionary social vision that 'would denote a return to the state of things in which the priest, the landlord, and the retainer, were the only elements of society', thereby rejecting the middle classes.[4] To a degree, the rejection of the middle classes can be seen legitimately through the Tractarian rejection of the rise of liberal capitalism. Maurice identifies this exclusionary attitude as a part of the 'curse' or 'evil' of the Oxford Movement: 'A tendency towards contradiction and denial was manifest in this school from the very first. From the first one could see that its members had a painful love of denouncing others for not making it, or for not perceiving its truth.'[5] At the same time, though, Maurice recognizes, paradoxically, the way in which the Movement's assertion of 'a permanent communion ... not created by human hands' worked to establish a sense of practical, pragmatic duty to one's community. This vision can be seen outworked through the lives of the poets I address, biographically as well as articulated through their literary works.

Much criticism has acknowledged the charitable work of these poets to varying degrees, but in terms of examining their everyday religious practice through their poetry, the majority of the scholarship has turned the focus towards daily devotion, defined as prayer practice, liturgical preferences, reading the Bible or other devotional materials, or frequency of church attendance. While the reading of poetry in spiritual terms has been useful – in particular, for instance, in reclaiming Christina Rossetti not just as a devotional poet but as a theologian[6] – little work has been done that connects their poetry directly to the dual influence of their personal social activism and their religious convictions. Emma Mason has acknowledged that, given the 'clear privileging of feeling in faith, social activism and lyric expression is not readily addressed in literary studies as it stands', but contends that this is because literary studies on the whole is 'a field preoccupied not with the intangible and religious, but with the material and secular'.[7] I would nuance this claim to suggest that while the emphasis is on the secular, even when religious poetry is studied, it is largely *restricted* to the intangible, creating a false impression of religion as only concerned with spiritual matters and not with the practical outworking of faith. In a similar vein, Susan Colón suggests 'it seems that ethics has been allowed back into the literary-critical conversation on the condition that it is divorced from religion', but at the same time that 'the growing number of studies on Victorian religion in literature have tended to leave ethics out of view'.[8]

To an extent, this division may be due to a hesitancy towards combining poetic form and social form, or aesthetics and the material, a distinction that Caroline Levine has substantially broken down in *Forms* (2015). My approach seeks to continue to interrogate the divide between the religious and the material, showing how the Tractarian ritual aesthetic flowed into the ethos of social activism. I adhere to Mason's perspective that poetry does not need to 'oppose the political and the personal, instead regarding social action as being motivated by the ... connection between feeling, virtue and social responsibility'.[9] Given that for the Tractarians and their Anglo-Catholic descendants there was no separation between poetry, aesthetics, social duty and religious practice, in my study, the fusion of aesthetics and the practical outworking of faith – looking outward, not merely upward – is at the core of Tractarian poetics.

The purpose of this chapter is not to give biographical accounts of the poets in regard to their social activism, although there is much excavation still to be done in that area. Rather I am interested in a triangulation between the Tractarian social vision, the poets' community-focused work, and the way in which the doctrinal context and their personal, practical experience of encountering the poor and vulnerable directly informs their literary work. I am including in my definition of social activism Tennyson's awareness of his social and political agency, which would see him become Poet Laureate, and Patmore's political journalism. Although not social activism in the same sense as, for example, Rossetti's work with fallen women or Hopkins's work as a Jesuit priest in the poorest communities, I argue that through these literary means Tennyson and Patmore both sought to use their influence to change conceptions of social inequality and social responses to poverty. This kind of educative process is a slow form of social activism that is not as obvious as physically working in a community; yet it is crucial to changing cultural positions, and works alongside the more immediate forms of activism. It was also a part of the agenda of Rossetti, Meynell and Procter, seen in their prose works, which show a fluidity between literary output and literal social work. This fusion of social and literary activism was central to Tractarian writing. In an 1839 essay for the High Anglican journal *The British Critic*, John Henry Newman wrote,[10]

> Premises imply conclusions; germs lead to developments; principles have issues; doctrines lead to action. As well might you invert a pitcher of water, and expect the contents to eschew the ground ... as fancy that men will not carry out the truths which they have gained, whether from their own minds, or from our divines, or from the Fathers.[11]

The interaction between the ideal, or theoretical, and the active outworking is made clear in the way that the broader idea of 'principles' is made present and practical in 'issues', while even more importantly, Newman sees doctrine not just as a theological stance, but as a motive for action. Like gravity, he expects faith to be grounded in practical living. Even more directly in relation to recognizing and confronting poverty, for the same journal in the following year, Simon Bosanquet challenged the complacency and distance that had arisen in comfortable society:

> Human life can be learned only by practice and personal experience. But no one now is willing to acquaint himself in this way; and least of all, in this country at least, with the classes below that one in which he moves. It is far easier to sit at home and read returns, and reports, and evidence on oath, and figures, and statistics, and to work out problems of society by a table or a machine, mathematically certain and demonstrable, and squaring all to a fraction, than to pry into dirty courts and lanes, and dismal rooms and cellars, full of vermin, and filth and infection, and to converse with the low-minded, the vulgar, the dying, the drunken, the discontented, the miserable. This may be the way to very creditable philosophy, but it is not the road to truth.[12]

This deliberate critique of the statistical turn in political economy and its subsequent move to distancing the social conscience would become a familiar perspective within Anglo-Catholicism. Such distancing is also resonant with abstract theological debates that were more concerned about intellectual prowess than addressing social concerns. As much as the Tractarian movement was theological, it adamantly sought to position itself as relevant, practical and actively working to improve communities at the parish level. Bosanquet's article is as much sermon as political critique, designed to challenge readers not just in terms of their intellectual understanding of poverty, but in their individual sense of responsibility towards their community. Importantly, the 'road to truth' is one that leads to proximity with the poor, rather than to intellectual abstraction.

Simon Skinner notes that in *The British Critic*, particularly under Newman's editorship, there was a preoccupation with enlightening the broader readership with the plight of the suffering. This agenda was driven by the writers' personal engagement with the community, and helping the poor was seen as much as a spiritual act as prayer or church attendance: 'A corresponding feature of later Tractarian commentary was an affirmation of the Church's role as the guardian of the poor, realized for example in the journal of criticism of the working conditions of the urban and rural workforce.'[13] In this chapter, I am extending

Skinner's perspective through Tractarian poetics; for, as G. B. Tennyson argues specifically in relation to Rossetti, 'most of what the Tractarians advocated in theory and sought to put into practice came to fruition in [her] poetry',[14] which was consciously influenced by Rossetti's own social work. This same motivation can be read through the other poets to varying degrees, inflected through their proximity to the poor, their personal politics, and the ways in which they envisaged literary activism speaking to the social. The social and the literary are intertwined, undergirded by the Tractarian social vision regarding care for the most vulnerable members of the community.

## Considering the lilies: Working with vulnerable women

In *The Face of the Deep* (1893), Rossetti writes: 'complicated civilization produces or amasses riches: and the riches come to nothing except as accusers, and the lives cannot be silenced in the day of account. In that day many luxuries may turn out to have been unlawful, and the price of blood'.[15] This criticism of an age that selfishly hoards and accumulates, often at the expense and impoverishment of others, is at the heart of the biblical verse from which she derives her title for '"Consider the Lilies of the Field"',[16] which speaks directly to the Tractarian emphasis on trusting in God's daily provision: 'And why take ye thought for raiment? Consider the lilies of the field, how they grow; they toil not, neither do they spin; And yet I say unto you, That even Solomon in all his glory was not arrayed like one of these' (Mt. 6:28-9).[17] It is evident that Rossetti saw a correlation between the dispossession and vulnerability of the poor and the selfish accumulation of the wealthy. King notes in his reading of Rossetti's 'Son, Remember' (1893) the poet's conviction that 'actions toward the oppressed and vulnerable bear directly on one's participation in the new world'.[18] The haunting yet tangible presence of hunger can be read through the poem's reference to the parable of the rich man and the poor man in Luke 6:19-31: 'I laid beside thy gate, am Lazarus: | *See me or see me not I still am there,* | Hungry and thirsty, sore and sick and bare' ('Son, Remember', 1–3; emphasis added).

Mary Arseneau notes that the 'Rossetti women expressed their faith in devotional practices, in religious social work, in their vocal interest in church politics, in their lively engagement with Tractarian literature, and in their own adaptations of Tractarian poetics',[19] while Jill Rappoport observes that Anglican sisterhoods, like the ones the Rossetti women were involved in, 'differentiate[d]' themselves from 'their cloistered, Catholic counterparts, [by] emphasizing their unpaid social service over contemplative behavior'.[20] My purpose here is to entwine these facets of Rossetti's vision even closer to her poetry. King refers to Rossetti's 'sustained commitment' to social justice, shown through both the literary activism of letter writing as well as her personal involvement in 'aiding victimized women, educating the poor ... and defending minors sexually abused in London's human trafficking network',[21] and suggests that 'Son, Remember' can be read in relation to Rossetti's response to the overwhelming poverty in London. In a similar manner, '"Consider the Lilies of the Field"' speaks not merely to a spiritual encounter with God, but a physical encounter with the downtrodden. While Dinah Roe recognizes the aesthetic of the Doctrine of Reserve in '"Consider the Lilies of the Field"', she reads the poem in relation to the individual's devotion to God – an upward trajectory: 'God is not addressed directly, but is a presence alluded to in an analogical description of nature.'[22] My reading does not reject this upward trajectory, but contends that the outward trajectory is just as present, and just as much a spiritual devotion. I argue that Rossetti's vision for the poem is derived from her concern for fallen women and their vulnerable social and economic position within nineteenth-century Britain. In this way, she re-envisages ideas of morality and judgement, shifting, to a degree, the sense of responsibility from the woman herself towards the society who shuns her.

Rossetti volunteered at St Mary Magdalene Home for Fallen Women in Highgate between 1859 and 1870, so although '"Consider the Lilies"' was composed before she began this work, it was published in the midst of her time there. Arseneau suggests Rossetti's interest in working with fallen women was established well before this time, from the work her sister, Maria, did with Mrs Chambers' Young Women's Friendly Society in their parish. Mrs Chambers opened a refuge for fallen women in 1852, the year before '"Consider the Lilies"' was composed.[23] Moreover, it was published in the volume named for 'Goblin Market', which is often read as a fallen-woman narrative, and is followed in that volume by 'The World', an ironic sonnet that depicts the sensual temptations of the temporal world as the unattainable mistress:

By day she wooes me, soft, exceeding fair:
>But all night as the moon so changeth she;
>Loathsome and foul with hidden leprosy
And subtle serpents gliding in her hair.
By day she wooes me to the outer air,
>Ripe fruits, sweet flowers, and full satiety:
>But thro' the night, a beast she grins at me,
A very monster void of love and prayer.
By day she stands a lie: by night she stands
>In all the naked horror of the truth
With pushing horns and claws and clutching hands.
Is this a friend indeed; that I should sell
>My soul to her, give her my life and youth,
Till my feet, cloven too, take hold on hell?

Although the form of the sonnet is Petrarchan, the tone is more resonant with Shakespeare's Sonnet 130, 'My mistress's eyes are nothing like the sun' (1), but Rossetti transforms Shakespeare's image of love for the imperfect into a love for the monstrous. Shakespeare's 'If hairs be wires, black wires grow on her head' (4) becomes, in the corresponding line, a reference to Medusa: 'And subtle serpents gliding in her hair' (4). In this way, Rossetti rewrites both the Italian and English sonnet to evoke the dangerous pull of the temptations of worldly things as satanic: the 'pushing horns' and 'clutching hands' juxtaposed to condemn greed, while the 'Ripe fruits, sweet flowers, and full satiety' connote illicit sexual encounters. The connection to physical hunger in this reference cannot be ignored: while some have the privilege of 'full satiety', others, through starvation, are drawn into criminal activities, such as prostitution, in order to feed their families. The excesses of the world, both in luxuries and in want, are as leprous as venereal disease.

Reading '"Consider the Lilies"' in conversation with 'The World' grounds the former poem in Rossetti's material concern for fallen women, and the intended audience becomes the society that would condemn them. The first line, then, 'Flowers preach to us if we will hear: –' (1) subversively positions the fallen women (the flowers) with the authority of the priest: a significant hierarchical shift that should not be ignored, given Rossetti's Anglo-Catholic persuasion. Furthermore, as in 'Up-Hill', discussed in Chapter 2, the lack of quotation marks to distinguish speakers conflates the speaker and listener in this poem, a structure that gives equal standing to the fallen women within their supposedly more virtuous community. Beginning with roses, the flower most traditionally associated with beauty and love, Rossetti acknowledges that there is curse inherent in feminine beauty: 'I am most fair; | Yet all my loveliness is born | Upon a thorn' (3–5). The short line lends the intensity of an internal rhyme, reflecting the closeness to which women are tied to the dangers of sexual predators. To this extent, the reading seems fairly conventional: beautiful women led astray by men who are captivated by their beauty. But the sermon of the poppies takes a subversive turn in its visceral vitality:

> The poppy saith amid the corn:
> Let but my scarlet head appear
> And I am held in scorn;
> Yet juice of subtle virtue lies
> Within my cup of curious dyes. (6–10)

While in the Catholic tradition poppies symbolize sleep and indifference, often used in depictions of the disciples sleeping while Christ grieves in the Garden of Gethsemane, these symbolic roots exist also in Greek mythology. In *Flora Symbolica* (1870), John Ingram connects the understanding of the poppy as a signifier of the consolation of sleep, 'created by Ceres whilst in search of her daughter Proserpine, as a soother of her grief ... The well-known somniferous qualities of the poppy is adduced as another reason why it should be deemed symbolic of consolation, and of oblivion'.[24] In terms of Rossetti's poem, the evocation of oblivion can be read as that of those who turn their back on the fallen women: those who have provision – represented by the corn, which also recalls the Eucharist and therefore the Communion of the Saints – have the luxury of being able to be oblivious and indifferent. They blame the women for their own state, rather than acknowledging their own investment in the social and economic structures that lead women into such dire situations. Then, by virtue of this oblivion, the fallen woman is no longer visible. Like the Lady of Shalott, discussed in Chapter 3, she becomes a figure or metaphor rather than a literal human being in want. In this sense, the sleep of oblivion reflects the complacency of a self-interested society.

Yet even more significant is that Rossetti deliberately refers to *scarlet* poppies. Apart from the well-trodden cultural connotations of 'scarlet', most obviously the 'scarlet woman', that the poppies are red is crucial: Robert Tyas, in his *Handbook of the Language & Sentiments of Flowers* (1850), makes a critical move in distinguishing between red and white poppies. While white poppies hold the conventional symbolism of consolation and sleep, red poppies are separated out as representative of 'evanescent pleasure'.[25] From the Anglo-Catholic perspective, any of the pleasures of the world would be considered evanescent in comparison to eternity in heaven; yet Rossetti also plays subversively on what Dominic Janes identifies as 'hard-line Protestant opinion' in the nineteenth century, in which flowers were considered an inappropriate adornment in church buildings because flowers are, essentially, 'reproductive bodies'[26] and, as 'markers of desire', they equated the Catholicizing of the church as both a sexual and doctrinal threat.[27] Antony Harrison notes the 'elaborate pun' on the cup of the poppy and the Eucharistic chalice, yet while he sees this image as reinforcing the idea of Christ's sacrifice,[28] it also reinforces suspicion and danger. The 'juice' of the poppies, with their 'subtle virtue' (9), conjures the same opulent sexual deviance as 'suck my juices' in 'Goblin Market' (468), as well as the obvious reference to opium, the drug of forgetting, rife not only among prostitutes, but among the impoverished more generally. It was common, for instance, for mothers to give their own portion of food to their starving children and take laudanum to dull their own hunger pains, just as it was also common for mothers to give their starving babies laudanum in order to try to soothe them to sleep.[29] Hunger, want and drugged deviance are conflated in the poppy's 'cup of curious dyes' (10), breaking down the divisions between the so-called deserving and undeserving poor.

While the poppies are seen as deviant, the violets, for all their representation of modesty and humility, are in no sounder position:

> The violets whisper from the shade
> Which their own leaves have made:
> Men scent our fragrance on the air,
> Yet take no heed
> Of humble lessons we would read. (13–17)

The violets are potentially the most subversive flowers in Rossetti's poem. Rossetti overturns the assumption that all fallen women are prostitutes; the violets 'whisper from the shade' of their modesty – their attempts to protect themselves – yet their leaves were not able to hide their 'fragrance' from men. Importantly, Rossetti observes that the men who share in evanescent pleasures of the body do not have to 'take ... heed' of the same 'humble lessons' as the women who find themselves cast out, sometimes pregnant, due to unsanctioned sexual encounters. Importantly the poppies and the violets are bridged by the lilies: 'The lilies say: Behold how we | Preach without words of purity' (11–12). In this sense, the lilies of the field are the women working with the fallen women, like those at St Mary Magdalene, and the idea of considering the lilies turns to taking up the example of the lilies. In preaching 'without words of purity', Rossetti suggests that actions speak louder than words, while simultaneously challenging the ideas of female purity that would see these women ostracized.

Line 18 creates a break, not just in stanza, but in the rhyme scheme: it ironically stands alone, as no other line in the poem rhymes with 'But not alone the fairest flowers:' (18). The jolt of this transition is meant to create an awakening, reinforced by the colon, perhaps from the indifference towards the poppies. The reference to 'The merest grass | Along the roadside where we pass' (19–20) recalls the parable of the Good Samaritan and is intended to convict those who would merely pass by the vulnerable, impoverished women. The 'sturdy weed' (21) again recalls Christ's Passion, and that the disciples slept while Jesus wept. Rossetti's poem ends with a call to be willing to be one with God's nature, like the grass, lichen and moss, to 'Tell of His love who sends the dew, | The rain and sunshine too, | To nourish one small seed' (22–4). The final three lines refer both to the Parable of the Sower and Christ's metaphor of faith as the size of a mustard seed. The conflation of these two references speaks to the Tractarian vision of being willing to do even something small, but in that, having faith in a greater impact. Crucially, Rossetti works in this poem to break down the assumptions and stereotypes of what constitutes a 'fallen' woman, and the ways in which these assumptions bar her from being able to break free from poverty and social exclusion.

Considering the content of a number of the poems, Rossetti's *Goblin Market and Other Poems* can be seen in part as a means by which Rossetti is able to use her literary scope to influence and speak to her age regarding the way in which vulnerable members of the community were viewed or, what was worse, made invisible. '"Consider the Lilies"' was, importantly, included in the section of Devotional Pieces. Adelaide Procter's *A Chaplet of Verses* (1862), published in the same year as *Goblin Market*, takes this vision a step further in that it was specifically produced in order to raise money for the Providence Row Night Refuge for Homeless Women and Children, opened in 1860 by Father Daniel Gilbert and the Sisters of Mercy in East London as the first shelter to offer refuge to Roman Catholics. The funds raised by Procter's publication sales enabled the shelter to move into a larger premises in Spitalfields, thereby offering relief to larger numbers of the homeless.[30] Arguably, Procter was able to use her prominence as a literary figure to market the *Chaplet*, for, as Mason suggests, apart from Tennyson, Procter 'sold more poetry than any of her contemporaries',[31] and this prominence was in spite of the fact that Procter died at the age of 38, two years after the publication of the *Chaplet*, of tuberculosis, which was most likely contracted, it has been suggested, through her work with London's poor.[32]

Procter's social activism went much further than the conventional understandings of visiting the sick and poor to being heavily involved in organizations, such as the Society for the Promotion of the Employment of Women, which was designed to train women in employable skills and help them to find occupations.[33] Gill Gregory observes that the *Chaplet* is evidence of 'Procter's concern that her religion should be an active one ... and not content to stay complacently within an aesthetically pleasing church',[34] and therefore in her poetry, as Mason suggests, the Doctrine of Reserve operates to encourage her readers 'to think and feel at the same time'.[35] The way in which Karen Dieleman suggests that Procter's imaginary was more concerned with the Body of Christ than the social body[36] resonates with Rossetti's conviction regarding the Community of Saints; and with this emphasis, Procter intends to evoke a response that moves the reader beyond appreciating the aesthetics of church form, to using that aesthetic to moderate the emotional response to poverty, and then to act in a material, practical way. The poetry in the *Chaplet* is meant to elicit a spiritual response through its mirroring of Catholic rites, but in a way that leads to a meditation not on the wonders of God, but on the depths of abject poverty and how one should remedy it.

While the use of rosaries or chaplets in Roman Catholic devotional practice is fairly well understood, the use of prayer beads in Anglo-Catholic practice is less documented. Arseneau mentions the 'string of black beads and cross' worn by both Maria and Christina Rossetti in their respective work within

Anglican sisterhoods, which seems to suggest rosary practices within Anglo-Catholicism across at least several orders.[37] It is evident, then, that Procter's evocation of chaplets in the form of her poetry in *A Chaplet of Verses* would have been familiar to Anglo-Catholic readers, and perhaps a part of her own Anglo-Catholic roots before her conversion to Romanism. Dieleman also notes that Procter's choice of 'chaplet' rather than 'rosary' is significant. She argues that the use of 'chaplet' suggests that Procter was aiming at a 'lay readership' because 'members of a religious house used the rosary (fifteen decades of aves) for devotions, while lay Catholics used a chaplet (fewer beads, for shorter devotions). Procter's term, therefore, signals her intention to be populist rather than elitist or exclusive'.[38] The poems in the volume are designed each to be a decade in the chaplet, while the stanzas represent the aves. Two of the poems in particular, 'Our Daily Bread' and 'A Beggar', lend themselves to this understanding through their use of opening and closing refrains that are repeated in each stanza, closing the space of each stanza like an individual bead. Both poems are preoccupied with daily provision, but while 'Our Daily Bread' is directed upward, borrowing from The Lord's Prayer, a common part of the rosary, with the opening refrain 'Give us our daily Bread' and the closing 'To be our daily Bread', 'A Beggar' places more emphasis on the outward direction: giving voice to a beggar, each stanza beginning 'I beg of you' and closing 'Pray for me'.

Given Procter's intended audience of the middle to wealthy classes, 'Our Daily Bread' functions in a way similar to 'Give', discussed in Chapter 1, in that it is meant to provide a reminder of God's daily provision in order to moderate fears of loss or lack so that one feels able to share one's bounty with others. The bread transitions through the poem from 'the bread of strength' (2) in the first stanza to the 'bitter bread of grief' (10) in the second. Yet the bread of grief is not due to sufferings accrued due to no fault of one's own, but because 'We sought earth's poisoned feasts | For pleasure and relief; | We sought her deadly fruits' (11–13). These lines resonate with both Rossetti's 'Goblin Market' and 'The World', emphasizing the dangers of luxury and excess. The third stanza then moves towards repentance and atonement, asking for bread 'To cheer our fainting soul; | The feast of comfort ... | For we are sick of tears, | The useless tears we shed: –' (18–19, 21–2). These lines express a process of spiritual purification, following the repentance from the pleasures of the world, but even more important is the recognition of the uselessness of tears. In Procter's Catholic vision, tears of repentance are not enough; atonement must be active. The final stanza, calling upon the 'Bread of Angels' (26), recalls the Eucharist, and is written in such a way as to challenge the reader to take up Christ's example and image:

> Broken, betrayed, adored:
> His Body and His Blood; –
>    The feast that Jesus spread:
> Give Him – our life, our all –
>    To be our daily Bread! (28–32)

Although the poem is a plea for Christ, the separation out in line 31 of 'our life, our all' complicates what is being given and to whom. While it could be a parenthetical description of the Him that precedes us, the break could also emphasize 'Give Him' as a command to give to Christ one's life and actions in order to contribute to the daily bread of others.

It is in this respect that 'A Beggar' intervenes powerfully in Procter's vision:

> I beg of you, I beg of you, my brothers,
>    For my need is very sore;
> Not for gold and not for silver do I ask you,
>    But for something even more:
> From the depths of your hearts pity let it be –
>    Pray for me. (1–6)

Dieleman argues that Procter fails to give voice to the poor in this poem, instead reinforcing middle-class moral superiority. This perspective comes from the beggar not asking for money, but for prayer, seemingly for moral rejuvenation: in line with the way political economy had fused with much religious thought, if the beggar was as moral as the wealthier middle classes, then he would not be in need of food and shelter. It becomes an indirect message that the middle classes just need to pray, not actually give of their own wealth to help the poor any further than the taxes they pay. Dieleman concludes that had 'Procter envisioned the beggar asking for food and shelter or even demanding them on the grounds of religious equality before God, she might have avoided this ultimately patronizing note'.[39] While this reading is valid, I would suggest that in the beggar asking for prayer, he is going beyond the external needs of food, clothing and shelter to the core demand for human recognition. Not only is he physically hungry and homeless, the wealthier members of the community, uncomfortable with the beggar's abject state, seem compelled to walk past him as if he were not even there. Yet to pray sincerely for someone is to acknowledge their humanity and, from that position, ideally, be inspired with more practical means of assistance. In Procter's poem, the beggar, standing on the doorstep of the church, asks not for charity, but to be visible. It is one thing to throw a few coins at the beggar, but another to recognize him as a part of the community, towards whom one is responsible before God. The verses ironically refer to the 'robes of radiant whiteness' (7) and the 'calm souls' (13) of the parishioners, as well as the 'anointed hands' (26) of the priests, revealing the hypocrisy of those who enter the church to worship but ignore the starving literally at the door. Procter recalls the biblical verse that persists through Tractarian social thought, in which Christ says 'Inasmuch as ye have done it unto one of the least of these my brethren, ye have done it unto me' (Mt. 25:40) and conflates it with Christ's appeal 'Behold I stand at the door and knock' (Rev. 3:20) in order to challenge the reader to recognize Christ in the beggar. It is as though it is Christ who says 'I am standing on your doorstep as a Beggar | Who will not be turned away' (39–40), an idea that is emphasized in the way that the word 'Beggar' is capitalized in the same manner as pronouns and nouns are capitalized to designate holiness or divinity; therefore, if the reader denies the beggar, they are denying Christ himself.

In a similar manner, the final poem in the *Chaplet*, 'Homeless', criticizes the willingness to dismiss poverty by channelling it into social narratives of criminality. Cheri Lin Larsen Hoeckley sees 'Homeless' as primarily about the equalizing need for divine forgiveness for the 'fair lady' who is the listener in the poem and the homeless figure on the street whom the lady disregards. While Larsen Hoeckley initially argues that Procter saw 'forgiveness as a phenomenon with both sufficient accessibility and sufficient complexity to address the Victorian social ills of sexual inequalities and economic injustice',[40] it is important that she goes on to nuance this understanding by recognizing that Procter's vision of forgiveness is not equally accessible in the poem because of the attitudes of the poem's subjects: 'The fair lady must shift from complacency to a fuller understanding of some of the despair around her before she can experience forgiveness herself' and, further, 'if there is forgiveness for even the pitilessness of the fair lady in response to the suffering at her doorstep, the extent of that forgiveness is wide'.[41] The fair lady is in more need of forgiveness than the homeless figure, and Procter is less willing to bestow it upon her. Indeed, Procter implies that the actual sin of the middle class in judging the poor is far less forgivable than the perceived sins of the homeless. Importantly, Larsen Hoeckley recognizes that '"Homeless" demonstrate[s] that forgiveness – though universally available – is not universally experienced'.[42] Dieleman's suggestion that the poem is a 'dialogue ... lack[ing] genuine exchange' reinforces this inequality, but turns the responsibility back more forcibly on the more socially privileged, housed figure.[43] Larsen Hoeckley notes a kind of reserve in the 'break in a clear path of communication between human and God', but this kind of reserve adds to the sins of the 'fair lady', rather than pointing her towards heaven.[44] The lady's failure to acknowledge her own need for forgiveness, alongside her failure to recognize her moral equality with the homeless, is what excludes her from forgiveness. This failure is reinforced by the slippage in pronouns throughout the poem that Larsen Hoeckley identifies.[45]

'Homeless' provides a profound punctuation at the end of Procter's volume. From the opening lines it is established that the homeless figures referred to are children, and the evocation to 'listen | To that patter of tiny feet' (1–2) ironically normalizes the children outside in the cold of midnight as if it were the patter of the fair lady's own children in the warm domestic space. Yet instead of continuing the comparison to her own children, the poem turns the comparison to the lady's dogs, asking if they are 'Shut out in the snow and the sleet?' (6). The rapid movement from children to animals reinforces the lady's empathetic distance, which is also reinforced in the quietening mode of parentheses: '(Those are only the homeless children | Who are wandering to and fro)' (11–12). The parentheses are followed, however, with the very active command to 'Look out in the gusty darkness' (13), a momentum that is again halted by the seeming resolution, 'It is surely some criminal lurking | Out there in the frozen rain?' (17–18). The use of question marks reflects the unconvincing attempts of the lady to reinforce social narratives of criminality in order to justify turning a blind eye and deaf ear to the impoverished on the doorstep, this time of the domestic space rather than the religious doorstep in 'A Beggar'. Twice in the poem the command to 'Look out' is turned back through similar narratives; and twice the poetic voice sardonically responds 'Nay' to reject the social narrative: criminals are sheltered in prisons, 'pitied and taught and fed' (20), and so the poor are treated worse than criminals. The second 'Nay' drives home the horror of this treatment through an ironic reference to the waste of the wealthy: 'Nay; – goods in our thrifty England | Are not left to lie and grow rotten, | For each man knows the market value | Of silk or woollen or cotton …' (31–4). Not only are the homeless criminalized for being poor, they are blamed for the weathering and destruction of the few goods they have because they should know to look after them better: if they cannot care for them, they do not deserve to possess them. Procter importantly follows the ellipses in line 34 with 'But in counting the riches of England | I think our Poor are forgotten' (35–6). In this way she challenges the myths of political economy that speak statistically of the nation's wealth, dehumanizing poverty or, at least, refusing to count the human cost of such prosperity. It is therefore important that Procter again lends the impoverished divine importance through the capitalization of 'Poor' and insists on them being counted among the riches – the valuables – of the nation.

Just as Gill Gregory recognizes Procter's concern with 'women's formlessness' and her 'anonymous status and what it suggests' in regard to fallen women,[46] it is evident that this concern carries through to other vulnerable figures on London's streets. The final lines of 'Homeless' speak prophetically to the nation, again alluding to a biblical judgement that belies the idea of forgiveness for the pitiless:

> Our Beasts and our Thieves and our Chattels
>     Have weight for good or for ill;
> But the Poor are only His image,
>     His presence, His word, His will –
> And so Lazarus lies at our doorstep
>     And Dives neglects him still. (37–42)

The capitalization of 'Beasts', 'Thieves' and 'Chattels' suggests that these are the gods of the age, while the Poor are again equated with Christ, driven home through the anaphoric 'His image, | His presence, His word, His will'. By referencing Christ's parable of the rich man and the beggar, the reader who does not act is condemned by Procter to the fate of hell.

## Social narratives of complacency and exhaustion

Hopkins's vision of the beggar is somewhat more hopeful than Procter's, even though he similarly recognized the problems of human complacency and self-serving, as well as being, perhaps, more conflicted in his personal response to the poor. Robert Bernard Martin suggests that Hopkins's attitude towards the poor after he became a Jesuit priest 'vacillated between a kind of sentimental belief in the nobility of poverty when he was living in Bedford Leigh, and a dislike, amounting almost to contempt, for the drunken, lawless lower classes of Liverpool'.[47] This division of social narratives between the rural poor and the urban poor is not unfamiliar, with rural poverty seeming more palatable: the pastoral setting provides a romantic relief that could not be afforded to the abject urban slums. Yet for Hopkins there is perhaps a more entrenched aesthetic in this division, in the idea that whereas he could find God – Christ's inscape – in nature, God seemed invisible in the urban setting. As F. R. Leavis contended in the middle of the twentieth century, Hopkins had 'a habit of seeing things as charged with significance', and that significance was 'not a romantic vagueness, but a matter of explicit and ordered conceptions regarding the relations between God, man and nature'.[48] With a stronger connection to nature through the pastoral, it is possible to read Hopkins's view through the idea that poverty is moderated by the hope that through nature one can connect with the divine. In the urban setting, poverty is unmitigated by such hope, which is ironic considering the number of people who fled to towns and cities in search of employment when they could find none in their own rural parish. Yet the hopelessness of the city is compounded by the lack of nature, and therefore a lack of access to God.

Dennis Sobolev argues that it is impossible to account for Hopkins's poetry without understanding the importance of the motifs of 'the temporality of human existence, the acute feeling of mortality, [and] the irrationality of pain, despair, and poverty'; moreover, it is the paradox of a seemingly 'unchangeable world of serene and eternal vision' that is 'permeated with the signs of historicity' that encompasses the incongruence of Hopkins's understanding of his personal temporality in light of his faith in eternity.[49] From this perspective, Hopkins's ambivalent response to abject poverty can be seen as his personal struggle to maintain faith and action in the face of overwhelming want. His concern regarding poverty and privilege was well-established even when he was an undergraduate at Oxford, with accounts of the lavish breakfasts and 'wines' enjoyed by the undergraduates, but also of his personal resolutions and abstentions as a form of spiritual discipline. In his famous Lenten penance in 1866, the year he would convert to Roman Catholicism, his resolutions conflate food, physical comfort, his love of poetry, and work practices:

> For Lent. No pudding on Sundays. No tea except if to keep me awake and then without sugar. Meat only once a day. No verses in Passion Week or on Fridays. No lunch or meat on Fridays. Not to sit in an armchair except if can work in no other way. Ash Wednesday and Good Friday bread and water.[50]

It is reasonable to suggest that the elitism of Oxford contributed to Hopkins's conversion; and the stressing of 'emotion and intellect' in the Jesuit order, which Angus Easson sees as paralleling 'poetic discipline',[51] provided a path for him to be able to adopt reserve effectively in order to be able to serve the poor without sacrificing his poetry, which is infused with the emotional outworking of his ministry. Indeed, his poetic outflow is necessary to the emotional reserve that preserves him for his ministerial labour. His perspective is one of intimate engagement: his poetry on poverty is not merely an expression of philosophical or theological ponderings, but the visceral response of a man struggling with the incongruence between faith in a divine Good, and the abjection of the lives of the people to whom he was ministering. The influence of the Doctrine of Reserve persists in both 'Summa', written while Hopkins was an undergraduate at Oxford, before his conversion, and the much later 'Cheery Beggar' (1879). Given that much of Hopkins's poetry remained unpublished until after his death, it is less possible to see traces of the literary social activism evident in other poets like Rossetti or Procter; however, where his poetic work intervenes is that it provides insight into the heart and mind of one trying to alleviate poverty, rather than using poetry to try to provoke a response in others. In this way, these poems reflect a more traditional lyric mode. The discipline of poetry in these works allows Hopkins to find a way to moderate his emotional response in order to connect intimately with the poor, rather than psychologically distancing himself from them and the horror of their situation. In this way, he provides a vision of social justice that is predicated through communal connection, rather than the destabilizing effect of excessive emotional fervour.

Hopkins uses the space of the poem to reflect the potential space of action that the individual has within his or her community. Tontiplaphol makes the important observation that Hopkins is concerned about the 'art's infrastructure, the internal "organization" that "penetrates" the textual enclosure', arguing that the internal patterns and forms of Hopkins's poetry are crucial in the way they 'secure' the reader 'within [the] boundaries' of the poem's world.[52] There is a crucial space represented in both 'Summa' and 'Cheery Beggar', a space in which it is the poet's responsibility, and effectively becomes the reader's responsibility, to respond and act. The second quatrain of 'Summa' expresses the scope between God and man, a seemingly insurmountable polarization in 'Man is most low, God is most high' (5), but this line does not just create a distance between humanity and the divine; it creates a mediatory space. The polarization, rather than creating disconnection, creates an expansion of possibilities. The rhythm of 'As sure as heaven is | There must be something to supply | All insufficiencies' (6–8) presents a call to action: in all the space between God and man, there must be a means and a way to bridge the gaps of inequality. Similarly, in the space of the extended first line of 'Cheery Beggar', which refers to 'a place called there the Plain', Hopkins again evokes a space between God and humanity that calls for action: it is on that plain that the poetic speaker meets with the beggar and, in the transient moment, gives him 'poor pence of mine' (9).

I draw these two poems together in their recognition of an active space between God and humanity, but will now address them separately in terms of the way they use that space: their different poetic and political tones, reflected in the urban setting of 'Summa' and the more pastoral 'Cheery Beggar'. 'Summa', as a comprehensive treatise (which its Latin title suggests), uses its active space as a bridge between two states of existence: one a heavenly ideal in which 'souls that might have blessed the time | And breathed delightful breath' (9–10), the other an abject existence in which these souls 'In sordidness of care and crime | The city tires to death' (11–12). Rather than the people, it is the city that is tired, overwhelmed by its numbers. The exhaustion of poverty, with its incongruence with the divine ideal, calls for a moderation of emotion, as much as the diffusion of excitement, which is enacted through the transferred epithet in the desire to distance the exhaustion from the people who experience it. Exhaustion is problematic in the religious vision, which calls for sustained faith. Further problematic is the conclusion of Hopkins's treatise, where instead of maintaining poetic convention by returning to the ideal glory of the holy trinity expressed in the opening lines of the poem, he eschews any tendency towards aestheticized poverty: the faces of the poor 'Are never known for fair' (16). The absolute that the poem leaves behind is a negative – 'never' – rather than the positive action or ideal of the divine. The double entendre of fair as beautiful and also as just brings together in the final word the tension of this abject world. In this way, Hopkins seems to be resisting the Doctrine of Reserve, mirrored in the way that the heavenly ideal in the first quatrain is the only part of the poem that does not have unsettled rhythms. But at the same time, the poem is contained through rhyme – 'fair' and 'sweet air', for example – which gives a sense of a safety-valve release of emotion, similar to that espoused by Keble in his *Lectures on Poetry*. Hopkins, like his fellow Victorian religious poets, speaks of faith in 'steady and regular rhythms' and doubt in 'irregular, unsteady, unbalanced rhythms';[53] but the end of 'Summa' is not so much a matter of doubt, but a jarring challenge, designed to awaken either the poet or the reader to social problems, rather than lull them into contentment with their own salvation. In this way, Hopkins is prompting his reader, or perhaps himself, in Anglo-Catholic terms, to look outward to the space between heaven and earth that is occupied by the community, and to do something to intervene.

'Cheery Beggar' assumes this outward perspective from the outset and, from this stance, is much more stable in rhythm and rhyme. In the more pastoral scene, there is a sense of hope in the lush repetition of 'In Summer, in a burst of summertime | Following falls and falls of rain' (2–3) that enters into the sense of seasonal, natural and therefore divine order. In this sense, the poem evokes Christ's inscape, his presence in the natural world, in contrast to 'Summa', in which the focus of the poem is on the impoverished urban figure. However, I argue that the difference goes further, in that whereas in 'Summa' there is a mass of souls who have been reduced to sordidness, the overwhelming problem of poverty tiring the city, in 'Cheery Beggar' there are two discrete humans – without names, but with equal and separate identities – encountering each other as subjects. There is a human recognition in and of this space, a recognition that enables communion and intimacy. The pollen referred to in the first stanza as the 'flown fineflour' (4) connects to 'The motion of that man's heart is fine' (6), creating the notion that as pollen is tiny, yet necessary to create life and food, the motion of the man's heart to do something seemingly tiny, in giving his 'poor pence' to just one other person, is also an act of pollination, fertilizing the community and, by extension, the nation. In this way, Hopkins, now as a Jesuit priest, calls on individual humans to act within their community: what they do for one another may seem small and insignificant, but corporately these acts would move the nation much more effectively than a change in legislation.

It is evident that Hopkins was fully conscious of the enormity of the problem of poverty and social inequality within England. He found vent through poetry – in the expression of feeling, contained in the written word, restricted by form and feeling – but this attitude, wrapped up in the Doctrine of Reserve, also manifested through his philosophy and actions. As Robert Lowth claimed over a century earlier that the role of poetry was first to incite and then to temper the passions, 'not to extinguish them',[54] a chronological reading of 'Summa' and 'Cheery Beggar' reveals Hopkins's emotional progression from paralysing emotion to small, yet effective, community-based action, which was the touchstone of the Tractarian social mission. In his Jesuit ministry, Hopkins can be seen in some ways to parallel John Keble, who left his professorship at Oxford to return to parish ministry. Like Keble, Hopkins exemplifies a mission that focuses on the greater effectiveness of human intimacy and connection to alleviate social injustice, as opposed to the apathetic deferral to institutions and opaque social structures.

Tennyson's time at Cambridge University predates the height of Tractarianism, but his involvement with the Cambridge Apostles shows his engagement with social and theological thought that would be seen as both resonant with and sympathetic to the Oxford Movement. Tennyson's involvement with the Apostles remains somewhat ambivalent, with some critics suggesting apathy, while others see his reticence as shyness.[55] His ecumenical friendships would suggest further that he did not wish to be associated too closely with any one group, but maintained a truly broad and liberal view of religious and social thought, being willing to explore different modes and ideas. His involvement with the founding of the Metaphysical

Society in London in 1869 furthers this perspective.[56] Tennyson maintained a deliberate critical distance; and his willingness to embrace paradox is a key element of his work that resonates with the Tractarian poetic mode.

Paradoxes can both create unrest in their disjunction as well as operate as a means towards emotional and intellectual reserve. Within his deliberate distance, Tennyson enacts reserve through his willingness to listen while not holding too tightly to any theological or intellectual dogma. At the same time, through his poetry, he enacts paradoxical conflicts that convey the inequities and injustices in human society. Isobel Armstrong refers to 'The Lotos-Eaters'[57] as being 'at once the culminating expression of the poetry of sensation and its greatest critique'.[58] I take this dualistic vision into Tennyson's response to the elitism and decadence of life as a Cambridge student. John Batchelor suggests that 'The Lotos-Eaters' particularly 'express[es] the languor and pleasure that these young men at Cambridge enjoyed'[59] and sees the 1842 revisions as those of Tennyson revising 'his young man's visions': the 'irresponsibility enjoyed by Ulysses' companions in the first, luxuriant version of this poem was replaced by a rather more sober state of mind, appropriate to an older man but losing the playfulness and freshness of the original undergraduate vision'.[60] He goes on to acknowledge that a 'certain amount was gained by this mature decision-making, but much was lost. Tennyson had forced his imagination to grow up prematurely'.[61]

All versions of 'The Lotos-Eaters' express a mutual attraction and aversion towards the pleasures of the island. The desire to escape from the abject is an affective state that is both empathized with and scorned, following a trajectory of recognizing the horror of poverty, inequality and injustice for some, while others live in hoarded prosperity; having a desire to do something to change this state; feeling powerless to do so; and finally being overwhelmed and paralysed by the enormity of the problem. The loss of imaginative innocence in the 1842 version that Batchelor laments becomes not only necessary in the development of Tennyson's understanding of the world, but also shows a capacity to move beyond being burnt out through emotional exhaustion to recognition of the abject, even though the poem still maintains an escapist end. The revisions give more space to the justifiable reasons for wanting to escape, which helps to balance, sympathetically, the escapist response. Armstrong notes the obvious reference to opium eaters in the poem, and its expression of 'the addictive desire in which drug requires further drugging' and the 'conditions under which the unhappy consciousness and the unhappy body come into being'.[62] However, I want to take this reading further in the broader sense of what opium addiction represented in nineteenth-century British society: as noted above regarding Rossetti's work with vulnerable women, it was not just the decadent university students, who perhaps came from wealthy families and were ruined through addiction, who were taking opium; it was also the poor, desiring to escape literal hunger pains through the drug, who found themselves destructively addicted. The implications of these two classes of addiction can be read in parallel throughout 'The Lotos-Eaters', provocatively challenging the motive of escape: it is not always a matter of laziness; rather, the evocation of the laziness at Cambridge is the feature of the poem that Tennyson uses most powerfully to confront complacency, a challenge that persists and becomes even more pointed in the revised versions. Batchelor writes that 'Tennyson worked hard ... at the effect of laziness', giving an example of the ironic intellectual effort in Tennyson's own words: '"The 'strand' was, I think, my first reading," he explained many years later, "but the no rhyme of 'land' and 'land' seemed lazier." It is a delicious form of escape.'[63]

Although the most significant revisions were made in the 1842 version, and most of my discussion will centre on the changes made between 1832 and 1842, each revision reveals Tennyson's growing understanding of, and preoccupation with, the social trauma of the nation and the increasing apathy and disconnection of society within and towards itself. The loss of community that coincides with economic precarity explicitly brings together the social and physical hungers that operate in many of Tennyson's poems, such as 'The Lady of Shalott', discussed in the previous chapter. Even in times of seeming prosperity, the memory of scarcity and *expectations* of scarcity, alongside watching the persistence of poverty throughout the nation, create both economic and psychological depression. Indeed, to position the key moments of Tennyson's text, 1832 saw the Reform Act, which followed devastating national riots in 1831; in 1842 the nation was in the midst of Chartism; while in 1851, not only had Tennyson been made Poet Laureate the year before, which required careful political thought in revisions, the Great Irish Famine as well as Continental riots known as the Springtime of the People in 1848 meant that even those desiring to escape, to be complacent and blind to the international devastation, could no longer ignore the impact of these events on Britain. Hope was hard to find. Therefore, one of the revisions of 1851, which seems minor in comparison to the 1842 revisions, is extremely telling: the first line of the final stanza in both the 1832 and 1842 versions reads 'The Lotos blooms below the flowery peak:' (145). However, in the 1851 version, 'flowery' becomes 'barren'. Thus the 'winding creek' (146) no longer seems winnowing and free, but has connotations of twisting strain, if not strangulation, which complicates the attraction of 'the spicy downs' around which the 'Lotos-dust is blown' (149), in itself a strangling internal half-rhyme. This complication fits with the reading of addiction, but also of a devastated society searching desperately for hope in the midst of turmoil.

The addition of lines 114–32 in the 1842 version shifts the focus of the 'half-shut eyes ever to seem | Falling asleep in a half-dream!' (100–1) from the oblivion of Lotos intoxication to the very realities from which they wish to escape. Instead of merely suggesting that 'Eating the Lotos day by day' (105) lends their 'hearts and spirits wholly | To the influence of mild-minded melancholy' (108–9), from which the 1832 version quickly moves to the sensuous luxury of 'Or propt on lavish beds of amaranth and moly, | How sweet (while warm airs lull us, blowing lowly)' (1832: 114–15; 1842: 133–4), the 1842 version dwells spatially within those memories over which Ulysses' men 'muse and brood' (110):

> Dear is the memory of our wedded lives,
> And dear the last embraces of our wives
> And their warm tears: but all hath suffer'd change:
> For surely now our household hearths are cold:
> Our sons inherit us: our looks are strange:
> And we should come like ghosts to trouble joy.
> Or else the island princes over-bold
> Have eat our substance, and the minstrel sings
> Before them of the ten years' war in Troy,
> And our great deeds, as half-forgotten things.
> Is there confusion in the little isle?
> Let what is broken so remain.
> The Gods are hard to reconcile:
> 'Tis hard to settle order once again.
> There *is* confusion worse than death,

> Trouble on trouble, pain on pain,
> Long labour unto aged breath,
> Sore task to hearts worn out by many wars
> And eyes grown dim with gazing on the pilot-stars. (114–32)

Batchelor reads the 1842 version as showing an awareness of 'the human condition that [Ulysses' men] have left behind and they make a judgement, namely that it is better to leave it'.[64] Yet while I agree with this conclusion to an extent, Dennis Taylor's observation regarding Tennyson's empathy for 'the unresolved complexities of the human condition' is crucial at this point.[65] There seems in the ending of the poem, whether the 'Oh! islanders of Ithaca, we will return no more' in 1832, or the 1842 'O rest ye, brother mariners, we will not wander more', that there is intended to be a level of discomfort in the subjugation of the men to their plight: they are unable to hold onto 'Courage!', the first word of the poem. Readers are not meant to be satisfied with the adventurers deserting them, while the idea of travelling and not returning could be linked to the colonial venture and the attached myths and dangers.

Although writing about an imagined elsewhere, the added lines of 1842 can be read as a vision of Britain. Travelling from beyond could speak to the sense of dislocation from one's own place, a now foreign place, given that 'all hath suffer'd change' (116). The use of colons after 'And their warm tears' (116) and 'Our sons inherit us' (118) has a dual purpose in creating a caesuraic break, which gestures towards the temporality of life, but also balances the lines of the familiar figures of home with the unknown or unfamiliar – 'our looks are strange' (118). In this way, the men try to justify their disconnection as if they were already beyond death; but this is a level of hopelessness where they feel that it is better for them not to return – not to reconnect – which conveys the extent of their emotional exhaustion. They believe that 'we should come like ghosts to trouble joy' (119). They further enter into a depressed state in which they believe that their previous deeds no longer hold impact, merely sung of as myths by minstrels as 'half-forgotten things' (123).

It is within the question, 'Is there confusion in the little isle?' (124), that the resonance with Britain is most strongly portrayed. The question is answered emphatically with 'There *is* confusion worse than death' (128; Tennyson's emphasis), and even the gods seem unable 'to settle order once again' (127). The compounding of 'Trouble on trouble, pain on pain' (129) and the alliterative weariness and oscillating assonance of 'Long labour unto aged breath' (130) express the incessant exhaustion of the nation. It is in the desire to escape in death, but not being able to do so, that the need to escape through the Lotos is made palpable; and therefore the sensuality of the isle becomes something darker, conjuring the desolation that makes its existence both attractive and necessary. That the Lotos is addictive, drawing the men away from their home lives and thus from community connections, speaks of the dangers of escapism: the desire to disconnect, to be half-seeing through the 'half-dropt eyelids still' (135), is perpetuated and increased, particularly in a world that is increasingly fraught. Furthermore, complacent, wilful denial of turmoil only increases the turmoil's power.

The 1832 ending maintains a determined vision of order within the sensual pleasure, projecting the aesthetic beauty of the Lotos isle as an escape from the wearied world. Yet the constriction of form into tetrameter embodies the mythical nature of this belief in order. The men determine that, having 'had enough of motion, | Weariness and wild alarm,' they will remain in the Lotos-land:

> Men of Ithaca, this is meeter,
> In the hollow rosy vale to tarry,
> Like a dreamy Lotos-eater, a delirious Lotos-eater!
> We will eat the Lotos, sweet
> As the yellow honeycomb,
> In the valley some, and some
> On the ancient heights divine;
> And no more roam,
> On the loud hoar foam,
> To the melancholy home
> At the limit of the brine,
> The little isle of Ithaca, beneath the day's decline.[66]

The play on 'meeter' and 'metre' suggests that through aesthetic and poetic order the men can justify their indulgence in the Lotos and the myth of freedom from Ithaca. Importantly, the emphasis in the 1832 version is on the men and their perceived need to escape, whereas the 1842 ending turns outward. Although the men still selfishly and complacently look to their own comfort through escapism, it is made uncomfortable for the reader who might envy such escape through detailed reference to what they are escaping: the inequities of the excessive opulence of some in contrast to the poverty of others, and the paralysing chaos that belies myths of order. The men still vow to live 'In the hollow Lotos-land' (154) – importantly morally empty in its aestheticism – but they do so with disturbing awareness of what they are leaving others to face, namely their own wives and children whom they have already referenced.

The shift to heptameter in the revised ending reflects the opulence and excess, as well as the languid complacency of the men. As the embodiment of capitalist individualism, they decide to live

> On the hills like Gods together, careless of mankind.
> For they lie beside their nectar, and the bolts are hurl'd
> Far below them in the valleys, and the clouds are lightly curl'd
> Found their golden houses, girdled with the gleaming world:
> Where they smile in secret, looking over wasted lands.
> Blight and famine, plague and earthquake, roaring deeps and fiery sands,
> Clanging fights, and flaming towns, and sinking ships, and praying hands.
> (155–61)

Batchelor observes that it is striking that Tennyson capitalized 'Gods' when he was writing about a pagan time; yet it is evident that Tennyson uses the mythological to speak to his own time, much as he did in 'The Victim', discussed in Chapter 2, and many other works. Consistent with his growing critique of capitalism, the Gods on the hills can represent the complacent wealthy classes, as well as political and social institutions, including the church. That Ulysses' men are positioned as those who have the power to act but choose not to do so becomes a powerful social critique. The poem goes on to speak of the 'enduring toil' of the poor, who 'Storing yearly little dues of wheat, and wine and oil; | Till they perish and suffer' (166–8), recalling the Holy Communion: the poor labour for the salvation of the rich in a perverse contortion of the church community. Ulysses' men are condemned in their vision because in spite of being able to see these injustices, they choose their own comfort – sweetness – over seeking to do anything to bring about social change: 'Surely, surely, slumber is more sweet than toil, the shore | Than labour in the deep mid-ocean, wind and wave and oar; | Oh rest ye, brother mariners, we will not wander more' (171–3). Tennyson evokes the excessive laziness of the men through the lulling consonance of 'wind and wave' that melds into the rhyme of 'shore' and 'oar'. The turning inward remains unforgiven in the absolute apathy of the men; in the 1832 version, although the last three lines are similar, there is more of a sense of actual labour in the action of 'rowing with the oar', which was replaced with 'wind and wave and oar'. In the revised version, the men buy into the myth of the world acting upon them, rather than being actors within the world, and therefore they believe that they cannot do anything, and so they do not try; and in the assumption of this position they become the epitome of the capitalist greed that Tennyson resisted.

## Conservatism, socialism and community interdependence

Coventry Patmore, like Tennyson, used his literary reach in an attempt to effect social change. They both saw the need for courage in politics – the need to maintain principle and a moral conscience, rather than giving way to self-indulgence and complacency. While Cornelia Pearsall notes that 'The Lotos-Eaters' does present to a degree 'something like discursive and presumably social equality', in that the Lotos-Eaters were 'leaderless, exempted from the orders of a "Hero-King"',[67] this lack of leadership is indicative of a Britain in which capitalist individualism was extending its ground, and politics seemed increasingly morally fluid. Like Ulysses' men on their prolonged voyage, the nation seemed to be floating aimlessly at sea. Patmore uses his journalism primarily to critique this lack of leadership and the way it legitimated the abdication of individual human responsibility, which arguably contributed to the destabilization of the nation. J. C. Reid suggests that Patmore 'stood aloof' in the age of humanitarian reforms, concluding that his 'chief blindnesses in social matters were a certain lack of compassion, and a disbelief in the value of active works of benevolence'.[68] However, his further observation that Patmore's 'friends and family unite in asserting, he was *personally* the most charitable of men' hints at a different picture.[69] While Reid judges according to institutional reforms, he ignores the Anglo-Catholic ethos that focused on individual action, the same narrow criticism that condemned the Tractarians. Elliot Oliver shows a more nuanced understanding of Patmore's social stance when he acknowledges Patmore's criticism of political structures in general. In terms resonant with the early Tractarians, Oliver recognizes Patmore's emphasis on the need to reform individuals rather than trying to change institutions: 'More than most of his contemporaries he foresaw that the coming crisis would be one of conviction rather than political or social organization.'[70]

Although it has received little critical attention, Patmore's journalism provides a crucial context for his poetry in terms of the way in which his social vision impacted and entered into dialogue with his creative output. He freelanced as a journalist from 1844 to 1846, and then between 1885 and 1888 contributed over one hundred articles to *St James's Gazette*.[71] The articles are simultaneously personal and politically focused, as Patmore seeks to address the heart of late-nineteenth-century Britain's moral, social and economic depression. In 'Manifest Destiny', first published in *St James's Gazette* on 26 December 1885, he writes,

> Every one must have experienced seasons of depression of spirits, during which the smallest cloud of threatening adversity seems to blot out sun, moon, and stars, and weigh down the soul as with a spiritual malaria. Whole nations, it appears, are subject to these periods of depression, as much as individuals; and there is nothing out of which crafty politicians may obtain more fatal advantages. It is in vain that persons or peoples are reminded how such ghosts have been driven back to limbo by the exorcism of a single bold deed.[72]

The short essay observes the complacency of the nation towards church, government and society as evidence of Britain's inability to act with moral consciousness and decision. 'The country is ready to fall into this fatalistic stupor about everything which the Radicals assert "must come"', which is, in Patmore's view, evidence of the mindlessness and self-focus he sees as the disease of the nation.[73] Furthermore, it is the apathy of individualism and complacency of capitalism that Patmore sees as potentially leading to a civil war:

> This emasculate condition of the national mind is probably due in great part to our long-continued and unparalleled material prosperity. It would disappear at once at the tonic touch of a great misfortune. There are not a few, and those not among the least wise and patriotic among us, who begin to look forward to some such misfortune with hope, and in whose eyes few

calamities can be more terrible than the panic apathy under which a great part of their fellow-countrymen are content to be led by ambitious knaves and giddy fools towards a clearly discerned destruction. The Radicals are counting too much upon this apathy if they imagine that it would continue after the first blow had been struck in the civil war they seem so anxious to figure in, after the manner of the heroes of the French Revolution.[74]

The 'material prosperity' he refers to is, of course, not for every individual, but the blindness created by statistical economic thinking washes over the very real poverty experienced by many. By evoking the French Revolution, much as members of parliament and journalists had done so frequently throughout the century, Patmore draws attention to the disaffection created by ignoring the poor for the sake of one's own comfort and ambition.

Such critique of political and economic ambition is even more explicitly expressed in a later essay, 'Courage in Politics' (1888).[75] Criticizing the Conservative government, he suggests that had they 'shown themselves above being frightened by a temporary loss of office, they would now, almost beyond doubt, have been in a strong and independent majority, with no necessity for adopting pillage as a principle' and that 'Men lose the power of seeing the truth when they drop the custom of obeying it – that is to say, when they cease to be ready, if called upon, to make personal sacrifices for it. The habit of courage, once lost, is very hard of recovery, and the loss of reputation for it is still more difficult to overcome.'[76] This attitude is what undergirds the death of the nation in his poem 'England', which opens with the nation lying feverishly near death, 'with hasty pulse and hard, | Her ancient beauty marr'd' (2–3),[77] recalling the nostalgia for England's medieval Catholic past. The conceit of the fevered nation continues:

> Sole vigour left in her last lethargy,
> Save when, at bidding of some dreadful breath,
> The rising death
> Rolls up with force;
> And then the furiously gibbering corse
> Shakes, panglessly convuls'd, and sightless stares,
> Whilst one Physician pours in rousing wines,
> One anodynes,
> And one declares
> That nothing ails it but the pains of growth. (6–15)

The irregular metre expresses a nation in chaos; yet even more disturbing than the feverish state near death is the ignorance and complacency of the physicians, as well as the excess of self-indulgent, useless treatment. The suggestion of multiple dosages of the dulling effects of alcohol and painkillers, most likely opiates, gestures back to the escapism of Tennyson's Lotos-Eaters; yet most troubling is the grossly inaccurate diagnosis: instead of seeing the approach of inevitable death, one physician declares the nation to be growing. Who the physicians represent is not made clear, but it is reasonable to read them as the key defining social and intellectual structures of church, government and political economy, all of which can be seen to embody compromised principle for the sake of individual political and economic gain.

Patmore is not without hope that the nation's leaders 'might again learn to face, for honour and patriotism, the reality of risk, and become worthy to govern in times when real and enormous risks have either to be faced or ruinously ignored',[78] but as it stands, the nation is being led down a path of mercenary selfishness that has little connection to standing by established principles of moral or social benefit. He writes that '[m]odern democracy means nothing but the possession of the elective power by ignorant aristocrats: by those who desire that the best should govern, but who have no sufficient means of discovering the best'.[79] Patmore sees this mode of ignorance, wrapped up in selfishness, as the core of political corruption:

> They make him the master of their persons and purses, and let him deal with laws and constitutions as if none before him had ever been wise; and even the grossest self-contradictions, perpetrated, as seems to the less simple, with the most manifestly selfish motives, fail to shake the confidence he has once secured in the minds of those who more or less conscious weakness and ignorance render them, as a rule, ridiculously suspicious.[80]

In a kind of self-cannibalization, the end result of such selfish ignorance is the abdication of one's own freedom to those political powers. Greed and ambition, whether for money or power, are the manacles of late-Victorian society.

The antidote to this self-destructive attitude lies within the emotional moderation of the Doctrine of Reserve, a reserve that recognizes God's provision in terms of gratefulness, rather than being absorbed into a scarcity mentality of never having enough. In 'Heaven and Earth'[81] Patmore writes,

> How long shall men deny the flower
>     Because its roots are in the earth,
> And crave with tears from God the dower
>     They have, and have despised as dearth,
> And scorn as low their human lot,
>     With frantic pride, too blind to see
> That standing on the head makes not
>     Either for ease or dignity!
> But fools shall feel like fools to find
>     (Too late inform'd) that angels' mirth
> Is one in cause, and mode, and kind
>     With that which they profaned on earth. (1–12)

Patmore addresses the inability of humans to recognize their wealth and the inclination in the capitalist narrative to see wealth as 'dearth': they never have enough. The reference to the wealth on earth as 'the dower' is a reminder of the Church as the Bride of Christ and the imperative to acknowledge the responsibilities to the earth designated by that position. The world is out of order – 'standing on the head' – because of the preoccupation with gaining more wealth for oneself, rather than looking outward to the vulnerable in one's community. The final lines, in their expression of the disorder on earth as profanity, suggest that heaven will be hell for those who live on earth in self-serving 'frantic pride'; what is enjoyed and revered by angels is the opposite of what has been valued by those men on earth, who tell themselves they are seeking higher purposes.

Although Reid suggests that Patmore was caught up in the 'Golden Age' imagined in eighteenth-century social theories,[82] Patmore's vision is not to return to an idyllic Tory feudalism, but for liberal small government. Although he had converted to Roman Catholicism by the time he was writing for the *Gazette*, his social and political vision remains very much influenced by the ideals of Tractarianism in his views of charity and the way in which he grapples with impersonal intimacy. In 'Minding One's Own Business',[83] Patmore expresses the general need and failure to 'know one's own business, with quiet persistence to forward it, and to mind nothing else', which he affirms as 'the true way to carry on the work of life'.[84] Yet his idea of minding one's own business is not simply to ignore the plight of others as not one's own business – that it is their problem, or even their fault, in the persistent narratives of the undeserving poor. He does talk about 'wasting sympathy', which relates to the Tractarian reserve of emotion, but sympathy is defined as wasted when it is exhausted 'upon sorrows and evils which it cannot remove or alleviate. Ills, either in his own condition or in that of others, which his conduct cannot affect, are really no business of his'.[85] Patmore's appraisal of such wasted emotion goes further:

> Sympathy which does not mean action of some sort is not much of a virtue in any man; while in those humane persons who habitually indulge in sympathy for its own sake, it is apt to become nauseous and vicious effeminacy … In proportion to a man's good sense will be his readiness to confess that his sphere of direct and real usefulness – which is his business – is, as a rule, extremely limited. The old-fashioned limitation of usefulness, that of neighbourhood, is a sound one.[86]

Patmore's extreme of parochialism is problematic in the way that he argues that it is better to give 'a five-pound note' to someone in his acquaintance who you know will use it well, than ten times that amount to strangers in need because of the risk of misuse. But from his perspective, he is attempting to rebuild the idea of neighbourhood or community. Rather than reading his dismissal of charity towards the stranger as a personal affront to unknown vulnerable people, his attack could be read as an attack on the governmental systems and institutions put in place with the purpose of alleviating poverty. Patmore suggests it is safer for individuals to cut out the political, institutional middleman. While this move would seem to reduce the impact, his argument resonates with the Tractarian social vision that sees the consistent small giving of all within the community as a more effective means of alleviating social distress than pouring funds into ineffective administrative institutions.

Both Patmore and Meynell were heavily influenced by Anglo-Catholicism before their conversions to Roman Catholicism, and much of their social vision adheres closely to the Tractarian vision of each individual being actively engaged and responsible in their local community (or neighbourhood, in Patmore's words). Their intense friendship could seem incongruous due to Patmore seeming more conservative while Meynell was essentially a socialist, not to mention their extremely different views on women's suffrage. Yet in spite of their differing political perspectives, the similarities of their religious views caused them essentially to draw the same conclusions in regard to the individual's responsibility to act within their community. Both use the aesthetics of poetry to evoke an emotional response in their readers that is checked by reserve: there is a desire to emote a passion that is tempered by the intellect, so that the emotion does not run wild and subsequently burn out. Sustained commitment (social, intellectual, emotional, spiritual and economical) is the motive of reserve. Meynell's persistent mode of reserve and suspicion of emotional excess can be seen in her response to the Suffragette protests. Although committed to the suffrage movement, and seen by many in that movement as a leading force within it, she was ambivalent towards what she referred to as 'militant suffragism'. Badeni notes that Meynell's 'anger was very real' and that when 'her own sex [was] being slighted or insulted or patronized she was there to do battle', but 'she could not approve' of militant suffragism: 'the window-smashers did not have her support; but she worked for this cause that was so near her heart, writing and speaking and marching with the suffragettes'. The ambivalence emerges in her correspondence, where on the one hand she writes of one event that the newspaper reports were inaccurate – 'wretched reports' – that it was 'a magnificent meeting', but in the following sentence, 'the house crammed, unanimous, and (I am sorry to say) militant. They made me sit in the front of the platform, but you know that I am *not* militant'.[87]

Meynell's reticence towards being the public face of women's suffrage, but willingness to write to the press in its defence, is a manifestation of reserve in a Tractarian sense: it removes the spectacle and potential violence, the social unrest, and instead engages through the mediated written word. Importantly, she facilitates the periodical press, the most powerful instrument of community-building and knowledge-building in the nineteenth century. As discussed in Chapter 2, it is in the press that conversations take place; the spectacle of protest is only the catalyst. It is also consistent with Meynell's pacifism and her desire to maintain a critical distance from any kind of excess that leads to unrest on local, national and international scales. F. Elizabeth Gray notes that while Meynell is 'deeply engaged with contemporary debates on suffragism and pacifism, she is simultaneously a participant in the religious conversations of the Victorian age'.[88] She argues that the use of sacramental language enables Meynell to investigate the 'mutually constitutive relationship between individual and society' and that through 'emphasizing the participatory function of uttering religious language, Meynell can incorporate feminist and socialist ideas within a Christian context', and in this way, she 'explores the ways in which ritualistic language disperses power and creates community in a provocative reassessment of religious experience as both personal and politically charged'.[89]

In this vein, Meynell's 'A General Communion' (1911)[90] explicitly engages across social, aesthetic and ritualistic lines, from the depiction of 'the throng' (1) to their imaginative transformation into a field of daisies in the last two stanzas:

> I saw the throng, so deeply separate,
>     Fed at one only board –
> The devout people, moved, intent, elate,
>     And the devoted Lord.
>
> Oh struck apart! not side from human side,
>     But soul from human soul,
> As each asunder absorbed the multiplied,
>     The ever unparted whole.
>
> I saw this people as a field of flowers,
>     Each grown at such a price
> The sum of unimaginable powers
>     Did no more than suffice.
>
> A thousand single central daisies they,
>     A thousand of the one;
> For each, the entire monopoly of day;
>     For each, the whole of the devoted sun. (1–16)

Within the moment of Eucharistic ritual, in which they are 'Fed at one only board', Meynell violently conveys the social disparity of the community: 'O struck apart! not side from human side, | But soul from human soul.' The biblical command to go forth and multiply (Gen. 9:7) is satirized in the division of 'As each asunder absorbed the multiplied, | The ever unparted whole'. The whole is fraught in its internal division, yet in the final stanza this violence is aestheticized through the representation of the people as a field of daisies: 'A thousand single daisies they, | A thousand of the one.' Each flower is a part of the whole, yet of discrete and equal value, 'Each grown at such a price' that even the 'sum of unimaginable powers' could only 'suffice' to represent.

In the reference to the price, Meynell is clearly referring to Christ on the Cross; however, it also evokes ideas of consumerism and exchange within the nineteenth-century context. The reference to daisies, the flower of innocence, is ironic in this picture because they embody the selfish individualism that Meynell critiqued. The field of flowers is no longer a collective, but 'a thousand single central daisies': they stand alone, each claiming the 'monopoly of day' and 'the whole of the devoted sun'. The same people who claim religious devotion are the ones who express greed and selfish isolation; and it is to this inconsistency that the world owes its social disparities. Although Meynell writes on the cusp between the nineteenth and twentieth centuries, her poetry and social ethos reflects the influence early in the nineteenth century that emerged within the Oxford Movement. Regenia Gagnier refers to Meynell's 'intense explorations of interdependence' in her literary works,[91] which express her understanding of community as being predicated on human relationships that, while acknowledging disparity, individuals seek to alleviate the difficulties and distress of others. Within this vision, there emerges an 'ethical aesthetic', or 'an economy of self',[92] that seeks to moderate one's own expenditure out of a moral conviction regarding ideas of necessity and the obscenity of excess when others are starving. Meynell's *ascesis* comes from the Tractarian theological and poetic aesthetic that sees no separation between religion, poetry and social action, where poetry becomes God's ordering force in humanity. While social justice remains fraught, there is a way to find order and forward-moving action: 'If life is not always poetical, it is at least metrical.'[93]

# Conclusion: 'Seeing, touching, tasting are in thee deceived': Responding to the fragmentation of poetry, community and the senses

*Visus, tactus, gustus in te falliur.*
– St Thomas Aquinas, 'Adoro te devote' (c. 1264), 5[1]

Gerard Manley Hopkins's search for Christ's inscape in the fragmented world is reflected in his poetic translation of Aquinas's eucharistic hymn. The 'poignantly unrequited love for Christ' that Hilary Fraser identifies in his poetry[2] is not so much evidence of the position Hopkins envisages for himself in relation to Christ, but more of a triangulation between himself, God and the world. As much as John Ruskin wrote to Charles Norton in 1861 of the 'abysses of life and pain' and 'every one important in its own sight and a grain of dust in its Creator's' making him 'giddy and desolate beyond all speaking',[3] Hopkins despaired over God's seeming 'invisibility in His world'.[4] For Hopkins, not being able to see evidence of God means that he cannot experience the material world accurately: his senses are deceived and disoriented. His sense of disorientation looks both forward and back, and seems imbibed with the kind of modernist angst that emerged throughout the nineteenth century. Some fin-de-siècle poets like Alice Meynell attempted to reassert the divine into the material world through the actions of the church, such as in 'Messina, 1908' (1909), written as an ode in the wake of a devastating earthquake at the Sicilian port. While in the first stanza God is the 'Destroyer' (5) who has 'crushed [His] tender ones' (1), in the second stanza, those who go to the aid of the survivors are the actual hands of God, and the '*Im*mediate, *un*intelligible hand' (6; emphasis added) is moderated by 'Thy mediate and intelligible hand' (12), demonstrated in the work of those who sped to the port in ships and trains to assist their fellow human beings.

Meynell's poetic transformation of the Hand of God from a distant, vengeful actor to the proximate hands of humans working selflessly operates within the Tractarian aesthetic of reserve: while it cannot be known why such a disaster had to occur (or even if there is a reason), what can be known is that it is the responsibility of God's people on earth to do what they can to help the community. Just as Ruskin saw 'the spiritual poverty of modern Europe ... thrown into sharp distinction by the enduring value of [the Psalms as] poetry of praise',[5] Meynell looks for a sense of divine purpose and, importantly, tangible presence, through the aesthetic order and containment of poetry. The paradox of immediate/mediate and unintelligible/intelligible speaks directly to the Doctrine of Reserve in its purest theological form, and is used poetically to moderate the emotional response to a devastating natural disaster that saw over 100,000 people lose their lives in an occurrence of less than a minute.

Meynell's divine hand demonstrates a persistent desire to reconcile the paradox of God's mutual distance and proximity to the world in the early twentieth century that resonates with T. S. Eliot's sense of dislocation and alienation in *The Wasteland* (1922). Written before his conversion from Unitarianism to Anglo-Catholicism in 1927, *The Wasteland* evokes a spiritual and social hunger for order within the chaos of the world – an order he would come to locate in Anglican liturgy and ritual. There is an absence of taste, touch and sight that evokes the absence of God. Although self-consciously read back through Eliot's later conversion, the emptiness of the world without Christ's inscape is evident:

> The river's tent is broken; the last fingers of leaf
> Clutch and sink into the wet bank. The wind
> Crosses the brown land, unheard. The nymphs are departed.
> Sweet Thames, run softly, till I end my song.
> The river bears no empty bottles, sandwich papers,
> Silk handkerchiefs, cardboard boxes, cigarette ends
> Or other testimony of summer nights. The nymphs are departed.
> And their friends, the loitering heirs of City directors;
> Departed, have left no addresses.
> By the waters of Leman I sat down and wept ...
> Sweet Thames, run softly till I end my song,
> Sweet Thames, run softly, for I speak not loud or long.

> But at my back in a cold blast I hear
> The rattle of bones, and chuckle spread from ear to ear. (173–86)[6]

Reserve lies under the surface of this desolation. Importantly, the figure of the Thames resonates with the Tractarian preoccupation with channelling emotion, feeling and knowledge; yet in Eliot, the channel is corrupted. The wetness of the bank suggests its fragility, while the enjambed, 'unheard' wind is a perversion of the silences of poetic reserve. The ironic repetition of 'Sweet Thames' is a cry to the divine that remains unanswered, and instead of death opening into the promise of an afterlife and continued connection to the community of saints, there is only the uncanny laughter of death, the 'rattle of bones', and the knowledge that such a community does not even exist on earth. Eliot's river is doubly empty: it 'bears no empty bottles' or any other sign that life had preceded the poem's space. There is no 'testimony' of life. The loss of history evoked in this image recalls the preoccupation of the Tractarians and Anglo-Catholics throughout the nineteenth century with the past and the desire to find human and spiritual connection through that past. This desire is reinforced through the recognition of the transience of life and the limited scope of the finite human being: 'for I speak not loud or long'. Yet it is then in the image of the river, albeit polluted, as the world is, that there remains hope in Tractarian terms: although broken, the river continues, suggesting a continued vision of humanity that gently encompasses that brokenness.

Within the fin de siècle, questions of 'how did individual needs and desires relate to the needs and desires of others; and how did nations or states relate to other nations or states?' became increasingly critical.[7] The globalization of the late nineteenth century presented a challenge to the parochial ideas of reserve and local government, with an impetus towards recognizing a global community. Remaining grounded in the Tractarian ideas of reserve and individual responsibility becomes more difficult in this level of engagement, yet it is evident that the poets I have addressed in this study were all to varying degrees ethically engaged beyond their local geographical space. Indeed, globalization enabled an increase of scope, once lessons of reserve established a capacity to acknowledge the limits of an individual human. In their focus on individual responsibility, they did not stop at that point, any more than the early

Tractarians had; indeed, the expectation was that by addressing individuals, and encouraging individuals to act, it would inevitably lead to broader action on national and international levels. Anglo-Catholicism persisted in its desire to respond to social concerns in the context of the Communion of the Saints and general Anglican focus on community, but this vision extended into a global picture, with the expectation that reserve would be maintained on that scale.

This extension into a global view, the idea of a global community, grew out of economic and political conversation throughout the nineteenth century. Interconnectedness and interdependence were established between politics, economics, war and relief. However, the concern for the Other place was not entirely new: the devastations in Continental Europe throughout the late eighteenth and first half of the nineteenth centuries impacted Britain in trade and migration, and therefore there was a degree of understanding of its impact domestically. Beyond Europe, the early Tractarians were active in the wake of the American wars and the subsequent implications for Britain's relationships with Spain and France, predominantly Roman Catholic nations. In the middle of the century, the impact of the American Civil War was felt profoundly by those who lived by the cotton mills in Britain's north. Religion, politics and economics converge into the question, 'Who is my neighbour?' Beyond these relationships, the extension of the British Empire contributed to a wider perspective with increasing family abroad and the fraught relationships enacted by colonization.

Engagement with the global community and its challenge to ideas of social responsibility emerge throughout the poetry of the nineteenth century. Tennyson's 'Charge of the Light Brigade' (1854), Procter's poetry about the Irish Famine, and Rossetti's 'In the Round Tower at Jhansi, June 8, 1857' (1862) show an outward vision beyond the local community from the middle of the century, one in which the extent of devastation is overwhelming. Continuing later into the century, Hopkins's 'The Wreck of the Deutschland' (comp. 1875; pub. 1918) and Patmore's '1880–85' (1890) speak of devastation elsewhere that impacts the British mindset, respectively a shipwreck and drownings of nuns trying to escape religious persecution, and a critique of Gladstone's liberal government and Britain's involvement in the first Anglo-Boer War. Patmore mocks Gladstone with 'Your kingly hands suit not the hangman's tools' (3) and writes, 'We saw the slaying and were not aghast' (92), powerfully evoking the complacency of human society within a global community at war. While addressing the challenge of how to extend empathy beyond the local, this image provides a dark vision of the breakdown of community lines. The move away from Keble's poetic order to the comparative chaos of modern verse mirrors a descent into hunger and destruction that the Tractarians sought to avoid by focusing on building local community connections.

One of the most influential Anglican intellectuals of the twentieth century, C. S. Lewis, wrote,

> I do not believe one can settle how much we ought to give. I am afraid the only safe rule is to give more than we can spare. In other words, if our expenditure on comforts, luxuries, amusements, etc., is up to the standard common among those with the same income as our own, we are probably giving away too little. If our charities do not at all pinch or hamper us, I should say they are too small …. For many of us the great obstacle to charity lies not in our luxurious living or desire for more money, but in our fear – fear of insecurity.[8]

Born two years before the end of the nineteenth century, being a soldier in the First World War, and then experiencing the subsequent Great Depression, Lewis lived in a time that seemed to epitomize the breakdown of community on both a national and international scale. Yet it bore a strong resemblance to the instability of the early nineteenth century, which was the world of the Tractarians. In the oscillations of human history, it is evident that between the incursions of war and disaster, the persistent problem is how to care for the community between the moments when emotional excess is the common response. After the initial outpouring of support burns out, the question remains as to what happens to those still devastated, but now forgotten. The Tractarians' vision of reserve, from the theological capacity to accept paradox to the desire to contain emotional fervour, not only influenced the religious, intellectual, creative and aesthetic production of the nineteenth century, but through its poetic constructs provided an alternative social vision to the incessant force of capitalist individualism. Reaching beyond the boundaries of Anglo-Catholicism, the individualism that focuses on responsibility rather than gain, and moderation rather than excess, emerges from the Tractarian lyric impulse to be present in the moment. Within the social theory of the responsibility of the part to the whole is the responsibility of one human to another; and for the Tractarians this vision is at the core of social justice.

# Notes

## Introduction: Containing hunger and doctrines of reserve

1. Translated from Catulle Mendès, 'L'heureux vagabond' (1892). Meynell's version first published in *Poems* (1913).
2. John Keble, *Lectures on Poetry, 1832-1841* (Oxford: Clarendon Press, [1844] 1913), 22. From Keble's Inaugural Oration.
3. Ibid., 11.
4. Emma Mason, 'Christina Rossetti and the Doctrine of Reserve', *Journal of Victorian Culture*, 7 no. 2 (2002): 196.
5. Nigel Yates, *Anglican Ritualism in Victorian Britain 1830-1910* (Oxford: Oxford University Press, 1999), 3.
6. Hilary Fraser, *Beauty and Belief: Aesthetics and Religion in Victorian Literature* (Cambridge: Cambridge University Press, [1986] 2008), 19.
7. Isobel Armstrong, *Victorian Poetry: Poetry, Poetics and Politics* (London: Routledge, [1993] 2006), 2-3.
8. Catulle Mendès, 'L'heureux vagabond' (1892). First published in *Lieds de France*, 21 (1892), most commonly known through the musical adaptation by Louis Charles Bonaventure Alfred Bruneau. The original of the extract cited from Meynell reads:

    Un pauvre sur le chemin,
       lirelin, un pauvre homme,
    m'a demandé mon pain blanc, lirelan.
    'Pauvre, prends toute la miche!
    J'ai dans mon coeur fleuri
    (chante, rossignol, chante si je ris!)
    j'ai dans mon coeur joli, lireli, ma mie!'

9. Karen Dieleman, *Religious Imaginaries: The Liturgical and Poetic Practices of Elizabeth Barrett Browning, Christina Rossetti, and Adelaide Procter* (Athens: Ohio University Press, 2012), 128.
10. Stewart J. Brown, *Providence and Empire 1815-1914* (London: Routledge, [2008] 2013), 108-9.
11. Lauren M. E. Goodlad, *Victorian Literature and the Victorian State: Character and Governance in a Liberal Society* (Baltimore, MD: John Hopkins University Press, 2003), vii.

12 Simon Skinner, 'Social and Political Commentary', in *The Oxford Handbook of the Oxford Movement*, ed. Stewart J. Brown, Peter B. Nockles and James Pereiro (Oxford: Oxford University Press, 2017), 333–48, 345.
13 Simon Skinner, *Tractarians and the 'Condition of England': The Social and Political Thought of the Oxford Movement* (Oxford: Clarendon Press, 2004), 121.
14 Ibid., 229.
15 Dominic Janes, *Victorian Reformation: The Fight over Idolatry in the Church of England, 1840–1860* (Oxford: Oxford University Press, 2009), 4. Emphasis added.
16 See Kirstie Blair, *Form and Faith in Victorian Poetry and Religion* (Oxford: Oxford University Press, 2012).
17 Ibid., 18.
18 Seth Koven, *Slumming: Sexual and Social Politics in Victorian London* (Princeton, NJ: Princeton University Press, 2004), 232.
19 Susan M. Griffin, *Anti-Catholicism and Nineteenth-Century Fiction* (Cambridge: Cambridge University Press, 2004), 62.
20 Dennis Taylor, 'Tennyson's Catholic Years: A Point of Contact', *Victorian Poetry*, 47, no. 1 (2009): 286.
21 Ibid., 287.
22 Published as tracts 80 and 87 in *The Tracts for the Times* (1833–41). The series, which gave the Tractarians their name, was ended by the Bishop of Oxford after the January 1841 publication of John Henry Newman's Tract 90 on the Thirty-Nine Articles of Faith, which raised extreme controversy and fears of Romanism.
23 Quoted in G. J. Cuming, *A History of Anglican Liturgy*, 2nd edn (London: Macmillan Press, [1969] 1982), 152.
24 Mary Arseneau, *Recovering Christina Rossetti: Female Community and Incarnational Poetics* (Basingstoke: Palgrave Macmillan, 2004), 32.
25 Jacques Derrida, *On Touching – Jean-Luc Nancy* [2000], trans. Christine Irizarry (Stanford, CA: Stanford University Press, 2005), 66.
26 Armstrong, *Victorian Poetry*, 27.
27 Ibid., 60.
28 Caroline Levine, *Forms: Whole, Rhythm, Hierarchy, Network* (Princeton, NJ: Princeton University Press, 2015), 74.
29 Ibid., 74.
30 Armstrong, *Victorian Poetry*, 3.
31 Marion Thain, 'Victorian Lyric Pathology and Phenomenology', in *The Lyric Poem: Formations and Transformations*, ed. Marion Thain (Cambridge: Cambridge University Press, [2013] 2016), 156–76, 165.
32 Emily Harrington, *Second Person Singular: Late Victorian Women Poets and the Bonds of Verse* (Charlottesville: University of Virginia Press, 2014), 1.

33  G. B. Tennyson, *Victorian Devotional Poetry: The Tractarian Mode* (Cambridge, MA: Harvard University Press, 1981), 117.
34  Emma Mason, 'Tractarian Poetry: Introduction', *Victorian Poetry*, 44, no. 1 (2006): 3.
35  Dieleman, *Religious Imaginaries*, 167.
36  Thain, 'Victorian Lyric Pathology', 165.
37  Kerry McSweeney, *The Language of the Senses: Sensory-Perceptual Dynamics in Wordsworth, Coleridge, Thoreau, Whitman, and Dickinson* (Montreal: McGill-Queen's University Press, 1998), 73. McSweeney's emphasis.
38  Brown, *Providence and Empire*, 159.
39  Levine, *Forms*, 6.
40  Skinner, *Tractarians and the 'Condition of England'*, 231.
41  Samuel Bosanquet, 'Private Alms and Poor Relief', *British Critic*, 28, no. 56 (October 1840): 441.
42  Skinner, *Tractarians and the 'Condition of England'*, 128.
43  Dieleman, *Religious Imaginaries*, 131.
44  Goodlad, *Victorian Literature and the Victorian State*, 25.
45  Brown, *Providence and Empire*, 102.
46  Coventry Patmore, 'Essay on English Metrical Law', *North British Review*, 27 (1857): 131.
47  Dieleman, *Religious Imaginaries*, 110.
48  Quoted in Robert Douglas-Fairhurst, 'Address', in *The Oxford Handbook of Victorian Poetry*, ed. Matthew Bevis (Oxford: Oxford University Press, 2013), 56–73, 59.
49  Blair, *Form and Faith*, 200.
50  Ibid., 10.
51  Dieleman, *Religious Imaginaries*, 170.
52  Goodlad, *Victorian Literature and the Victorian State*, 33.
53  Alice Meynell, *The Poor Sisters of Nazareth: An Illustrated Record of Life at Nazareth House, Hammersmith* (New Delhi: Isha Books, [1889] 2013), 44–5.

# 1 Economizing emotion and moderating hunger

1  First published in *All the Year Round*, 2, no. 27 (1859): 13–14.
2  Ruth Kenyon, 'The Social Aspect of the Catholic Revival', in *Northern Catholicism: Centenary Studies in the Oxford and Parallel Movements*, ed. N. P. and C. Harris (London: SPCK, 1933), 367–400, 368.

3  Keble, 'Inaugural Oration', *Lectures on Poetry, 1832–1841*, 2 vols. (Oxford: Clarendon Press, 1912), vol. 1, 13–14.
4  Armstrong, *Victorian Poetry*, 175.
5  John Henry Newman, *The Arians of the Fourth Century, Their Doctrine, Temper, and Conduct, Chiefly as Exhibited in the Councils of the Church, between A.D. 325 & A.D. 381* (Oxford: Rivington, 1833), 276–8.
6  Armstrong, *Victorian Poetry*, 175.
7  Stephen Prickett, 'Keble's Creweian Oration of 1839: The Idea of a Christian University', in *John Keble in Context*, ed. Kirstie Blair (London: Anthem Press, 2004), 19–31, 20.
8  See, for example, S. C. Carpenter, *Church and People 1789–1889* (London: SPCK, 1933), who Prickett takes as his authority.
9  Skinner, *Tractarians and the 'Condition of England'*, 222.
10  Ibid., 140, 144.
11  Carpenter, *Church and People*, 306.
12  Derrida, *On Touching*, 11.
13  Ibid., 6.
14  Adam Smith, *An Inquiry into the Nature and Causes of the Wealth of Nations*, 8th edn (London: A. Strahan, T. Cadell, and W. Davies, [1776] 1796), 3 vols. Vol. 1, 43–4.
15  Thomas R. Malthus, *Principles of Political Economy*, ed. John Pullen (Cambridge: Cambridge University Press, [1820] 1989), 448.
16  Edward B. Pusey, *The Danger of Riches: Seek God First, and Ye Shall Have All. Two Sermons Preached in the Parish Church of St. James, Bristol* (Oxford: John Henry Parker, 1850), 20–1.
17  Samuel Bosanquet, 'The Age of Unbelief', *British Critic*, 31, no. 61 (January 1842): 94.
18  Thomas R. Malthus, *Essay on the Principle of Population*, ed. Antony Flew (London: Penguin, [1798] 1985), 2 vols, vol. 2, 660.
19  Jeff Nunokawa, *The Afterlife of Property: Domestic Security and the Victorian Novel* (Princeton, NJ: Princeton University Press, 1994), 7, 122.
20  G. J. Cuming, *A History of Anglican Liturgy*, 2nd edn (London: Macmillan Press, [1969] 1982), 149.
21  W. J. Conybeare, 'Church Parties', *Edinburgh Review*, 98, no. 200 (October 1853), 309. Quoted in Skinner, *Tractarians and the 'Condition of England'*, 167–8.
22  First published in *Household Words*, 10, no. 243 (1854): 324–5.
23  Armstrong, *Victorian Poetry*, 337.
24  Dieleman, *Religious Imaginaries*, 22.
25  First published in *A Pageant and Other Poems* (London: Macmillan, 1881).

26  David Howes and Constance Classen, *Ways of Sensing: Understanding the Senses in Society* (London: Routledge, 2014), 5.
27  Blair, *Form and Faith*, 1.
28  Andrew D. Armond, 'Limited Knowledge and the Tractarian Doctrine of Reserve in Christina Rossetti's *The Face of the Deep*', *Victorian Poetry*, 48, no. 2 (2010): 220.
29  Betsy Winakur Tontiplaphol, *Poetics of Luxury in the Nineteenth Century: Keats, Tennyson, and Hopkins* (Farnham: Ashgate, 2011), 159.
30  Adam Smith, *The Theory of Moral Sentiments* (London: George Bell, [1759] 1907), 263.
31  Ibid., 263.
32  Quoted in Tontiplaphol, *Poetics of Luxury*, 144.
33  David Howes and Marc Lalonde, 'The History of Sensibilities: Of the Standard of Taste in Mid-Eighteenth Century England and the Circulation of Smells in Post-Revolutionary France', *Dialectical Anthropology*, 16 (1991): 127.
34  Mark M. Smith, *The Smell of Battle, the Taste of Siege: A Sensory History of the Civil War* (Oxford: Oxford University Press, 2015), 90–1.
35  Armstrong, *Victorian Poetry*, 421.
36  Blair, *Faith and Form*, 203.
37  Tontiplaphol, *Poetics of Luxury*, 21.
38  Composed 27 June 1854, first published in *Goblin Market and Other Poems* (London: Macmillan, 1862).
39  Armstrong, *Victorian Poetry*, 95.
40  Isaac Williams, 'On Reserve in Communicating Religious Knowledge', *Tracts for the Times*, 80 (Oxford: Rivington and Parker, 1838), 5.
41  Ibid., 54.
42  Ibid., 35.
43  Tontiplaphol, *Poetics of Luxury*, 107–8.
44  Ibid., 107.
45  First published in *The Victories of Love and Other Poems* (London: Cassell, 1888).
46  First published in *Poems, Chiefly Lyrical* (London: Effingham Wilson, 1830).
47  Blair, *Form and Faith*, 29.
48  Williams, 'On Reserve': 53.
49  F. Elizabeth Gray, *Christian and Lyric Tradition in Victorian Women's Poetry* (New York: Routledge, 2010), 138.
50  Ibid., 138–9.
51  Harrington, *Second Person Singular*, 1.
52  Derrida, *On Touching*, 66–7. Emphasis added.
53  Harrington, *Second Person Singular*, 11.

54 Derrida, *On Touching*, 67. Derrida's emphasis.
55 Ibid., 67. Derrida's emphasis.
56 George Henry Lewes, *The Physiology of Common Life* (Edinburgh: Blackwood, 1859), 1.
57 Williams, 'On Reserve': 53.
58 Ibid., 43–4.
59 Keble, *Lectures on Poetry*, 1: 12.
60 Ibid.
61 First published in Meynell's *Later Poems* (London: John Lane, 1901).
62 Harrington, *Second Person Singular*, 3–4.
63 Emma Mason, 'Christina Rossetti and the Doctrine of Reserve', *Journal of Victorian Culture*, 7, no. 2 (2002): 197.
64 Joshua Taft, 'The Forms of Discipline: Christina Rossetti's Religious Verse', *Victorian Poetry*, 51, no. 3 (2013): 311–12.
65 Mason, 'Christina Rossetti and the Doctrine of Reserve', 200.
66 Unpublished. Composed 3 December 1845.
67 'Sweet Death' first appeared in *The Germ* in March 1850 and was later published in *Goblin Market and Other Poems* in 1862.
68 Tontiplaphol, *Poetics of Luxury*, 5, 7.

## 2  Looking outward: The moment of lyrical connection

1 First published in *The Examiner*, 3126 (28 December 1867), 826 and *Good Words*, 9 (1 January 1868), 17–19.
2 Theodor W. Adorno, 'On Lyric Poetry and Society', in *Notes to Literature, Volume 1*, trans. Shierry Weber Nicholsen, ed. Rolf Tiedemann (New York: Columbia University Press, 1991), 37–54, 43.
3 Caroline Levine, *Forms: Whole, Rhythm, Hierarchy, Network* (Princeton, NJ: Princeton University Press, 2015), xi. Levine's emphasis.
4 Ibid., 74.
5 Adorno, 'On Lyric Poetry', 40.
6 Hilary Fraser, 'Aesthetics, Visuality and Feelings in the Natural Theology of Gerard Manley Hopkins and Alice Meynell', in *Form and Feeling in Modern Literature: Essays in Honour of Barbara Hardy*, ed. William Baker and Isobel Armstrong (London: Taylor and Francis, 2013), 87–99, 97.
7 Adorno, 'On Lyric Poetry', 38.
8 Charlotte Boyce, 'Representing the "Hungry Forties" in Image and Verse: The Politics of Hunger in Early-Victorian Illustrated Periodicals', *Victorian Literature and Culture*, 40 (2012): 421.

9 Ibid., 422.
10 Elaine Scarry, *The Body in Pain: The Making and Unmaking of the World* (Oxford: Oxford University Press, 1985), 3.
11 Thain, 'Victorian Lyric Pathology and Phenomenology', 165.
12 Rachel Crawford, *Poetry, Enclosure, and the Vernacular Landscape, 1770–1830* (Cambridge: Cambridge University Press, 2002), 67.
13 Ibid., 5.
14 Emma Mason, *Women Poets of the Nineteenth Century* (Tavistock: Northcote House, 2006), 10.
15 Armstrong, *Victorian Poetry*, 4–5.
16 Adorno, 'On Lyric Poetry', 41.
17 Joshua King, *Imagined Spiritual Communities in Britain's Age of Print* (Columbus: Ohio State University Press, 2015), 10–11.
18 Linda K. Hughes, 'What the "Wellesley Index" Left Out: Why Poetry Matters to Periodical Studies', *Victorian Periodical Review*, 40, no. 2 (2007): 92–3.
19 Ibid., 98.
20 Susan Stewart, *Poetry and the Fate of the Senses* (Chicago, IL: University of Chicago Press, 2002), 2.
21 Ibid.
22 Ibid., 43–4.
23 Hughes, 'What the "Wellesley Index" Left Out', 99.
24 Linda K. Hughes, *The Cambridge Introduction to Victorian Poetry* (Cambridge: Cambridge University Press, 2010), 90.
25 King notes in *Imagined Spiritual Communities* that Tennyson's *In Memoriam* (1850) provided a provocative Broad Church counterpoint to Keble's *Christian Year*. While *In Memoriam* was condemned by the High Church journal *The English Review*, its 'doctrinal minimalism' was appreciated by Evangelicals, Non-Conformists, liberal Christians and Anglo-Catholics alike, 'confirm[ing] a bedrock of faith within the human soul' (161). The minimalism suggested implies the aesthetic influence of the Doctrine of Reserve.
26 Joshua King, 'John Keble's *The Christian Year*: Private Reading and Imagined National Religious Community', *Victorian Literature and Culture*, 40 (2012): 402.
27 Linda K. Hughes and Michael Lund, *The Victorian Serial* (Charlottesville: University of Virginia Press, 1991), 10.
28 Ibid., 8–9.
29 Adorno, 'On Lyric Poetry', 37.
30 Meredith Martin, *The Rise and Fall of Meter: Poetry and English National Culture, 1860–1930* (Princeton, NJ: Princeton University Press, 2012), 2.

31 Laurel Brake, 'Writing, Cultural Production, and the Periodical Press in the Nineteenth Century', in *Writing and Victorianism*, ed. J. B. Bullen (London: Longman, 1997), 54–72, 54.
32 Hughes and Lund, *The Victorian Serial*, 9.
33 Kathryn Ledbetter, *Tennyson and Victorian Periodicals: Commodities in Context* (Farnham: Ashgate, 2007), 1.
34 Ibid., 102.
35 First published in *The Nineteenth Century*, 10, no. 57 (November 1881): 629–40.
36 Ledbetter, *Tennyson and Victorian Periodicals*, 94.
37 First published in the *Union Review*, 3 (1865): 579–80.
38 Edward B. Pusey, *Christ, the Source and Rule of Christian Love. A Sermon, Preached on the Feast of S. John the Evangelist, MDCCCXI., At St. Paul's Church, Bristol, in Aid of a New Church to be Erected in an Outlying District in that Parish; with a Preface on the Relation of our Exertions to Our Needs* (Oxford: John Henry Parker; London: J. G. F. and J. Rivington, 1841), 44. Emphasis added.
39 Ibid., 4–5.
40 'Sermon of Peter de Blois, FL A.D. 1167. Feast of St Michael and All Angels', *The Union Review*, 3 (1865): 581.
41 Ibid., 583.
42 Stewart, *Poetry and the Fate of the Senses*, 3.
43 Ibid., 5.
44 See Blair's *Form and Faith* and Dieleman's *Religious Imaginaries* for key authoritative studies on the connection between liturgical and poetic forms.
45 Mason, 'Christina Rossetti and the Doctrine of Reserve', 197.
46 Elizabeth Ludlow, *Christina Rossetti and the Bible: Waiting with the Saints* (London: Bloomsbury, 2014), 15.
47 Hughes, *Cambridge Introduction to Victorian Poetry*, 11.
48 First published in *Macmillan's Magazine*, 3 (1861): 325, later reprinted in *The English Woman's Journal*, *The Saturday Review* and *The Eclectic Review*.
49 First published in the *Shilling Magazine*, 2 (1865): 193.
50 J. M. Ludlow, 'Trade Societies and the Social Science of Association', *Macmillan's Magazine*, 3 (1861): 313.
51 Ibid., 318.
52 Hughes suggests that the respondent could be Rossetti as poet, or perhaps 'death itself, a possibility that displaces piety and religious assurance in favor of irony and alienation as the inquiring pilgrim confronts the supremely confident figure of death awaiting its inescapable harvest' (*Cambridge Introduction to Victorian Poetry*, 9).

53 Lines 481–540 of 'The Prince's Progress' were published in *Macmillan's Magazine*, 7 (May 1863): 36.
54 Ana Parejo Vadillo, *Women Poets and Urban Aestheticism: Passengers of Modernity* (Hampshire: Palgrave Macmillan, 2005), 110.
55 Dickens was a family friend of both the Procters and the Thompsons, so both poets were connected to this dominant figure of the periodical press from a young age.
56 Meynell was nominated twice for Poet Laureate, being overlooked first for Alfred Austin and then Robert Bridges.
57 Gill Gregory, *The Life and Work of Adelaide Procter: Poetry, Feminism and Fathers* (Aldershot: Ashgate, 1998), 9.
58 *Household Words*, 10, no. 253 (27 January 1855): 560–1.
59 'When London was Little', *Household Words*, 10, no. 253 (27 January 1855): 560.
60 Ibid.
61 Gregory, *Life and Work of Adelaide Procter*, 69.
62 First published in *The Outlook: A Weekly Review of Politics, Art, Literature, and Finance*, 17 (16 June 1906): 814. Later published in *Ceres' Runaway and Other Essays* (London: Constable, 1909), 1–3. References here are taken from Meynell's 1909 essay collection.
63 Ibid., 2.
64 Ibid.
65 Vadillo, *Women Poets and Urban Aestheticism*, 110.
66 Meynell, *Ceres' Runaway*, 3.
67 Ibid.
68 John S. Anson, '"The Wind is Blind": Power and Constraint in the Poetry of Alice Meynell', *Studia Mystica*, 9, no. 1 (1986): 46.
69 First published in *Later Poems* (1901), but reprinted in full in *The Athenæum*, 3877 (15 February 1902): 203, and *The Living Age: A Weekly Magazine of Contemporary Literature and Thought*, 233, no. 3013 (5 April 1902): 384.
70 Alice Meynell, 'A Modern Poetess', in *The Second Person Singular and Other Essays*, ed. Humphrey Milford (London: Oxford University Press, 1921), 18–24, 24.
71 Harrington, *Second Person Singular*, 11.
72 Ibid.
73 '*Later Poems*. By Alice Meynell', rev. in *The Athenæum*, 3877 (15 February 1902): 203.
74 'Mrs. Meynell's *Later Poems*', 647.
75 Vadillo, *Women Poets and Urban Aestheticism*, 110.
76 'Mrs. Meynell's *Later Poems*', 647–8.

77 Ibid., 647.
78 June Badeni, *The Slender Tree: A Life of Alice Meynell* (Padstow: Tabb House, 1981), 144–5.
79 Reprinted in *The General Baptist Repository, and Missionary Observer for 1863* (London: Marlborough, 1863), 410.

## 3 Embracing the community as one people

1 Robert Liddell, *Matins, Litany, and Holy Communion* (London: G. J. Palmer, 1852), 9. Liddell's emphasis.
2 George Herring, 'The Parishes', in *The Oxford Handbook of the Oxford Movement*, ed. Stewart J. Brown, Peter B. Nockles and James Pereiro (Oxford: Oxford University Press, 2017), 349–61, 355.
3 Dieleman, *Religious Imaginaries*, 106, 109. Dieleman's emphasis.
4 Julie Melnyk, *Victorian Religion: Faith and Life in Britain* (Westport, CT: Praeger, 2008), 26.
5 James K. A. Smith, *Desiring the Kingdom: Worship, Worldview, and Cultural Formation* (Grand Rapids, MI: Baker, 2009), 198.
6 Dieleman, *Religious Imaginaries*, 16.
7 Quoted in Brian Douglas, *A Companion to Anglican Eucharistic Theology. Volume 1, The Reformation to the 19th Century* (Boston: Brill, 2012), 454. Paget (1851–1911) was the Bishop of Oxford from 1901 until his death in 1911.
8 Dieleman, *Religious Imaginaries*, 16.
9 Ibid., 109.
10 Fraser, *Beauty and Belief*, 39.
11 Dieleman, *Religious Imaginaries*, 104.
12 King, *Imagined Spiritual Communities*, 242–3.
13 Fraser, 'Aesthetics, Visuality and Feelings', 95.
14 Ibid., 97.
15 Edward B. Pusey, *The Holy Eucharist a Comfort to the Penitent. A Sermon Preached before the University, in the Cathedral Church of Christ, in Oxford, on the Fourth Sunday after Easter* (Oxford: John Henry Parker; London: Rivingtons, 1843), iii–iv.
16 Ibid., iv.
17 Pusey, *Christ, the Source and Rule of Christian Love*, 4.
18 Edward Pusey, *God and Human Independence. A Sermon, Preached before the University of Oxford, on Sexagesima Sunday, 1876* (Oxford: James Parker; London: Rivingtons; New York: Pott, Young, 1876), 8.

19 Emmanuel Levinas, *Otherwise Than Being, or Beyond Essence*, trans. Alphonso Lingis (Pittsburgh, PA: Duquesne University Press, [1974] 1998), 47.
20 Alphonso Lingis, Translator's Introduction, *Otherwise Than Being*, xix.
21 Ibid., xx. Emphasis added.
22 Liddon was prebendary of Salisbury Cathedral before becoming professor of the Exegesis of Holy Scripture at Oxford in 1870.
23 H. P. Liddon, *Profit and Loss: A Sermon, Preached in Substance at St. Paul's Cathedral, at the Special Evening Service, on the 3rd Sunday after Epiphany, 1865* (London: Rivingtons, 1865), 14.
24 King, *Imagined Spiritual Communities*, 16.
25 Ibid.
26 Liddon, *Profit and Loss*, 12.
27 Levinas, *Otherwise Than Being*, 55–6. Emphasis added.
28 F. Elizabeth Gray, 'Making Christ: Alice Meynell, Poetry, and the Eucharist', *Christianity and Literature*, 52, no. 2 (2003): 168.
29 Ibid., 172. Gray's emphasis.
30 Pusey, *The Holy Eucharist a Comfort to the Penitent*, 5–6. Emphasis added.
31 McSweeney, *The Language of the Senses*, 73. McSweeney's emphasis.
32 First published in *Household Words*, 13, no. 323 (31 May 1856), 470.
33 Dieleman, *Religious Imaginaries*, 184.
34 Ibid., 110.
35 First Published in *Goblin Market and Other Poems* (London: Macmillan, 1862).
36 Arseneau, *Recovering Christina Rossetti*, 110–11.
37 First published in *The Saturday Review* (2 February 1907), 140.
38 Fraser, 'Aesthetics, Visuality and Feeling', 94.
39 Preface, 'In Portugal, 1912', *New Catholic World*, 94 (1912): 719.
40 Pusey, *The Holy Eucharist a Comfort to the Penitent*, 2.
41 Smith, *Desiring the Kingdom*, 198.
42 Mark M. Smith, *Sensing the Past: Seeing, Hearing, Smelling, Tasting, and Touching History* (Berkeley: University of California Press, 2007), 78.
43 Smith, *Sensing the Past*, 76.
44 Howes and Classen, *Ways of Sensing*, 96.
45 Levinas, *Otherwise Than Being*, 73.
46 Ibid., 74.
47 Blair, *Form and Faith*, 218.
48 Levinas, *Otherwise Than Being*, 72.
49 Finbarr Barry Flood, 'Bodies and Becoming: Mimesis, Mediation, and the Ingestion of the Sacred in Christianity and Islam', in *Sensational Religion: Sensory Cultures in Material Practice*, ed. Sally M. Promey (New Haven, CT: Yale University Press, 2014), 459–94, 493.

50  Constance Classen, *The Deepest Sense: A Cultural History of Touch* (Urbana: University of Chicago Press, 2012), 41.
51  Ibid.
52  Levinas, *Otherwise Than Being*, 90, 139.
53  Ibid., 16.
54  Ibid., 82.
55  Composed 28 June 1858, first published in *Goblin Market and Other Poems* (1862).
56  Arseneau, *Recovering Christina Rossetti*, 37.
57  King, *Imagined Spiritual Communities*, 237.
58  Richard A. Cohen, Foreword to *Otherwise Than Being* (Pittsburgh, PA: Duquesne University Press, 2016), xi–xvi, xv.
59  First published in *The Unknown Eros and Other Odes* (London: George Bell, 1877).
60  Liddon, *Profit and Loss*, 10.
61  Ibid., 11.
62  Blair, *Form and Faith*, 164. Although Tennyson's time at Cambridge ended before the Oxford Movement emerged, he was influenced by the High Church ideas that were stirring at both institutions, as well as a long-standing preoccupation with Roman Catholicism. See Dennis Taylor, 'Tennyson's Catholic Years: A Point of Contact', *Victorian Poetry*, 47, no. 1 (2009): 285–312.
63  Quoted in Armstrong, *Victorian Poetry*, 165.
64  Linda K. Hughes, 'Scandals of Faith and Gender in Tennyson's Grail Poems', in *The Grail: A Casebook*, ed. Dhira B. Mahoney (New York: Garland, 2000), 415–46, 425.
65  Written in 1831, published in 1832, but revised heavily for republication in 1842.
66  Tontiplaphol, *Poetics of Luxury*, 98.
67  Christina Rossetti, 'Goblin Market', first published in *Goblin Market and Other Poems* (1862).
68  Charlotte Boyce, '"Mighty through thy Meat and Drinks Am I": The Gendered Politics of Feast and Fast in Tennyson's *Idylls of the King*', *Victorian Poetry*, 52, no. 2 (2014): 227.
69  Ibid., 227.
70  First published in *All the Year Round*, 3 (1860): 180.

# 4  Social action demonstrated

1  F. D. Maurice *On Right and Wrong Methods of Supporting Protestantism. A Letter to Lord Ashley, Respecting a Certain Proposed Measure for Stifling the Expression of Opinion in the University of Oxford* (London: John W. Parker, 1843), 10–11.

2  Maurice's Broad Church affiliation places him in a complex relationship to the Oxford Movement and later forms of Anglo-Catholicism. Jeremy Morris notes the appreciation that Newman and Pusey both had for Maurice's 1834 theological tract in defence of the Thirty-Nine Articles, *Letters on the Subscription no Bondage*, as well as the way in which his 'combination of conservatism and sympathy to contemporary intellectual trends made him an attractive figure for post-Tractarian Anglo-Catholics'. Yet the liberalism of his theological position meant that he was often viewed with suspicion by those of a more conservative Tractarian mode, such as Newman, Pusey and Liddon. See Jeremy Morris, 'Liberalism Protestant and Catholic', in *The Oxford Handbook of the Oxford Movement*, ed. Stewart J. Brown, Peter B. Nockles and James Pereiro (Oxford: Oxford University Press, 2017), 585–604, 593.
3  King, *Imagined Spiritual Communities*, 71.
4  Maurice, *On Right and Wrong*, 12.
5  Ibid.
6  See, for example, Lynda Palazzo's *Christina Rossetti's Feminist Theology* (2002).
7  Mason, *Women Poets*, 2.
8  Susan E. Colón, *Victorian Parables* (London: Continuum, 2012), xi.
9  Mason, *Women Poets*, 3.
10  Newman was the editor for *The British Critic 1838–1841*.
11  John Henry Newman, 'Prospects of the Anglican Church', in *Essays Critical and Historical* (London: Longmans, Green, 1897), 302–3.
12  Simon Bosanquet, 'Pauperism and Alms-Giving', *British Critic*, 28, no. 55 (July 1840): 201–2.
13  Simon Skinner, 'Social and Political Commentary', in *The Oxford Handbook of the Oxford Movement*, ed. Stewart J. Brown, Peter B. Nockles and James Pereiro (Oxford: Oxford University Press, 2017), 333–48, 343.
14  Tennyson, *Victorian Devotional Poetry*, 198.
15  Christina Rossetti, *The Face of the Deep: A Devotional Commentary on the Apocalypse*, 6th edn (London: SPCK, [1893] 1911), 474.
16  Composed 21 October 1853, first published in *Goblin Market and Other Poems* (1862).
17  The title has also been linked to Luke 12:27, 'Consider the lilies how they grow: they toil not, they spin not; and yet I say unto you, that Solomon in all his glory was not arrayed like one of these', but Luke's Gospel does not reference the field. Although the sentiment is the same, the field is a crucial element of the way in which I am reading Rossetti's poem, in which the field represents the scope for action one has in the temporal world.
18  King, *Imagined Spiritual Communities*, 247.
19  Arseneau, *Recovering Christina Rossetti*, 5.

20  Jill Rappoport, *Giving Women: Alliance and Exchange in Victorian Culture* (Oxford: Oxford University Press, 2012), 93.
21  King, *Imagined Spiritual Communities*, 247.
22  Dinah Roe, *Christina Rossetti's Faithful Imagination: The Devotional Poetry and Prose* (Basingstoke: Palgrave Macmillan, 2007), 16.
23  Arseneau, *Recovering Christina Rossetti*, 27.
24  John Ingram, *Flora Symbolica; or, the Language and Sentiment of Flowers* (London: Frederick Warne, 1870), 140.
25  Robert Tyas, *The Handbook of the Language & Sentiments of Flowers, Containing the Name of Every Flower to Which a Sentiment Has Been Assigned: with Introductory Observations* (London: Houlston & Stoneman, 1850), 29.
26  Dominic Janes, '"The Catholic Florist": Flowers and Deviance in the Mid-Nineteenth-Century Church of England', *Visual Culture in Britain*, 12, no. 1 (2011): 78.
27  Ibid., 77. Janes importantly notes that in the Anglo-Catholic Church, 'restrained, formal and symmetrical arrangement of flowers was crucial' (83), and thus even the flowers were contained within the Doctrine of Reserve.
28  Antony H. Harrison, *Christina Rossetti in Context* (Chapel Hill: University of North Carolina Press, 1988), 74.
29  I discuss narratives of opium and alcohol abuse in *Hunger Movements in Early Victorian Literature* (London: Routledge, 2016), 74–6, in which Harriet Martineau's Mrs. Kay in *Sowers Not Reapers* (1833) and Elizabeth Gaskell's John Barton in *Mary Barton* (1847) both succumb to earlier laudanum habits due to ongoing dearth.
30  Mason, *Women Poets*, 98.
31  Ibid., 3.
32  Cheri Lin Larsen Hoeckley, 'The Dynamics of Poetics and Forgiveness in Adelaide Procter's "Homeless"', *Literature Compass*, 11, no. 2 (2014): 96.
33  Ibid., 95.
34  Gregory, *Life and Work of Adelaide Procter*, 70.
35  Mason, *Women Poets*, 4.
36  Dieleman, *Religious Imaginaries*, 213.
37  Arseneau, *Recovering Christina Rossetti*, 27.
38  Dieleman, *Religious Imaginaries*, 235.
39  Ibid., 248–9.
40  Larsen Hoeckley, 'The Dynamics of Poetics', 94.
41  Ibid., 97.
42  Ibid., 98.
43  Dieleman, *Religious Imaginaries*, 247.
44  Larsen Hoeckley, 'The Dynamics of Poetics', 99.
45  Ibid.

46  Gregory, *Life and Work of Adelaide Procter*, 165.
47  Robert Bernard Martin, *Gerard Manley Hopkins: A Very Private Life* (London: Flamingo, [1991] 1992), 218.
48  F. R. Leavis, *The Common Pursuit* (Harmondsworth: Penguin, [1952] 1969), 51–2.
49  Dennis Sobolev, 'Semantic Counterpoint and the Poetry of Gerard Manley Hopkins', *Victorian Literature and Culture*, 35 (2007): 87.
50  Quoted in Martin, *Gerard Manley Hopkins*, 125.
51  Angus Easson, *Gerard Manley Hopkins* (London: Routledge, 2011), 22.
52  Tontiplaphol, *Poetics of Luxury*, 143.
53  Blair, *Form and Faith*, 1.
54  Robert Lowth, *Lectures on the Sacred Poetry of the Hebrews* (1753), quoted in Emma Mason, 'Tractarian Poetry: Introduction', *Victorian Poetry*, 44, no. 1 (2006): 1.
55  See Batchelor, *Tennyson* (2012) and Taylor, 'Tennyson's Catholic Years' (2009).
56  Taylor, 'Tennyson's Catholic Years', 300.
57  First published in 1832; heavily revised in 1842, with subsequent revisions in 1851, 1865 and 1872. See Christopher Ricks, ed., *The Poems of Tennyson* (London: Longmans, 1969), 429–38. Unless otherwise marked, line references refer to Tennyson, *Selected Poems* (London: Penguin, 2007).
58  Armstrong, *Victorian Poetry*, 87.
59  John Batchelor, *Tennyson: To Strive, to Seek, to Find* (London: Vintage Books, [2012] 2014), 75.
60  Ibid., 121.
61  Ibid.
62  Armstrong, *Victorian Poetry*, 87.
63  Batchelor, *Tennyson*, 75.
64  Ibid., 121.
65  Taylor, 'Tennyson's Catholic Years', 286.
66  Ricks marks the line numbers of the 1832 version quoted here as 11–22. See *The Poems of Tennyson*, 436.
67  Cornelia D. J. Pearsall, *Tennyson's Rapture: Transformation in the Victorian Dramatic Monologue* (Oxford: Oxford University Press, 2008), 196.
68  J. C. Reid, *The Mind and Art of Coventry Patmore* (London: Routledge & Kegan Paul, 1957), 218.
69  Ibid. Emphasis added.
70  Elliot J. Oliver, *Coventry Patmore* (New York: Sheed and Ward, 1956), 145.
71  Reid, *The Mind and Art of Coventry Patmore*, 15–16, 173.
72  Coventry Patmore, 'Manifest Destiny', in *Courage in Politics and Other Essays, 1885-1896* (London: Humphrey Milford and Oxford University Press, 1921), 9.

73  Ibid., 10.
74  Ibid., 10–11.
75  19 March 1888. Coventry Patmore, 'Courage in Politics', in *Courage in Politics and Other Essays, 1885–1896* (London: Humphrey Milford and Oxford University Press, 1921), 11–17.
76  Patmore, 'Courage in Politics', 14–15.
77  In *Poetry of Pathos and Delight: From the Works of Coventry Patmore*, ed. Alice Meynell (New York: G.P. Putnam, 1896).
78  Patmore, 'Courage in Politics', 16.
79  Ibid., 11.
80  Ibid.
81  In *The Poetry of Pathos and Delight*.
82  Reid, *The Mind and Art of Coventry Patmore*, 216.
83  First published in *St James's Gazette*, 21 April 1886. In *Courage in Politics and Other Essays*, 17–20.
84  Patmore, 'Minding One's Own Business', 17.
85  Ibid., 17–18.
86  Ibid., 18–19.
87  Badeni, *The Slender Tree*, 210.
88  F. Elizabeth Gray, 'Making Christ: Alice Meynell, Poetry, and the Eucharist', *Christianity and Literature*, 52, no. 2 (2003): 161.
89  Ibid.
90  First published in *The Living Church*, 46 (1911): 537 and *The Dublin Review*, 149, no. 299 (1911): 303. Later reprinted in Meynell's *Collected Poems* (1913) and *The Living Age*, 277 (1913): 386.
91  Regenia Gagnier, *Individualism, Decadence and Globalization: On the Relationship of Part to Whole, 1859–1920* (Basingstoke: Palgrave Macmillan, 2010), 75.
92  Ibid., 77.
93  Alice Meynell, 'The Rhythm of Life', in *The Rhythm of Life and Other Essays* (London: Elkin Matthews and John Lane, 1893), 1.

# Conclusion: 'Seeing, touching, tasting are in thee deceived': Responding to the fragmentation of poetry, community and the senses

1  Gerard Manley Hopkins translated Aquinas' 'Adoro te devote' as 'Seeing, touching tasting are in thee deceived' in 'Lost, All in Wonder' (c. 1866).

2  Fraser, 'Aesthetics, Visuality and Feelings', 89.
3  John Ruskin, *The Works of John Ruskin*, ed. E. T. Cook and Alexander Wedderburn, 39 vols (London: George Allen, 1903–12), vol. 36, 380.
4  Fraser, 'Aesthetics, Visuality and Feelings', 90.
5  Andrew Tate, ' "Sweeter also Than Honey": John Ruskin and the Psalms', *The Yearbook of English Studies*, 39 (2009): 114.
6  T. S. Eliot, 'The Fire Sermon', *The Wasteland* (1922), in *The Wasteland and Other Poems* (London: Penguin, 2003), 61–6.
7  Gagnier, *Individualism, Decadence and Globalization*, 3.
8  C. S. Lewis, *Mere Christianity* (New York: HarperCollins, [1952] 1980), 86.

# Bibliography

Abbott, C. C., ed. *The Letters of Gerard Manley Hopkins to Robert Bridges*. Oxford: Oxford University Press, 1970.

Adorno, Theodor W. 'On Lyric Poetry and Society'. In *Notes to Literature, Volume 1*, translated by Shierry Weber Nicholsen, edited by Rolf Tiedemann, 37–54. New York: Columbia University Press, 1991.

Anson, John S. '"The Wind is Blind": Power and Constraint in the Poetry of Alice Meynell'. *Studia Mystica* 9, no. 1 (1986): 37–50.

Armond, Andrew D. 'Limited Knowledge and the Tractarian Doctrine of Reserve in Christina Rossetti's *The Face of the Deep*'. *Victorian Poetry* 48, no. 2 (2010): 219–41.

Armstrong, Isobel. *Victorian Poetry: Poetry, Poetics and Politics*. London: Routledge, [1993] 2006.

Arseneau, Mary. 'Incarnation and Interpretation: Christina Rossetti, the Oxford Movement, and "Goblin Market"'. *Victorian Poetry* 31, no. 1 (1993): 79–93.

Arseneau, Mary. *Recovering Christina Rossetti: Female Community and Incarnational Poetics*. Basingstoke: Palgrave Macmillan, 2004.

Arseneau, Mary, Antony H. Harrison and Lorraine Janzen Kooistra, eds. *The Culture of Christina Rossetti: Female Poetics and Victorian Contexts*. Athens: Ohio University Press, 1999.

Attridge, Derek. 'A Return to Form'. *Textual Practice* 22 (2008): 563–75.

Austin, Alfred. *The Poetry of the Period*. London: Richard Bentley, 1870.

Austin, Linda M. 'Self against Childhood: The Contributions of Alice Meynell to a Psycho-Physiology of Memory'. *Victorian Literature and Culture* 34, no. 1 (2006): 249–68.

Badeni, June. *The Slender Tree: A Life of Alice Meynell*. Padstow: Tabb House, 1981.

Barker, Juliet. *The Brontës*. London: Phoenix Press, 1994.

Batchelor, John. *Tennyson: To Strive, to Seek, to Find*. London: Vintage, 2012.

Bateman, Bradley W., and H. Spencer Banzhaf. *Keeping Faith, Losing Faith: Religious Belief and Political Economy*. Durham: Duke University Press, 2008.

Bell, Amy. 'Women's Politics, Poetry, and the Feminist Historiography of the Great War'. *Canadian Journal of History* 42, no. 3 (2007): 411–37.

Bevis, Matthew, ed. *The Oxford Handbook of Victorian Poetry*. Oxford: Oxford University Press, 2013.

Blair, Kirstie. *Form and Faith in Victorian Poetry and Religion*. Oxford: Oxford University Press, 2012.

Blair, Kirstie. 'John Keble and the Rhythm of Faith'. *Essays in Criticism* 53, no. 2 (2003): 129–50.

Blair, Kirstie, ed. *John Keble in Context*. London: Anthem Press, 2004.

Blyth, Caroline. *Decadent Verse: An Anthology of Late-Victorian Poetry, 1872–1900*. London: Anthem Press, 2011.

Borg, Ruben Paul, Sebastiano D'Amico, and Pauline Galea. 'Earthquake and People: The Maltese Experience of the 1908 Messina Earthquake'. In *Earthquakes and Their Impact on Society*, edited by Sebastiano D'Amico, 533–61. Geneva: Springer, 2016.

Bosanquet, Samuel. 'The Age of Unbelief'. *British Critic* 31, no. 61 (January 1842): 91–123.

Bosanquet, Samuel. 'Pauperism and Alms-Giving'. *British Critic* 28, no. 55 (July 1840): 195–257.

Bosanquet, Samuel. 'Private Alms and Poor Relief'. *British Critic* 28, no. 56 (October 1840): 441–70.

Bosworth, R. J. B. 'The Messina Earthquake of 28 December 1908'. *European Studies Review* 11 (1981): 189–206.

Boyce, Charlotte. '"Mighty through thy Meats and Drinks Am I": The Gendered Politics of Feast and Fast in Tennyson's *Idylls of the King*'. *Victorian Poetry* 52, no. 2 (2014): 225–49.

Boyce, Charlotte. 'Representing the "Hungry Forties" in Image and Verse: The Politics of Hunger in Early-Victorian Illustrated Periodicals'. *Victorian Literature and Culture* 40 (2012): 421–9.

Brake, Laurel. 'Writing, Cultural Production, and the Periodical Press in the Nineteenth Century'. In *Writing and Victorianism*, edited by J. B. Bullen, 54–72. London: Longman, 1997.

Brown, Stewart J. *Providence and Empire, 1815–1914*. London: Routledge, [2008] 2013.

Brown, Stewart J., Peter B. Nockles and James Pereiro, eds. *The Oxford Handbook of the Oxford Movement*. Oxford: Oxford University Press, 2017.

Brzenk, Eugene J. '"Up-hill" and "Down-" by Christina Rossetti'. *Victorian Poetry* 10, no. 4 (1972): 367–71.

Bump, Jerome. 'Hopkins' Imagery and Medievalist Poetics'. *Victorian Poetry* 15, no. 2 (1977): 99–119.

Bump, Jerome. 'Victorian Religious Discourse as Palimpsest: Hopkins, Pusey, and Müller'. *Religion and the Arts* 5, nos 1–2 (2001): 13–33.

Burrows, Henry W. *The Half-Century of Christ Church, St. Pancras, Albany Street.* London: Skeffington, 1887.

Carlyle, Thomas. *Signs of the Times*. 1829. In *Essays: Collected and Republished by Thomas Carlyle*. 4 vols. Vol. 2, 3rd edn. London: Chapman and Hall, 1847.

Carpenter, S. C. *Church and People 1789–1889*. London: SPCK, 1933.

Castellani, Luigi. 'Correspondence: A Photographic Appeal for the Children made Orphans by the Messina Earthquake'. *The British Journal of Photography* 56, no. 2546 (19 February 1909): 149–50.

*The Churches, The People, and The Pew-System*. By a Layman. Manchester: A. Ireland, 1859.

Chapman, Raymond. *Faith and Revolt: Studies in the Literary Influence of the Oxford Movement*. London: Weidenfeld, 1970.

Clarke, Micael M. 'Charlotte Brontë's *Villette*, Mid-Victorian Anti-Catholicism, and the Turn to Secularism'. *ELH* 78, no. 4 (2011): 967–89.

Classen, Constance, ed. *The Book of Touch*. Oxford: Berg, 2005.

Classen, Constance. *The Deepest Sense: A Cultural History of Touch*. Urbana: University of Illinois Press, 2012.

Clifford, David, and Laurence Roussillon, eds. *Outsiders Looking in: The Rossettis Then and Now*. London: Anthem Press, 2004.

Colón, Susan E. *Victorian Parables*. London: Continuum, 2012.

Conn, Walter E. *Conscience and Conversion in Newman: A Developmental Study of Self in John Henry Newman*. Milwaukee: Marquette University Press, 2010.

Crawford, Rachel. *Poetry, Enclosure, and the Vernacular Landscape, 1770–1830*. Cambridge: Cambridge University Press, 2002.

Cronin, Richard, Alison Chapman and Antony H. Harrison, eds. *A Companion to Victorian Poetry*. Oxford: Blackwell, 2002.

Cuming, G. J. *A History of Anglican Liturgy*. 2nd edn. London: Macmillan Press, [1969] 1982.

D'Amico, Diane. *Christina Rossetti: Faith, Gender, and Time*. Baton Rouge: Louisiana State University Press, 1999.

D'Amico, Diane, and David A. Kent. 'Rossetti and the Tractarians'. *Victorian Poetry* 44, no. 1 (2006): 93–104.

Dau, Duc. *Touching God: Hopkins and Love*. London: Anthem Press, 2013.

Davies, Walford, ed. *Gerard Manley Hopkins: Poetry and Prose*. London: J. M. Dent, 1998.

Derrida, Jacques. *On Touching—Jean-Luc Nancy*. Translated by Christine Irizarry. Stanford: Stanford University Press, [2000] 2005.

Dickens, Charles. *A Christmas Carol*. London: Penguin, [1843] 2014.

Dickens, Charles. *Oliver Twist*. London: Penguin, [1837–9] 2003.
Dieleman, Karen. *Religious Imaginaries: The Liturgical and Poetic Practices of Elizabeth Barrett Browning, Christina Rossetti, and Adelaide Procter.* Athens: Ohio University Press, 2012.
Douglas, Brian. *A Companion to Anglican Eucharistic Theology. Volume 1, The Reformation to the Nineteenth Century*. Boston: Brill, 2012.
Easson, Angus. *Gerard Manley Hopkins*. London: Routledge, 2011.
Eliot, T. S. *The Wasteland and Other Poems*. Edited by Frank Kermode. London: Penguin, 2003.
Erskine-Hill, Howard, and Richard A. McCabe, eds. *Presenting Poetry: Composition, Publication, Reception*. Cambridge: Cambridge University Press, 1995.
Faught, C. Brad. *The Oxford Movement: A Thematic History of the Tractarians and Their Times*. University Park: Pennsylvania State University Press, 2003.
Felluga, Dino. 'Tennyson's *Idylls*, Pure Poetry, and the Market'. *Studies in English Literature, 1500–1900* 37, no. 4 (1997): 783–803.
Fraser, Hilary. 'Aesthetics, Visuality and Feelings in the Natural Theology of Gerard Manley Hopkins and Alice Meynell'. In *Form and Feeling in Modern Literature: Essays in Honour of Barbara Hardy*, edited by William Baker and Isobel Armstrong, 87–99. London: Taylor and Francis, 2013.
Fraser, Hilary. *Beauty and Belief: Aesthetics and Religion in Victorian Literature*. Cambridge: Cambridge University Press, 1986.
Frawley, Maria. ' "The Tides of the Mind": Alice Meynell's Poetry of Perception'. *Victorian Poetry* 38, no. 1 (2000): 62–76.
Frith, Richard. ' "Heartsease I Found": Rossetti, Analogy, and the Individual Believing Subject'. *Literature & Theology* 28, no. 1 (2014): 29–44.
Fulford, Tim. 'Apocalyptic Economics and Prophetic Politics: Radical and Romantic Responses to Malthus and Burke'. *Studies in Romanticism* 40 (2001): 345–68.
Furse Jackson, Vanessa. ' "Tides of the Mind": Restraint and Renunciation in the Poetry of Alice Meynell'. *Victorian Poetry* 36, no. 4 (1998): 443–64.
Gagnier, Regenia. *Individualism, Decadence and Globalization: On the Relationship of Part to Whole, 1859–1920*. Basingstoke: Palgrave Macmillan, 2010.
Gagnier, Regenia. *The Insatiability of Human Wants: Economics and Aesthetics in Market Society*. Chicago, IL: University of Chicago Press, 2000.
Gaskell, Elizabeth. *North and South*. London: Penguin, [1854–5] 2003.
Gelpi, Barbara Charlesworth. 'John Keble and Hurrell Froude in Pastoral Dialogue'. *Victorian Poetry* 44, no. 1 (2006): 7–24.
*The General Baptist Repository, and Missionary Observer for 1863*. London: Marlborough, 1863.

Goodlad, Lauren M. E., '"A Middle Class Cut into Two": Historiography and Victorian National Character'. *ELH* 67, no. 1 (2000): 143–78.

Goodlad, Lauren M. E. *Victorian Literature and the Victorian State: Character and Governance in a Liberal Society*. Baltimore: John Hopkins University Press, 2003.

Goodwin, Gregory H. 'Keble and Newman: Tractarian Aesthetics and the Romantic Tradition'. *Victorian Studies* 30, no. 4 (1987): 475–94.

Goody, Jack. 'The Secret Language of Flowers'. *Yale Journal of Criticism* 3, no. 2 (1990): 133–52.

Grafe, Adrian, ed. *Ecstasy and Understanding: Religious Awareness in English Poetry from the Late Victorian to the Modern Period*. London: Continuum, 2008.

Gray, F. Elizabeth. *Christian and Lyric Tradition in Victorian Women's Poetry*. New York: Routledge, 2010.

Gray, F. Elizabeth. 'Making Christ: Alice Meynell, Poetry, and the Eucharist'. *Christianity and Literature* 52, no. 2 (2003): 159–79.

Gray, F. Elizabeth. *Women in Journalism at the Fin de Siècle: Making a Name for Herself*. London: Springer, 2012.

Gregory, Gill. *The Life and Work of Adelaide Procter: Poetry, Feminism and Fathers*. Aldershot: Ashgate, 1998.

Griffin, Susan M. *Anti-Catholicism and Nineteenth-Century Fiction*. Cambridge: Cambridge University Press, 2004.

Griffiths, Eric. *The Printed Voice of Victorian Poetry*. New York: Clarendon Press, 1989.

Groves, Peter. 'Hopkins and Tractarianism'. *Victorian Poetry* 44, no. 1 (2006): 105–12.

Guite, Malcolm. *Faith, Hope and Poetry: Theology and the Poetic Imagination*. Farnham: Ashgate, 2012.

Hall, Jason D., ed. *Meter Matters: Verse Cultures of the Long Nineteenth Century*. Columbus: Ohio University Press, 2011.

Harrington, Emily. *Second Person Singular: Later Victorian Women Poets and the Bonds of Verse*. Charlottesville: University of Virginia Press, 2014.

Harrison, Antony H. *Christina Rossetti in Context*. Chapel Hill: University of North Carolina Press, 1988.

Harrison, Mary-Catherine. 'How Narrative Relationships Overcome Empathic Bias: Elizabeth Gaskell's Empathy across Social Difference'. *Poetics Today* 32, no. 2 (2011): 255–88.

Harrison, Mary-Catherine. '"The Great Sum of Universal Anguish": Statistical Empathy in Victorian Social-Problem Literature'. In *Rethinking Empathy through Literature*, edited by Meghan Marie Hammond and Sue J. Kim, 135–49. New York: Routledge, 2014.

Harrison, Mary-Catherine. 'The Paradox of Fiction and the Ethics of Empathy: Reconceiving Dickens's Realism'. *Narrative* 16, no. 3 (2008): 256–78.

Heimann, Mary. *Catholic Devotion in Victorian England*. Oxford: Clarendon Press, 1995.

Heurtley, Charles A. *The Doctrine of the Eucharist: Christ Present by Spirit and Grace: A Sermon Preached before the University of Oxford, on Sunday, January 27, 1867*. Oxford: James Parker, 1867.

Hill, Marylu. '"Eat Me, Drink Me, Love Me": Eucharist and the Erotic Body in Christina Rossetti's "Goblin Market"'. *Victorian Poetry* 43, no. 1 (2005): 455–72.

Hitchens, Robert. 'After the Earthquake'. *The Century Illustrated Monthly Magazine* 77, no. 6 (1909): 928–39.

Honeyman, Susan. 'Gingerbread Wishes and Candy(land) Dreams: The Lure of Food in Cautionary Tales of Consumption'. *Marvels & Tales* 21, no. 2 (2007): 195–215.

Hopkins, Gerard Manley. *Selected Poetry*. Edited by Catherine Phillips. Oxford: Oxford University Press, 1996.

Horne, Brian. 'Church and Nation: Newman and the Tractarians'. *International Journal for the Study of the Christian Church* 5, no. 1 (2005): 25–40.

Howes, David, and Constance Classen. *Ways of Sensing: Understanding the Senses in Society*. London: Routledge, 2014.

Howes, David, and Marc Lalonde. 'The History of Sensibilities: Of the Standard of Taste in Mid-Eighteenth Century England and the Circulation of Smells in Post-Revolutionary France'. *Dialectical Anthropology* 16 (1991): 125–35.

Hsiao, Irene. 'Calculating Loss in Tennyson's *In Memoriam*'. *Victorian Poetry* 47, no. 1 (2009): 173–96.

Hu, Esther T. 'Christina Rossetti, John Keble, and the Divine Gaze'. *Victorian Poetry* 46, no. 2 (2008): 175–89.

Hughes, Linda K. *The Cambridge Introduction to Victorian Poetry*. Cambridge: Cambridge University Press, 2010.

Hughes, Linda K. 'Media by Bakhtin/Bakhtin Mediated'. *Victorian Periodicals Review* 44, no. 3 (2011): 293–7.

Hughes, Linda K. 'Narrative Matters: Keynote Address, "Forms and Fashions": A Conference in Celebration of the Fiftieth Anniversary of *Victorian Poetry*'. *Victorian Poetry* 51, no. 4 (2013): 443–64.

Hughes, Linda K. 'Scandals of Faith and Gender in Tennyson's Grail Poems'. In *The Grail: A Casebook*, edited by Dhira B. Mahoney, 415–46. New York: Garland, 2000.

Hughes, Linda K. 'What the "Wellesley Index" Left Out: Why Poetry Matters to Periodical Studies'. *Victorian Periodicals Review* 40, no. 2 (2007): 91–125.

Hughes, Linda K., and Michael Lund. *The Victorian Serial*. Charlottesville: University of Virginia Press, 1991.
Humphries, Simon. 'The Uncertainty of "Goblin Market"'. *Victorian Poetry* 45, no. 4 (2007): 391–413.
Ingram, John. *Flora Symbolica; or, the Language and Sentiment of Flowers*. London: Frederick Warne, 1870.
Janes, Dominic. '"The Catholic Florist": Flowers and Deviance in the Mid-Nineteenth-Century Church of England'. *Visual Culture in Britain* 12, no. 1 (2011): 77–96.
Janes, Dominic. *Victorian Reformation: The Fight over Idolatry in the Church of England, 1840–1860*. Oxford: Oxford University Press, 2009.
Jasper, David, ed. *The Interpretation of Belief: Coleridge, Schleiermacher and Romanticism*. Houndmills: Macmillan, 1986.
Jay, Elisabeth. 'Charlotte Mary Yonge and Tractarian Aesthetics'. *Victorian Poetry* 44, no. 1 (2006): 43–60.
Johnson, Margaret. *Gerard Manley Hopkins and Tractarian Poetry*. Aldershot: Ashgate, 1997.
Johnson, Maria Poggi. 'The Reason for What Is Right: Practical Wisdom in John Keble and Charlotte Yonge'. *Literature & Theology* 20, no. 4 (2006): 379–93.
Johnson, Stephanie L. '"Home One and All": Redeeming the Whore of Babylon in Christina Rossetti's Religious Poetry'. *Victorian Poetry* 49, no. 1 (2011): 105–47.
Keble, John. *The Christian Year. Thought in Verse for the Sundays and Holydays Throughout the Year*. 2nd edn. Oxford: J. Parker, 1827.
Keble, John. *Keble's Lectures on Poetry, 1832–1841*. 2 vols. Oxford: Clarendon Press, [1844] 1912.
Keble, John. 'Sacred Poetry'. *The Quarterly Review* 32, no. 63 (1825): 211–32.
Kenyon, Ruth. 'The Social Aspect of the Catholic Revival'. In *Northern Catholicism: Centenary Studies in the Oxford and Parallel Movements*, edited by N. P. and C. Harris, 367–400. London: SPCK, 1933.
King, Joshua. *Imagined Spiritual Communities in Britain's Age of Print*. Columbus: Ohio State University Press, 2015.
King, Joshua. 'John Keble's *The Christian Year*: Private Reading and Imagined National Religious Community'. *Victorian Literature and Culture* 40 (2012): 397–420.
Knight, Mark, and Louise Lee, eds. *Religion, Literature and the Imagination: Sacred Worlds*. London: Bloomsbury, 2011.
Koven, Seth. *Slumming: Sexual and Social Politics in Victorian London*. Princeton, NJ: Princeton University Press, 2004.

Kreilkamp, Ivan. 'Victorian Poetry's Modernity'. *Victorian Poetry* 14 (2003): 603–11.

LaPorte, Charles. *Victorian Poets and the Changing Bible*. Charlottesville: University of Virginia Press, 2011.

Larsen Hoeckley, Cheri Lin. 'The Dynamics of Poetics and Forgiveness in Adelaide Procter's "Homeless"'. *Literature Compass* 11, no. 2 (2014): 94–106.

'Later Poems. By Alice Meynell'. Review. *The Athenæum* 3877 (15 February, 1902), 203.

[Latour, Charlotte]. *The Language of Flowers*. 2nd edn. Philadelphia, PA: Carey, Lea & Blanchard, [1834] 1835.

Lawler, Justus George. *Hopkins Reconstructed: Life, Poetry, and the Tradition*. New York: Continuum, 2000.

Leavis, F. R. *The Common Pursuit*. Harmondsworth: Penguin, [1952] 1969.

Ledbetter, Kathryn. *Tennyson and Victorian Periodicals: Commodities in Context*. Farnham: Ashgate, 2007.

Leder, Sharon and Andrea Abbott. *The Language of Exclusion: The Poetry of Emily Dickenson and Christina Rossetti*. New York: Greenwood Press, 1987.

Leighton, Angela. *On Form: Poetry, Aestheticism, and the Legacy of a Word*. Oxford: Oxford University Press, 2007.

Levinas, Emmanuel. *Humanism of the Other*. Translated by Nidra Poller. Urbana: University of Illinois Press, 2006.

Levinas, Emmanuel. *Otherwise than Being, or Beyond Essence*. Translated by Alphonso Lingis. Pittsburgh, PA: Duquesne University Press, 1998.

Levine, Caroline. 'Formal Pasts and Formal Possibilities in Victorian Studies'. *Literature Compass* 4 (2007): 1241–56.

Levine, Caroline. *Forms: Whole, Rhythm, Hierarchy, Network*. Princeton, NJ: Princeton University Press, 2015.

Levine, Caroline. 'Strategic Formalism: Toward a New Method in Cultural Studies'. *Victorian Studies* 48 (2006): 626–57.

Levinson, Marjorie. 'What Is New Formalism?' *PMLA* 122 (2007): 558–69.

Lewes, George Henry. *The Physiology of Common Life*. Edinburgh: Blackwood, 1859.

Lewis, C. S. *Mere Christianity*. New York: HarperCollins, [1952] 1980.

Liddell, Robert. *Matins, Litany, and Holy Communion*. London: G. J. Palmer, 1852.

Liddon, H. P. *Profit and Loss: A Sermon, Preached in Substance at St. Paul's Cathedral, at the Special Evening Service, on the 3rd Sunday after Epiphany, 1865*. London: Rivingtons, 1865.

Ludlow, Elizabeth. *Christina Rossetti and the Bible: Waiting with the Saints*. London: Bloomsbury, 2014.

Ludlow, J. M. 'Trade Societies and the Social Science of Association'. *Macmillan's Magazine* 3 (1861): 313–25.

Lysack, Krista. 'Goblin Markets: Victorian Women Shoppers at Liberty's Oriental Bazaar'. *Nineteenth-Century Contexts: An Interdisciplinary Journal* 27, no. 2 (2005): 139–65.

Lysack, Krista. 'The Productions of Time: Keble, Rossetti, and Victorian Devotional Reading'. *Victorian Studies* 55, no. 3 (2013): 451–70.

Malthus, Thomas R. *Essay on the Principle of Population*. Edited by Antony Flew. 2 vols. London: Penguin, [1798] 1985.

Malthus, Thomas R. *Principles of Political Economy*. Edited by John Pullen. Cambridge: Cambridge University Press, [1820] 1989.

Marsh, Jan. *Christina Rossetti: A Writer's Life*. New York: Viking, 1995.

Martin, Meredith. *The Rise and Fall of Meter: Poetry and English National Culture, 1860–1930*. Princeton, NJ: Princeton University Press, 2012.

Martin, Robert Bernard. *Gerard Manley Hopkins: A Very Private Life*. London: HarperCollins, 1992.

Mason, Emma. 'Christina Rossetti and the Doctrine of Reserve'. *Journal of Victorian Culture* 7, no. 2 (2002): 196–219.

Mason, Emma. 'Tractarian Poetry: Introduction'. *Victorian Poetry* 44, no. 1 (2006): 1–6.

Mason, Emma. *Women Poets of the Nineteenth Century*. Tavistock: Northcote House, 2006.

Mason, Emma, and Mark Knight. *Nineteenth-Century Religion and Literature: An Introduction*. Oxford: Oxford University Press, 2006.

Maurice, F. D. *On Right and Wrong Methods of Supporting Protestantism. A Letter to Lord Ashley*. London: John W. Parker, 1843.

McKelvy, William. *The English Cult of Literature: Devoted Readers, 1770–1880*. Charlottesville: University of Virginia Press, 2006.

McSweeney, Kerry. *The Language of the Senses: Sensory-Perceptual Dynamics in Wordsworth, Coleridge, Thoreau, Whitman, and Dickinson*. Montreal: McGill-Queen's University Press, 1998.

Melnyk, Julie. *Victorian Religion: Faith and Life in Britain*. Westport, CT: Praeger, 2008.

Mendoza, Victor Roman. '"Come Buy": The Crossing of Sexual and Consumer Desire in Christina Rossetti's *Goblin Market*'. *ELH* 73, no. 4 (2006): 913–47.

'The Messina Earthquake'. *Nature* 82, no. 2094 (16 December 1909): 203–4.

'The Messina Earthquake'. *School of Science and Mathematics* 9, no. 2 (February 1909): 180–2.

Meynell, Alice. *Ceres' Runaway and Other Essays*. London: Constable, 1909.

Meynell, Alice. *Later Poems*. London: John Lane, 1901.

Meynell, Alice. *The Poor Sisters of Nazareth: An Illustrated Record of Life at Nazareth House, Hammersmith*. New Delhi: Isha Books, [1889] 2013.

Meynell, Alice. *The Rhythm of Life and Other Essays*. London: Elkin Matthews and John Lane, 1893.

Meynell, Alice. *The Second Person Singular and Other Essays*. Edited by Humphrey Milford. London: Oxford University Press, 1921.

Meynell, Viola. *Alice Meynell: A Memoir*. London: Jonathan Cape, 1929.

Moeyes, Paul. 'The Eyre of the Whirlwind – The Poetry of Alice Meynell'. *Neophilogus* 80, no. 1 (1996): 149–59.

Moran, Maureen. *Catholic Sensationalism and Victorian Literature*. Liverpool: Liverpool University Press, 2007.

Morgan, Victoria and Clare Williams. *Shaping Belief: Culture, Politics and Religion in Nineteenth-Century Writing*. Liverpool: Liverpool University Press, 2008.

Mozley, Thomas. 'Agricultural Labour and Wages'. *British Critic* 33, no. 65 (January 1843): 247–74.

Mozley, Thomas. 'Pews'. *British Critic* 32, no. 64 (October 1842): 436–505.

Mozley, Thomas. 'Religious State of the Manufacturing Poor'. *British Critic* 28, no. 56 (October 1840): 334–71.

Mozley, Thomas. 'Temperance Societies'. *British Critic* 26, no. 51 (July 1839): 196–227.

'Mrs. Meynell's Later Poems'. Review. *The Academy* 62, no. 1548 (4 January 1902): 647–48.

Nelson, Holly Faith. *Through a Glass Darkly: Suffering, the Sacred, and the Sublime in Literature and Theory*. Waterloo, ON: Wilfried Laurier University Press, 2010.

Newman, Beth. 'Alice Meynell, Walter Pater, and Aestheticist Temporality'. *Victorian Studies* 53, no. 3 (2011): 495–505.

Newman, John Henry. *Apologia Pro Vita Sua*. London: Longman, Green, Longman, Roberts and Green, 1864.

Newman, John Henry. *The Arians of the Fourth Century, Their Doctrine, Temper, and Conduct, Chiefly as Exhibited in the Councils of the Church, between A.D. 325 & A.D. 381*. Oxford: Rivington, 1833.

Newman, John Henry. *Essays Critical and Historical*. London: Longmans, Green, 1897.

Nunokawa, Jeff. *The Afterlife of Property: Domestic Security and the Victorian Novel*. Princeton, NJ: Princeton University Press, 1994.

Oakeley, Frederick. 'Sacramental Confession'. *British Critic* 33, no. 66 (April 1843): 295–347.

O'Gorman, Francis. 'What Is Haunting Tennyson's *Maud* (1855)?' *Victorian Poetry* 48, no. 3 (2010): 293–312.

Oliver, Elliot J. *Coventry Patmore*. New York: Sheed and Ward, 1956.

Ong, Walter J. *Hopkins, the Self, and God*. Toronto: University of Toronto Press, 1986.

Palazzo, Lynda. *Christina Rossetti's Feminist Theology*. New York: Palgrave, 2002.

Patmore, Coventry. *Courage in Politics and Other Essays, 1885–1896*. London: Humphrey Milford, 1921.

Patmore, Coventry. 'Essay on English Metrical Law'. *North British Review* 27 (1857): 127–62.

Patmore, Coventry. *The Poetry of Pathos & Delight*. Edited by Alice Meynell. London: Wentworth Press, [1896] 2016.

Patmore, Coventry. *The Victories of Love and Other Poems*. London: Cassell, 1888.

Pearsall, Cornelia D. J. *Tennyson's Rapture: Transformation in the Victorian Dramatic Monologue*. Oxford: Oxford University Press, 2008.

Perret, Frank A. 'Preliminary Report on the Messina Earthquake of December 28, 1908'. *American Journal of Science* 27, no. 160 (April 1909): 321–34.

Peterson, Linda H. *Becoming a Woman of Letters: Myths of Authorship and Facts of the Victorian Market*. Princeton, NJ: Princeton University Press, 2009.

Peterson, Linda H. 'Victorian Poets, Politics, and Networks: Response'. *Victorian Studies* 55, no. 2 (2013): 309–16.

Pionke, Albert D. 'The Spiritual Economy of "Goblin Market"'. *Studies in English Literature, 1500–1900* 52, no. 4 (2012): 897–915.

Platt, Philip Wallace. *The Spiritual Vision of Coventry Patmore: A Study of His Religious Faith and Its Expression in His Work*. PhD diss., Toronto: University of Toronto, 1976.

Pond, Kristen. '"I Mistook the Faint Shadow": The Tractarian Ethos in Felicia Skene's Sensational Realism'. *Victorian Review* 42, no. 1 (2016): 85–105.

Poster, Carol. 'A Good Dissenter Speaking Well: William Enfield's Educational and Elocutionary Philosophies in Religious Context'. *Advances in the History of Rhetoric* 18, no. 1 (2015): 97–122.

Procter, Adelaide. *A Chaplet of Verses*. London: Longman, Green, Longman and Roberts, 1862.

Procter, Adelaide. *The Complete Works of Adelaide Procter*. Edited by Charles Dickens. London: George Bell, 1905.

Promey, Sally M., ed. *Sensational Religion: Sensory Cultures in Material Practice*. New Haven, CT: Yale University Press, 2014.

Pusey, Edward. *Christ, the Source and Rule of Christian Love. A Sermon, Preached on the Feast of S. John the Evangelist, MDCCCXI., At St. Paul's Church, Bristol, in Aid of a New Church to Be Erected in an Outlying District in That Parish; with a Preface on the Relation of our Exertions to Our Needs*. Oxford: John Henry Parker; London: J. G. F. and J. Rivington, 1841.

Pusey, Edward. *The Danger of Riches: Seek God First, and Ye Shall Have All. Two Sermons Preached in the Parish Church of St. James, Bristol*. Oxford: John Henry Parker, 1850.

Pusey, Edward. *God and Human Independence. A Sermon, Preached before the University of Oxford, on Sexagesima Sunday, 1876*. Oxford: James Parker & Co.; London: Rivingtons; New York: Pott, Young, 1876.

Pusey, Edward. *The Holy Eucharist a Comfort to the Penitent. A Sermon Preached before the University, in the Cathedral Church of Christ, in Oxford, on the Fourth Sunday after Easter*. Oxford: John Henry Parker; London: Rivington, 1843.

Rainof, Rebecca. 'Victorians in Purgatory: Newman's Poetics of Conciliation and the Afterlife of the Oxford Movement'. *Victorian Poetry* 51, no. 2 (2013): 227–47.

Rappoport, Jill. *Giving Women: Alliance and Exchange in Victorian Culture*. New York: Oxford University Press, 2012.

Rappoport, Jill. 'The Price of Redemption in "Goblin Market"'. *Studies in English Literature, 1500–1900* 50, no. 4 (2010): 853–75.

Rasmussen, Joel, Judith Wolfe and Johannes Zachhuber, eds. *The Oxford Handbook of Nineteenth-Century Christian Thought*. Oxford: Oxford University Press, 2017.

Reid, J. C. *The Mind and Art of Coventry Patmore*. London: Routledge & Kegan Paul, 1957.

Restifo, Giuseppe. 'Local Administrative Sources on Population Movements after the Messina Earthquake of 1908'. *Annali di Geofisica* 38, nos 5–6 (November–December 1995): 559–66.

Roberts, Michael J. D. 'Charity Disestablished? The Origins of the Charity Organisation Society Revisited, 1868–1871'. *Journal of Ecclesiastical History* 54, no. 1 (2003): 40–61.

Roe, Dinah. *Christina Rossetti's Faithful Imagination: The Devotional Poetry and Prose*. Basingstoke: Palgrave Macmillan, 2006.

Rossetti, Christina. *The Face of the Deep: A Devotional Commentary on the Apocalypse*. 6th edn. London: SPCK, [1892] 1911.

Rossetti, Christina. *Goblin Market and Other Poems*. London: Macmillan, 1862.

Rossetti, Christina. *A Pageant and Other Poems*. London: Macmillan, 1881.

Rossetti, Christina. *Selected Poems*. Edited by Dinah Roe. London: Penguin, 2008.

Rossetti, Christina. *Time Flies: A Reading Diary*. London: SPCK, 1897.

Rossetti, Christina. *Verses*. London: SPCK, 1893.

Ruskin, John. *The Works of John Ruskin*. Edited by E. T. Cook and Alexander Wedderburn, 39 vols. London: George Allen, 1903–12.

Saville, Julia F. *Victorian Soul-Talk: Poetry, Democracy, and the Body Politic*. Basingstoke: Palgrave, 2017.

Scarry, Elaine. *The Body in Pain: The Making and Unmaking of the World*. Oxford: Oxford University Press, 1985.

Schaffer, Talia. 'A Tethered Angel: The Martyrology of Alice Meynell'. *Victorian Poetry* 38, no. 1 (2000): 49–61.

Scheinberg, Cynthia. *Women's Poetry and Religion in Victorian England: Jewish Identity and Christian Culture*. Cambridge: Cambridge University Press, 2002.

Scholl, Lesa. *Hunger Movements in Early Victorian Literature: Want, Riots, Migration*. London: Routledge, 2016.

Schreuder, Deryck. *Gladstone and Kruger: Liberal Government and Colonial 'Home Rule' 1880–85*. London: Routledge, [1969] 2018.

Seeley, Tracy. 'Alice Meynell, essayist: Taking life "greatly to heart"'. *Women's Studies* 27, no. 2 (1998): 105–30.

'Sermon of Peter de Blois, FL A.D. 1167. Feast of St Michael and All Angels'. *The Union Review* 3 (1865): 581–84.

Shelton Reed, John. *Glorious Battle: The Cultural Politics of Victorian Anglo-Catholicism*. Nashville, TN: Vanderbilt University Press, 2000.

Shipton, Irene A. M. 'Christina Rossetti: The Poetess of the Oxford Movement'. *The Church Quarterly* 116 (1933): 219–29.

Skinner, Simon. 'Liberalism and Mammon: Tractarian Reaction in the Age of Reform'. *Journal of Victorian Culture* 4, no. 2 (1999): 197–227.

Skinner, Simon. *Tractarians and the 'Condition of England': The Social and Political Thought of the Oxford Movement*. Oxford: Clarendon Press, 2004.

Smith, Adam. *An Inquiry into the Nature and Causes of the Wealth of Nations*. 1776. 8th edn. 3 vols. London: A. Strahan, T. Cadell, and W. Davies, 1796.

Smith, Adam. *The Theory of Moral Sentiments*. 1759. London: George Bell, 1907.

Smith, James K. A. *Desiring the Kingdom: Worship, Worldview, and Cultural Formation*. Grand Rapids, MI: Baker, 2009.

Smith, Mark M. *Camille 1969: Histories of a Hurricane*. Athens: University of Georgia Press, 2011.

Smith, Mark M. *Sensing the Past: Seeing, Hearing, Smelling, Tasting, and Touching in History*. Berkeley: University of California Press, 2007.

Smith, Mark M. *The Smell of Battle, the Taste of Siege: A Sensory History of the Civil War*. Oxford: Oxford University Press, 2015.

Sobolev, Dennis. 'Semantic Counterpoint and the Poetry of Gerard Manley Hopkins'. *Victorian Literature and Culture* 35 (2007): 103–19.

Stern, Rebecca F. '"Adulterations Detected": Food and Fraud in Christina Rossetti's "Goblin Market"'. *Nineteenth-Century Literature* 57, no. 4 (2003): 477–511.

Stewart, Susan. *Poetry and the Fate of the Senses*. Chicago, IL: University of Chicago Press, 2002.

Strong, Rowan, and Carol Engelhardt Herringer, eds. *Edward Bourverie Pusey and the Oxford Movement*. London: Anthem Press, 2012.

Taft, Joshua. 'The Forms of Discipline: Christina Rossetti's Religious Verse'. *Victorian Poetry* 51, no. 3 (2013): 311–30.

Tate, Andrew. *Apocalyptic Fiction*. London: Bloomsbury, 2017.

Tate, Andrew. '"Sweeter also Than honey": John Ruskin and the Psalms'. *The Yearbook of English Studies* 39, nos 1/2 (2009): 114–25.

Taylor, Dennis. 'Tennyson's Catholic Years: A Point of Contact'. *Victorian Poetry* 47, no. 1 (2009): 285–312.

Tennyson, Alfred Lord. *Poems, Chiefly Lyrical*. London: Effingham Wilson, 1830.

Tennyson, Alfred Lord. *The Poems of Tennyson*. Edited by Christopher Ricks. London: Longmans, 1969.

Tennyson, Alfred Lord. *Selected Poems*. Edited by Christopher Ricks. London: Penguin, 2007.

Tennyson, G. B. *Victorian Devotional Poetry: The Tractarian Mode*. Cambridge, MA: Harvard University Press, 1981.

Thain, Marion. *The Lyric Poem and Aestheticism: Forms of Modernity*. Edinburgh: Edinburgh University Press, 2016.

Thain, Marion. ed. *The Lyric Poem: Formations and Transformations*. Cambridge: Cambridge University Press, [2013] 2016.

Thomas, Alan. *Value and Context: The Nature of Moral and Political Knowledge*. Oxford: Oxford University Press, 2006.

Thormählen, Marianne. *The Brontës and Religion*. Cambridge: Cambridge University Press, 1999.

Tontiplaphol, Betsy Winakur. *Poetics of Luxury in the Nineteenth Century: Keats, Tennyson, and Hopkins*. Farnham: Ashgate, 2011.

Tucker, Herbert F. 'Rossetti's Goblin Marketing: Sweet to Tongue and Sound to Eye'. *Representations* 83 (2003): 117–33.

Tucker, Herbert F. 'Tactical Formalism: A Response to Caroline Levine'. *Victorian Studies* 49 (2006): 85–95.

Turner, Frank M. *John Henry Newman: The Challenge to Evangelical Religion*. New Haven, CT: Yale University Press, 2002.

Tyas, Robert. *The Handbook of the Language & Sentiments of Flowers, Containing the Name of Every Flower to Which a Sentiment Has Been Assigned: with Introductory Observations*. London: Houlston & Stoneman, 1850.

Vadillo, Ana Parejo. *Women Poets and Urban Aestheticism: Passengers of Modernity*. Hampshire: Palgrave Macmillan, 2005.

Ward, Bernadette Waterman. 'The Kindly Light of Newman's Poetry'. *Renascence* 56, no. 2 (2004): 86–107.

Waterman, Andrew. 'A Cambridge "Via Media" in Late Georgian Anglicanism'. *Journal of Ecclesiastical History* 42, no. 3 (1991): 419–36.

Waterman, Andrew. 'The Ideological Alliance of Political Economy and Christian Theology, 1798–1833'. *Journal of Ecclesiastical History* 34, no. 2 (1983): 231–44.

Waterman, Catharine H. *Flora's Lexicon: An Interpretation of the Language and Sentiment of Flowers: With an Outline of Botany, and a Poetical Introduction*. Philadelphia, PA: Herman Hooker, 1839.

Weinstein, Ben. '"Local Self-Government Is True Socialism": Joshua Toulmin Smith, the State and Character Formation'. *The English Historical Review* 123, no. 504 (2008): 1193–228.

'When London was Little'. *Household Words* 10, no. 253 (27 January 1855): 558–60.

White, Norman. *Hopkins: A Literary Biography*. Oxford: Clarendon Press, 1992.

Williams, Isaac. 'On Reserve in Communicating Religious Knowledge'. *Tracts for the Times* 80. Oxford: Rivington and Parker, 1838.

Wolfson, Susan J. *Formal Charges: The Shaping of Poetry in British Romanticism*. Stanford, CA: Stanford University Press, 1997.

Wolfson, Susan J., and Marshall Brown, eds. *Reading for Form*. Seattle: University of Washington Press, 2006.

Yates, Nigel. *Anglican Ritualism in Victorian Britain 1830–1910*. Oxford: Oxford University Press, 1999.

Yonge, Charlotte. *A Book of Golden Deeds of All Times and All Lands*. London: Macmillan, 1864.

# Index

*Note*: Page numbers appearing in *italics* indicate that the reference appears in an endnote rather than in the main body of the volume.

Adorno, Theodor W. 61–2, 64–5, 67
aesthetics 2–3, 7, 10–16, 20, 27, 28, 34, 35, 40, 45, 49, 52–3, 58–9, 61–2, 65, 68, 70, 74, 83–5, 90–1, 93, 95, 100–2, 106, 110, 113, 117–20, 124, 126–34, 136–7, 140, 145, 151, 154, 160–1, 168–70, 172, 175, *183*
alcoholism 80, 87, 165, *190*
alienation 64–5, 117, 172, *184*
All Souls Day 117
allegory 28, 30, 34, 76
analogy 106, 115, 140
Anglicanism 4–6, 12, 15, 26, 74, 76–7, 96, 99–100, 108, 126, 135, 137, 140, 146, 172, 174, 175
    Anglican Revival 1
    *Book of Common Prayer* 15
    Communion of Saints 15, 108, 117, 134, 142, 174
Anglo-Boer War 175
Anglo-Catholicism 4–7, 28, 39, 41, 53, 55, 66, 70, 72, 76–7, 83, 84, 93, 96–7, 99, 101–5, 107, 109–10, 114, 117, 120, 121, 136–8, 141, 143, 145–6, 154, 162, 167, 172–4, 176, *183*, *189*, *190*
Aquinas, St Thomas 171, *192*
Armond, Andrew 29, 53
Armstrong, Isobel 2, 9, 20, 35, 38, 64, 156–7
Arseneau, Mary 7, 110, 139, 140, 145
asceticism 6, 34
austerity 34, 84, 93, 95, 104

Badeni, June 93, 168
Batchelor, John 156, 157, 159, 162
Blair, Kirstie 5, 15, 16, 29, 35, 41, 53, 57
Bosanquet, Samuel 12, 24, 64, 138
Boyce, Charlotte 62, 130
Brake, Laurel 68, 69

bread 1–3, 15, 31, 36, 44, 86, 100, 101, 104–8, 111–12, 114–16, 121, 122, 146–7, 152
    daily bread 44, 106–7, 132, 146–7
    of heaven 73
    of life 44, 106
Bridges, Robert 35, *185*
Bristol Riots 19, 72, 102
*British Critic, The* 137, 138, *189*
Broad Church 5–6, 45, 123, *183*, *189*

Cambridge Apostles, The 8, 155
capitalism 3, 23–4, 30, 34–5, 37, 38, 43, 62, 67, 71, 105–6, 124, 135, 161–2, 163
capitalist individualism 14, 34, 88, 104, 114, 122, 161, 162, 175
capitalist narrative 16, 166
Carlyle, Thomas 64
Chartism 32, 157
Christ's inscape 111–12, 151, 154, 171, 172
civilization 35, 76, 123, 131, 139
Classen, Constance 114, 116
Clough, Arthur Hugh 125
Colón, Susan 136
colonization 174
communal responsibility 8, 63–4, 67, 75, 79, 94, 102, 107
Communion of Saints (also Community of Saints) 15, 104, 107, 117, 145, 173, 174
community 1–4, 7–8, 9–16, 20–2, 26, 32, 34, 41, 43–4, 47–9, 51–2, 55, 59, 63–7, 70, 72–4, 75, 77–80, 82–3, 86, 89, 91, 93, 95–7, 99–105, 107–8, 111, 114, 116–7, 122, 124–5, 127, 134, 136–9, 142, 144, 145, 148, 153, 154–5, 157, 160, 161, 166–70, 172–5
    of faith 66, 77
    global 173, 174–5
    of grief 55

of readers 15, 65–7, 77, 96, 97
religious communities 93, 95
complacency 16, 37–8, 71, 72, 78, 81–2, 90, 97, 102, 104, 115, 116, 118, 123, 132, 138, 142, 148, 151, 157, 161, 162–3, 165, 175
   institutionalized 68–70
   social 14, 73, 116
consumer culture (also Consumerism) 83, 88, 91, 109, 170
Copyright Laws 68
Corn Laws 129
Crawford, Rachel 63
Crimean War 108

death 11, 23, 26, 30, 31, 33, 39–40, 43–7, 50–2, 54–9, 70, 77, 79, 81–2, 86–7, 90, 109, 117, 123, 130–3, 152, 153, 158–60, 164–5, 173, *184*
democracy 35, 63–5, 165
Derrida, Jacques 7–8, 23, 32, 42–3, 103, 126
   Law of Tact 7–8, 42–3, 103, 116
   *On Touching* 7–8, 23
Dickens, Charles 84, 85, 86, 87, *185*
   *A Christmas Carol* 87
   *Oliver Twist* 86
Dieleman, Karen 14, 16, 27, 99–100, 145, 146, 147, 149
Donne, John 39
   'A Valediction: Forbidden Mourning' 39
Dramatic Monologue 71, 82, 131

Easson, Angus 152
Eliot, T. S. 172
   *The Wasteland* 172–3
emotional paralysis 13, 23, 32, 33, 39, 59, 70, 71–2, 155, 156, 161
empathy 6, 13, 14, 15, 20, 22, 23, 25, 38, 41, 56, 71, 75, 149, 156, 159, 175
eucharist 14, 15, 41, 66, 73, 77, 83, 96–7, 99–134, 142, 143, 147, 169, 171
evangelicalism 2, 4, 5–6, 13, 25, 69, 70, *183*
excess 5, 24, 30–9, 46, 52, 53–8, 70, 74, 79–80, 83, 104, 118–19, 123, 124, 141, 146, 161–2, 165, 168, 170, 176
   and asceticism 6
   and decadence 2
   emotional 38, 41, 46, 48, 51, 54, 56, 67, 168, 175
   of hunger and poverty 11, 88

faith 2, 7, 25, 27–9, 33–4, 40, 43, 45–8, 50, 53, 54, 57–8, 77, 89, 109–11, 119, 121, 122, 135–8, 139–40, 144, 151–2, 154, *183*
   and doubt 29, 45, 48–9, 58
   excesses of 34, 58
   loss of 34, 71, 111
famine 3, 20, 43, 44, 61, 69, 71–2, 87, 108, 125, 161
   Great Irish, The 108, 114, 125, 157, 174
Flood, Finbarr Barry 115
*Flora Symbolica* 142
food 3, 11, 31, 35, 44, 57, 73, 82, 83, 88–9, 93, 94, 95–6, 104, 105, 112, 114–15, 116, 117, 118–9, 121, 124, 125, 130–1, 143, 147–8, 152, 155
Fraser, Hilary 62, 100, 101, 171
French Revolution 64, 111, 164
Froude, Hurrell 19
fruit 33, 37, 74, 81, 88, 118, 121–2, 125, 127, 141, 146

Gagnier, Regenia 36, 170
Gaskell, Elizabeth 85
   *North and South* 85, 86, *190*
*Germ, The* 56, *182*
Gladstone, William 174–5
globalization 173
Goodlad, Lauren 3
Gordon Riots 64
Gray, F. Elizabeth 41, 105, 168
Gregory, Gill 88, 145, 150
grief 14, 33, 39–41, 44–52, 54–9, 72, 142, 146

Hallam, Arthur 5, 8, 44
*Handbook of the Language & Sentiments of Flowers* 143
Harrington, Emily 7, 9, 41, 42, 52, 53, 76, 91, 103
   'impersonal intimacy' 7, 38, 43, 44, 49, 50, 52, 76, 91, 103, 166
Harrison, Antony 143
Holy Communion (*see also* Eucharist) 99, 114, 161
Hopkins, Gerard Manley 5, 13, 30, 34, 35–6, 38, 62, 101, 111, 118, 137, 151–3, 155, 171, *192*
   'A Soliloquy of One of the Spies' 34–7
   'Barnfloor and Winepress' 71–5

'Cherry Beggar' 153–5
'Easter' 118–20
'Easter Communion' 119–20
'New Readings' 120–1
'Summa' 153–4
'The Wreck of the Deutschland' 174
*Household Words* 44, 84, 85
Howes, David 35, 114
Hughes, Linda 65, 66, 67, 68, 69, 77, 125–6, *184*
human responsibility 72, 103, 121, 162
hunger 13, 14, 16, 21, 23, 28, 32, 33, 35, 36, 37, 39, 40, 42, 43, 47, 50, 51, 56–7, 59, 62–3, 67, 71, 75–6, 82, 87, 94, 95, 97, 104, 118, 133, 139, 143, 157, 175
  physical 3, 13, 44, 100, 107, 117, 125–6, 133, 141, 157
  and poverty 8, 11, 23, 83, 126
  social 3, 13, 34, 43, 44, 100, 117, 125–6, 133, 157, 172
  spiritual 44, 56, 57, 100, 107, 125, 172

idyll 67, 71, 82
imperialism 34, 70, 122–3
individualism 14, 20, 24, 34–5, 62, 67, 71, 88, 95, 104, 114, 122, 124, 161, 162, 163, 170, 175–6
isolation 3, 4, 20, 28, 32, 34–5, 43, 47, 117, 122, 123, 126–8, 131, 170

Janes, Dominic 4, 143, *190*

Keble, John 1–3, 7, 8, 12, 15, 16, 19–21, 48–9, 67, 100, 155, 175
  *Christian Year, The* 15, 66–7, *183*
  *Lectures on Poetry* 1, 154
Kenyon, Ruth 19
King, Joshua 65, 67, 100, 103, 135, 139, 140, *183*
Koven, Seth 5

Lalonde, Marc 35
Larsen Hoeckley, Cheri Lin 148–9
Leavis, F. R. 151
Ledbetter, Kathryn 69, 71
Levinas, Emmanuel 75–6, 103–4, 108, 115–16, 120, 126
Levine, Caroline 8, 11, 61, 136
Lewis, C. S. 175

Liddell, Robert 99
Liddon, Henry Parry 103–4, 122–3, 131, *187*, *189*
Liturgy 4, 15, 66, 71, 74, 75, 76–8, 99, 100, 101, 110, 124, 136, 172, *184*
Lowth, Robert 155
Ludlow, Elizabeth 77
luxury 3, 22, 31, 34, 36–7, 70, 72, 74, 79–80, 85, 88, 93, 118, 121, 125, 139, 141, 142, 146, 156, 158, 175
lyric 3, 9–10, 13, 14, 15, 16, 41, 52–3, 61–8, 70, 76, 83–4, 96, 110, 111, 112–13, 136, 152, 176

Malthus, Thomas 23–4
Malthusian 94
manna 35, 36, 105, 113–14
Martin, Meredith 68
Martin, Robert Bernard 151
Marxism 65
Mason, Emma 9, 53, 64, 76, 136, 145
Maurice, F. D. 5–6, 135–6, *189*
McSweeney, Kerry 10, 107
meat 30, 31, 37, 106, 152
Melnyk, Julie 99
Metaphysical Society, The 155
Meynell, Alice 1–3, 5, 9, 13, 14, 17, 83–5, 88, 90–5, 105, 107, 109, 110–3, 137, 167–70, 171–2, *177*, *185*
  'A Dead Harvest' 83, 90–1, 96
  'A General Communion' 169–70
  'Ceres' Runaway' 88–9
  'Fugitive, The' 111–12
  'In Portugal, 1912' 112–13
  'Joyous Wanderer, The' 1–3
  'Lady Poverty, The' 93–5
  'Messina 1908' 171–2
  'A Modern Poetess' 90
  *Sisters of Nazareth, The* 17
  'Two Poets, The' 49–50
Mill, John Stuart 15
modernity 3, 83, 85, 89–90, 92, 93, 171
mortality 14, 23, 28, 39–40, 47, 151
mature 9, 10, 11, 20, 34, 35, 39, 43, 48, 57, 65, 88, 90, 140, 144, 151

New Poor Law 4, 11–12, 21
Newman, John Henry 6–7, 8, 19, 126, 137, 138, *178*, *189*
Nunokawa, Jeff 24

Oliver, Elliot 162-3
opium 143, 156-7, *190*
Oxford Movement, The 1-2, 5-6, 7, 8, 12-13, 19, 126, 135-6, 155, 170, *188, 189*

paradox 7-8, 15, 27, 40, 49, 53, 64, 75-6, 92, 94, 103, 105, 109, 113, 116, 119, 135, 151, 156, 172, 175
Patmore, Coventry 5, 13, 95-6, 137, 162-7, 174-5
   '1880-85' 174
   'A Farewell' 39-40
   'An Essay on English Metrical Law' 13-14
   'Courage in Politics' 164-5
   'England' 164-5
   'Heaven and Earth' 165-6
   'Manifest Destiny' 163-5
   'Minding One's Own Business' 163-5
   'Victory in Defeat' 120
   'Zest of Life, The' 95-6
Pearsall, Cornelia 162
Periodical Press 14, 24, 59, 62, 65-9, 76, 77, 78, 83-4, 90, 96
pew rentals 25-6, 77, 117
philanthropy 21, 42
political economy 4, 16, 22-4, 27, 37, 43, 138, 147, 150, 165
political journalism 137
poor, the 1, 4, 6, 12, 15-17, 21-8, 32, 38, 58, 67, 73-5, 78, 85-9, 93, 94-5, 100, 102-3, 106-9, 119, 121-2, 128-9, 137, 138-40, 145, 147-55, 157, 161
   deserving and undeserving 11-12, 27-8, 94, 106, 143, 167
   dignity of 13, 63, 91, 95
   neglect of 22, 25, 35, 64, 72, 91, 114, 117
   proximity to 16, 22, 38, 103, 138-9
   suffering of 73-4
poverty 3, 8, 11, 13, 16, 21, 22-3, 26-8, 32, 63, 64, 72, 81, 83, 85-9, 91-5, 103, 107, 114, 126, 128-9, 132, 137-8, 140, 144, 145, 148, 150, 151-7, 161, 154, 167
   spiritual 74, 94, 95, 172
   vows of 94-5
Prayers for the Dead 131
Prickett, Stephen 21-2, *180*

Procter, Adelaide Anne 5, 13, 20, 27-8, 44, 50-2, 83-8, 107-9, 110, 111, 113, 123, 131-4, 137, 144-51, 152, 174, *185*
   'A Beggar' 146-8
   *A Chaplet of Verses* 144-50
   'Cradle Song of the Poor, The' 85-8
   'Give' 27, 146
   'Homeless' 148-50
   'Life in Death and Death in Life' 44, 50-2
   'Our Daily Bread' 146-7
   'Our Dead' 19, 26-7
   'Sowing and Reaping' 107-9
   'Too Late' 131-4
Providence Row Night Refuge for Homeless Women and Children 145
proximity 8, 9-11, 22, 38, 48, 52, 57, 86, 103-4, 113, 116, 120, 126-7, 130, 132, 138, 139, 172
psalter form 76-7
Pusey, Edward Bouverie 19, 22, 24, 67, 72-3, 93, 101-3, 105-6, 113-4, *189*

Rappoport, Jill 140
Real Presence, Doctrine of 15, 101-2, 105, 107, 112, 113
Reform Bill (1832) 19, 21, 32, 64, 71, 72, 157
Reform Bill (1867) 71
Reid, J. C. 162, 166
reserve 2-11, 14, 16, 27, 30, 31, 32-3, 34, 36, 38, 40-1, 43, 44-5, 47-9, 50, 52, 54-5, 58, 79, 91, 120, 123-4, 149, 152, 168, 173-4, 175
   aesthetic 11, 27, 113, 120, 133, 172
   doctrine of 2, 6-7, 13, 25, 38-9, 42, 43, 45, 52, 53, 58, 76, 90, 113, 134, 140, 145, 152, 154, 155, 165, 172, *183, 190*
   economic 3, 38
   emotional 2, 3, 11, 13, 14, 25, 27, 50-1, 74, 93, 156, 167, 168
   intellectual 5, 6-7, 102, 156
   poetic 2, 8, 9-11, 14, 28, 29, 30, 52-4, 76-7, 84-5, 106, 126, 173
   sensory 10-11
   spiritual 5, 13, 30, 74, 102
   theological 7
ritual 2, 5, 13-14, 15, 74, 76-7, 99, 100-1, 102, 105, 107, 110-11, 122, 125-6, 136, 169, 172

ritualism 2, 84, 96, 105, 126
Roe, Dinah 140
Roman Catholicism 4, 5–7, 15, 45, 74, 83, 84–5, 88, 89, 95, 96–7, 102, 108, 111, 120–1, 126, 145–6, 152, 166, 167, 174, *178*, *188*
Rosaries/Chaplets 145–6
Rossetti, Christina 4, 5, 13, 14, 16, 28–34, 35, 37–8, 52–8, 76–85, 91, 93, 103–4, 107, 109–11, 113, 117–8, 130–1, 136, 137, 139–46, 152, 157, *184*, *189*
  'Amen' 109–10
  'Amor Mundi' 7–8, 79–81, 82, 83, 94, 130–1
  'At Home' 117–18, 122, 126
  'Because he first loved us' 100
  '"Consider the Lilies of the Field"' 139–44
  *Face of the Deep, The* 139
  'Goblin Market' 82, 127, 129, 146
  *Goblin Market and Other Poems* 145
  'Hope in Grief' 54–6, 58
  'In the Round Tower at Jhansi, June 8, 1857' 174
  'Old World Thicket' 28–34
  *Poems* 78
  'Prince's Progress, The' 81–2, 123
  'Son, Remember' 139, 140
  'Sweet Death' 56–8
  *Time Flies* 66
  'Up-Hill' 77–9, 141
  *Verses* 66, 103–4
  'World, The' 37, 140–1, 146
Rossetti, Maria 93, 140, 145
Ruskin, John 171, 172

Scarry, Elaine 62–3
senses, the 10–11, 13, 25, 29, 34, 35, 40, 42, 50, 52, 57, 59, 63, 65, 74, 75–6, 80, 82, 86, 89, 99, 107, 110, 113–18, 126–7, 171
  sensory absence 10, 56, 89
  sensory assault 37
  sensory deprivation 28, 32, 50, 89, 91
  sensory excess 80
  sensory experience 10, 28, 57, 65, 80, 91, 107, 118, 126
  selective experience of 81, 86, 91
  sensory pleasure 89, 118, 158, 160
Shakespeare, William 141

Skinner, Simon 4, 12, 21–2, 25, 138–9
Slums 11, 13, 151
Smith, Adam 23, 24, 31–2
Smith, James K. A. 99, 113
Smith, Mark M. 35, 114
Sobolev, Dennis 151
social action/activism 3, 10, 13, 14, 15–16, 25, 44, 76, 77, 97, 100, 133, 135–70
social apathy 81, 82, 155, 157, 162, 163, 164
social responsibility 5, 12, 16, 63, 76, 136, 174
socialism 167, 169
Society for the Promotion of the Employment of Women 145
Society of Women Journalists 84
Sonnet 96, 119, 140–1
Springtime of the People 157
starvation 11, 21, 23, 24, 43, 44, 70, 73, 81, 82, 86, 87, 90, 109, 111, 114, 118, 122, 125, 126, 127, 129, 131, 133, 141, 143, 148, 170
*St James's Gazette* 163, 166
St Mary Magdalene Home for Fallen Women 140, 144
Stewart, Susan 65–6, 75
Suffrage 64, 167–8
sympathy 31, 66, 156, 167, *189*
synaesthesia 11, 52, 56–7

taste 10, 15, 24, 28, 32, 35, 36, 42, 48, 50, 56, 57–9, 63, 74, 89, 95–6, 101, 113–22, 172
Taylor, Dennis 6, 7, 159, *188*
Tennyson, Lord Alfred 5–8, 13, 30, 44–51, 52, 56, 61, 69–71, 84, 123–31, 132, 137, 145, 155–62, *183*, *188*, *191*
  'A Character' 123–5, 126
  'Charge of the Light Brigade' 174
  'Despair: A Dramatic Monologue' 71
  *Idylls of the King* 125
  *In Memoriam* 39
  'Lady of Shalott, The' 126–31, 132
  'Lotos-Eaters, The' 156–62, 165
  'Supposed Confessions' 40
  'Two Voices, The' 44–50, 56
  'Victim, The' 61, 69–71, 72
Tennyson, G. B. 9, 139
Thain, Marion 9, 63
Tontiplaphol, Betsy Winakur 30, 36, 39, 58, 126, 127, 153

touch 8, 10, 11, 23, 28, 32, 42–3, 51, 52, 59, 63, 64, 74, 75, 80, 82, 86, 87, 90, 94, 101, 103, 115, 117, 130, 172
Tractarianism 1–16, 19–26, 34, 38, 39, 43, 44, 45, 49, 53, 56, 58, 64, 69, 72, 88, 92, 99, 103, 104, 105, 116, 121, 122, 125, 135–7, 139, 144, 162–3, 166, 167, 168, 173–6, *178*, *189*
  aesthetics 5, 16, 84, 136–7, 172
  ethics 3, 5, 82
  ethos 126
  poetics 2, 4, 8, 9–10, 16, 19–21, 22, 29, 63, 66, 84, 106, 123, 138–9, 140, 156, 170, 176
  social mission 2, 4, 8, 9, 11, 15–16, 22–5, 63, 67, 76, 83, 100, 116, 136–9, 148, 155, 167
  theology 5–7, 15, 76, 107, 123, 138, 170

*Tracts for the Times* 38, *178*
Trade Unions 78
transubstantiation 15, 102, 112, 122

Unitarianism 6, 172

Vadillo, Ana Parejo 83, 88, 92

Williams, Isaac 7, 8, 38–9, 41, 43, 44
  'On Reserve in Communicating Religious Knowledge' 7, 38–9, 44
wine 15, 73, 74, 75, 100, 105–6, 110, 111–12, 113–14, 116, 118, 119, 121, 122, 152, 161, 164

Yates, Nigel 2
Yonge, Charlotte 69

www.ingramcontent.com/pod-product-compliance
Lightning Source LLC
Chambersburg PA
CBHW052039300426
44117CB00012B/1896